LANGUAGE /

Dorothy S. S
Celia Genishi and Dc
ADVISORY BOARD: *Richard Allingt*
Anne Haas Dyson, Carole Edelsky, Mary

Literacy Theory as Practice:
Connecting Theory and Instruction in K–12 Classrooms
LARA J. HANDSFIELD

Literacy and History in Action: Immersive Approaches to Disciplinary Thinking, Grades 5–12
THOMAS M. McCANN, REBECCA D'ANGELO, NANCY GALAS, & MARY GRESKA

Pose, Wobble, Flow:
A Culturally Proactive Approach to Literacy Instruction
ANTERO GARCIA & CINDY O'DONNELL-ALLEN

Newsworthy—Cultivating Critical Thinkers, Readers, and Writers in Language Arts Classrooms
ED MADISON

Engaging Writers with Multigenre Research Projects:
A Teacher's Guide
NANCY MACK

Teaching Transnational Youth—
Literacy and Education in a Changing World
ALLISON SKERRETT

Uncommonly Good Ideas—
Teaching Writing in the Common Core Era
SANDRA MURPHY & MARY ANN SMITH

The One-on-One Reading and Writing Conference:
Working with Students on Complex Texts
JENNIFER BERNE & SOPHIE C. DEGENER

Critical Encounters in Secondary English:
Teaching Literary Theory to Adolescents, Third Edition
DEBORAH APPLEMAN

Transforming Talk into Text—Argument Writing, Inquiry, and Discussion, Grades 6–12
THOMAS M. McCANN

Reading and Representing Across the Content Areas:
A Classroom Guide
AMY ALEXANDRA WILSON & KATHRYN J. CHAVEZ

Writing and Teaching to Change the World:
Connecting with Our Most Vulnerable Students
STEPHANIE JONES, ED.

Educating Literacy Teachers Online:
Tools, Techniques, and Transformations
LANE W. CLARKE & SUSAN WATTS-TAFFEE

Other People's English: Code-Meshing,
Code-Switching, and African American Literacy
VERSHAWN ASHANTI YOUNG, RUSTY BARRETT,
Y'SHANDA YOUNG-RIVERA, & KIM BRIAN LOVEJOY

WHAM! Teaching with Graphic Novels Across
the Curriculum
WILLIAM G. BROZO, GARY MOORMAN, & CARLA K. MEYER

The Administration and Supervision of Reading Programs, 5th Edition
SHELLEY B. WEPNER, DOROTHY S. STRICKLAND, & DIANA J. QUATROCHE, EDS.

Critical Literacy in the Early Childhood Classroom:
Unpacking Histories, Unlearning Privilege
CANDACE R. KUBY

Inspiring Dialogue:
Talking to Learn in the English Classroom
MARY M. JUZWIK, CARLIN BORSHEIM-BLACK,
SAMANTHA CAUGHLAN, & ANNE HEINTZ

Reading the Visual:
An Introduction to Teaching Multimodal Literacy
FRANK SERAFINI

Race, Community, and Urban Schools:
Partnering with African American Families
STUART GREENE

ReWRITING the Basics:
Literacy Learning in Children's Cultures
ANNE HAAS DYSON

Writing Instruction That Works:
Proven Methods for Middle and High School Classrooms
ARTHUR N. APPLEBEE & JUDITH A. LANGER, WITH KRISTEN CAMPBELL WILCOX, MARC NACHOWITZ, MICHAEL P. MASTROIANNI, & CHRISTINE DAWSON

Literacy Playshop: New Literacies, Popular Media, and Play in the Early Childhood Classroom
KAREN E. WOHLWEND

Critical Media Pedagogy:
Teaching for Achievement in City Schools
ERNEST MORRELL, RUDY DUEÑAS, VERONICA GARCIA, & JORGE LOPEZA

A Search Past Silence: The Literacy of Young Black Men
DAVID E. KIRKLAND

The ELL Writer:
Moving Beyond Basics in the Secondary Classroom
CHRISTINA ORTMEIER-HOOPER

Reading in a Participatory Culture:
Remixing *Moby-Dick* in the English Classroom
HENRY JENKINS & WYN KELLEY, WITH KATIE CLINTON, JENNA McWILLIAMS, RICARDO PITTS-WILEY, & ERIN REILLY, EDS.

Summer Reading:
Closing the Rich/Poor Achievement Gap
RICHARD L. ALLINGTON & ANNE McGILL-FRANZEN, EDS.

Real World Writing for Secondary Students:
Teaching the College Admission Essay and
Other Gate-Openers for Higher Education
JESSICA SINGER EARLY & MEREDITH DECOSTA

Teaching Vocabulary to English Language Learners
MICHAEL F. GRAVES, DIANE AUGUST, & JEANETTE MANCILLA-MARTINEZ

Literacy for a Better World:
LAURA SCHNEIDER VANDERPLOEG

Socially Responsible Literacy
PAULA M. SELVESTER & DEBORAH G. SUMMERS

Learning from Culturally and Linguistically Diverse
Classrooms: Using Inquiry to Inform Practice
JOAN C. FINGON & SHARON H. ULANOFF, EDS.

Bridging Literacy and Equity
ALTHIER M. LAZAR ET AL.

continued

For volumes in the NCRLL Collection (edited by JoBeth Allen and Donna E. Alvermann) and the Practitioners Bookshelf Series (edited by Celia Genishi and Donna E. Alvermann), as well as other titles in this series, please visit www.tcpress.com.

Language and Literacy Series, *continued*

"Trust Me! I Can Read"
SALLY LAMPING & DEAN WOODRING BLASE

Reading Girls
HADAR DUBROWSKY MA'AYAN

Reading Time
CATHERINE COMPTON-LILLY

A Call to Creativity
LUKE REYNOLDS

Literacy and Justice Through Photography
WENDY EWALD, KATHARINE HYDE, & LISA LORD

The Successful High School Writing Center
DAWN FELS & JENNIFER WELLS, EDS.

Interrupting Hate
MOLLIE V. BLACKBURN

Playing Their Way into Literacies
KAREN E. WOHLWEND

Teaching Literacy for Love and Wisdom
JEFFREY D. WILHELM & BRUCE NOVAK

Overtested
JESSICA ZACHER PANDYA

Restructuring Schools for Linguistic Diversity,
Second Edition
OFELIA B. MIRAMONTES, ADEL NADEAU, & NANCY L. COMMINS

Words Were All We Had
MARÍA DE LA LUZ REYES, ED.

Urban Literacies
VALERIE KINLOCH, ED.

Bedtime Stories and Book Reports
CATHERINE COMPTON-LILLY & STUART GREENE, EDS.

Envisioning Knowledge
JUDITH A. LANGER

Envisioning Literature, Second Edition
JUDITH A. LANGER

Writing Assessment and the Revolution in Digital Texts
and Technologies
MICHAEL R. NEAL

Artifactual Literacies
KATE PAHL & JENNIFER ROWSELL

Educating Emergent Bilinguals
OFELIA GARCÍA & JO ANNE KLEIFGEN

(Re)Imagining Content-Area Literacy Instruction
RONI JO DRAPER, ED.

Change Is Gonna Come
PATRICIA A. EDWARDS ET AL.

When Commas Meet Kryptonite
MICHAEL BITZ

Literacy Tools in the Classroom
RICHARD BEACH ET AL.

Harlem on Our Minds
VALERIE KINLOCH

Teaching the New Writing
ANNE HERRINGTON, KEVIN HODGSON, & CHARLES MORAN, EDS.

Children, Language, and Literacy
CELIA GENISHI & ANNE HAAS DYSON

Children's Language
JUDITH WELLS LINDFORS

"You Gotta BE the Book," Second Edition
JEFFREY D. WILHELM

Children's Literature and Learning
BARBARA A. LEHMAN

Storytime
LAWRENCE R. SIPE

Effective Instruction for Struggling Readers, K–6
BARBARA M. TAYLOR & JAMES E. YSSELDYKE, EDS.

The Effective Literacy Coach
ADRIAN RODGERS & EMILY M. RODGERS

Writing in Rhythm
MAISHA T. FISHER

Reading the Media
RENEE HOBBS

teaching**media***literacy*.com
RICHARD BEACH

What Was It Like?
LINDA J. RICE

Research on Composition
PETER SMAGORINSKY, ED.

The Vocabulary Book
MICHAEL F. GRAVES

New Literacies in Action
WILLIAM KIST

Teaching English Today
BARRIE R.C. BARRELL ET AL., EDS.

Bridging the Literacy Achievement Gap, 4–12
DOROTHY S. STRICKLAND & DONNA E. ALVERMANN, EDS.

Out of This World
HOLLY VIRGINIA BLACKFORD

Critical Passages
KRISTIN DOMBEK & SCOTT HERNDON

Making Race Visible
STUART GREENE & DAWN ABT-PERKINS, EDS.

The Child as Critic, Fourth Edition
GLENNA SLOAN

Room for Talk
REBEKAH FASSLER

The Brothers and Sisters Learn to Write
ANNE HAAS DYSON

The Testing Trap
GEORGE HILLOCKS, JR.

"Why Don't They Learn English?"
LUCY TSE

Conversational Borderlands
BETSY RYMES

Inquiry-Based English Instruction
RICHARD BEACH & JAMIE MYERS

LITERACY THEORY AS PRACTICE

CONNECTING THEORY AND INSTRUCTION IN K–12 CLASSROOMS

LARA J. HANDSFIELD

Foreword by Annemarie Sullivan Palincsar

TEACHERS COLLEGE PRESS

TEACHERS COLLEGE | COLUMBIA UNIVERSITY

NEW YORK AND LONDON

Published by Teachers College Press, 1234 Amsterdam Avenue, New York, NY 10027

Copyright © 2016 by Teachers College, Columbia University

All rights reserved. No part of this publication may be reproduced or transmitted in any form or by any means, electronic or mechanical, including photocopy, or any information storage and retrieval system, without permission from the publisher.

Library of Congress Cataloging-in-Publication Data is available at loc.gov

Handsfield, Lara Jean, 1969-
    Literacy theory as practice : connecting theory and instruction in K–12 classrooms / Lara J. Handsfield ; foreword by Annemarie Sullivan Palincsar.
        pages cm — (Language and literacy series.)
    Includes bibliographical references and index.
    ISBN 978-0-8077-5705-5 (pbk. : alk. paper) —
    ISBN 978-0-8077-5706-2 (hardcover : alk. paper) —
    ISBN 978-0-8077-7414-4 (ebook)
        1. Reading. 2. Literacy. I. Title.
    LB1573.H1718 2015
    372.4—dc23   2015025259

ISBN 978-0-8077-5705-5 (paper)
ISBN 978-0-8077-5706-2 (hardcover)
ISBN 978-0-8077-7414-4 (ebook)

Printed on acid-free paper
Manufactured in the United States of America

For Granny, a.k.a. Pearl Louise Hunter Weber (1878–1975)

"All knowledge, all thinking really worthy of the name, ends in reaction, implicit or explicit. Only so can knowledge be power. Knowledge that is all ready to eventuate in reaction is power-ful but it is not yet power. It comes to the same thing to say that the final stage in any complete act of knowledge is application, which is the true climax of intellect." (Weber, 1922, para. 2)

Contents

Foreword   *Annemarie Sullivan Palincsar*   xi

Acknowledgments   xiii

1. **Introduction**   1

    Conceptualizing Theory   1

    Situating Praxis Within a Conceptual Continuum   5

    Content and Organization of This Book   7

**PART I: INTRODUCTION TO THEORETICAL FRAMES
OF READING AND LITERACY**   13

2. **Correspondence Theories**   15

    Grounding Curricular Model:
      Heggerty's Phonemic Awareness Curriculum   16

    Behaviorism   17

    Information-Processing Theories   21

    Stage Theories of Word Recognition and
      Spelling Development   33

    Concluding Thoughts   36

3. **Coherence Theories, Take 1: Cognitive Constructivism**   38

    Foundations of Cognitive Constructivist Theories   39

    Grounding Curricular Model:
      Transactional Strategies Instruction   40

    Schema Theory   42

    Psycholinguistic Theory   45

    Construction–Integration Model   48

Transactional/Reader Response Theory   50

Concluding Thoughts   55

4. **Coherence Theories, Take 2: Social Constructivism**   **57**

Vygotsky's Impact on Teaching and Learning   57

Grounding Curricular Model:
    Lucy Calkins's Units of Study for Writing   60

Sociocultural-Historical Theory   62

Sociolinguistic Theory   66

Emergent Literacy Theory   70

Concluding Thoughts   73

5. **Coherence to Incoherence:**
    Social Constructionist Theories   **75**

Social Constructionism   76

Grounding Curricular Model:
    Youth Participatory Action Research   78

Critical Literacy Theory   79

New Literacy Studies   83

Multiliteracies/New Literacies Theory   86

Critical Sociocultural Theory   89

Critical Race Theory   92

Concluding Thoughts   97

PART II: EXPLORING PRAXIS AND BRINGING THEORIES TO LIFE   **99**

6. **Cracking the Code:**
    Skills Instruction and Developing Concepts of Literacy   **101**

Skills Instruction Across the K–12 Grade Span   101

Word Sorting in a 3rd-Grade Multilingual Classroom   103

Making Valentines at Home from Pre-K to 1st Grade   109

Manipulating Sentences in a 9th-Grade English Class   114

7. **Constructing Meaning with Texts**   **121**

Fluency, Vocabulary, and Comprehension Instruction   121

Fluency Instruction with a 3rd-Grade Reader
in a One-on-One Tutoring Context 124

Strategic Reading and Word Identification in
a Literature Discussion Group 129

8. **Literature Discussion, Response, and Critique** 139

Literature Discussion, Response, and Critique
in K–12 Classrooms 139

Responding to Literature About Civil Rights
in a 1st-Grade Classroom 141

Literature Discussion in an 11th-/12th-Grade
Modern World Literature Class 145

Stepping into Another's Shoes in a 6th-Grade
Language Arts Classroom 151

9. **Writing and Writing Development:
Authoring Texts, Authoring Lives** 158

Writing Instruction in K–12 Classrooms 158

Small Moments Writing in a 1st-Grade Monolingual Classroom 160

Autobiographical Writing in a 4th-Grade Bilingual Classroom 166

10. **Disciplinary Literacies in the Content Areas** 174

Teaching Disciplinary Literacies 174

Charting Plant Growth in a 4th-Grade Bilingual Classroom 176

Researching Japanese Internment in a
Culturally Diverse 10th-Grade History Class 182

11. **Teacher Inquiry and Praxis** 190

One Teacher's Pedagogical and Theoretical Shifts Over Time 190

Teacher Inquiry 193

Concluding Thoughts: Praxis and Useful Inquiry 197

References 199

Index 213

About the Author 226

Foreword

Lara Handsfield begins this remarkable text with a reference to Marge Piercy's iconic poem, *To Be of Use*. She uses Piercy's words to convey her own commitment to rendering theory useful to educators, to support teachers to understand and communicate what they do in educational contexts through the use of theory, and also to support teachers to undertake change in their practice in guided and principled ways.

This is not a new refrain in the education literature. In 1904, John Dewey decried teachers' lack of intellectual independence and urged teachers to take intellectual responsibility for their practice—a responsibility that could only be assumed if teachers experienced the study of theory *and* practice in their preparation. Scholars of teacher education continue to wrestle with the relationship between theory and practice, and teacher education programs struggle to redesign programmatic features and specific forms of pedagogy to acknowledge and build on the integrated nature of theory and practice.

The powerful approach that Lara has used (in Part I of this volume) to demonstrate this integration is to foreground instructional strategies and curricular models and use them as entrées for illustrating theories and epistemologies. This approach brings a richness to (1) the abstract principles that describe and explain how reading, writing, and oral language develop in home, school, and community contexts and (2) the real-world experiences of teachers and students. The catholic approach that Lara has taken to the theoretical frameworks that she presents in Part I befits the complexities of literacy learning and development. Lara helps the reader understand that the value of any particular frame cannot be judged in the absence of understanding the knowledge and skill one aspires to teach or cultivate and the role of context in that process of acquisition and development.

The strength of Part I of this volume is the access it provides to conceptual tools that have the power to facilitate teachers' framing and interpretations of practice; but it is in Part II that Lara leads the reader through the process of seeing how the conceptual tools can be applied as solutions for negotiating the dilemmas that arise at the intersection of teaching, learning, and curriculum enactment.

In Part II, Lara presents a broad range of cases that support educators in examining teaching, learning, and classroom dynamics together using the multiple perspectives and theoretical frameworks to which the reader was introduced in Part I. As a teacher educator, I am especially appreciative of this resource because the vignettes make it possible for the learning community that is my class to access rich and complex accounts that mirror what happens in classrooms, but may not, in fact, be experienced in practicum placements. The cases are current, multidimensional, and often poignant; they interweave the conceptual tools presented in Part I, which are general in nature, with practical tools that are specific, concrete, and designed for enactment in classrooms.

Furthermore, these cases support the development of visions of classrooms and visions of teacher practice. This is important because we know that one of the most robust predictors of teachers' commitment to teaching is a sense of efficacy; that is, a belief that one can make a positive difference in what happens to children and youth. Providing prospective as well as in-service teachers with generative visions can support educators in surfacing and exploring their beliefs, examining assumptions that underlie their practice, and provide a means for educators to address gaps between their aspirations and specific practices.

I close this foreword with another reference to Piercy's poem in which she extolls the merits of people who "strain . . . with massive patience . . . to move things forward" (1982, p. 106). Lara has done just this, resulting in a text that supports the process of taking action in practice; action that is informed and justified by thought, as advocated by Freire (1970) when he called for praxis. In these times, when teachers are maligned in both the popular press and professional literature and subject to the vagaries of the sociopolitical contexts in which education unfolds, a volume such as this offers the potential to provide intellectual freedom in the complex work of teaching.

—Annemarie Sullivan Palincsar

Acknowledgments

As Bakhtin (1981) argued, thought and language are dialogic, constructed from multiple voices that are in constant dialogue with one another. This book is truly a fusion of many voices—those of teachers and theorists who have influenced my thinking and teaching over the years, and those of people who assisted me more directly in writing this book. I am indebted to all of them.

First and foremost, I wish to recognize the teachers—past, present, and future—enrolled in Illinois State University's Masters in Reading program. Their willingness to venture into new theoretical and pedagogical territory, coupled with their continual questioning of the value of different theoretical ideas for informing and explaining real classrooms with real students, inspired me to write this book. In particular, I am grateful to those who took TCH 462 (Connecting Literacy Theory, Research, and Practice) with me in spring 2015. Not only did they serve as guinea pigs, using a draft version of this book as their course text, but they did so without an index and without complaint. Their thoughtful commentary and feedback were invaluable in my process of revision and editing.

Special thanks also go out to the many teachers who have invited me into their classrooms over the years. I especially want to recognize Kay Coulson and Patricia Valente. Their classroom practices are spotlighted in Chapter 9, but their influence on me as an educator is vast. Their pedagogical intellect, care, and energy have touched the lives of so many children and families, including my own. The world is simply a better place because of their dedication and skill.

In addition, I want to express my gratitude to Tom Crumpler, Marcelle Haddix, George Hruby, and Terry Husband, whose thoughtful contributions on specific theories of reading and literacy and instructional practices directly enrich the ideas expressed within this book. Their voices expand the theoretical and pedagogical possibilities that I have tried to highlight in the ensuing pages.

I would like to thank several individuals who provided critical feedback on drafts of chapters and vignettes, as well as mind-bending theoretical conversation and debate. These include my colleagues in the collective brain that is my writing group: Christopher Hansen, Carolyn Hunt, Sonia Kline,

Kara Lycke, Deborah MacPhee, Sandra Osorio, Jay Percell, and Sherry Sanden. Linda Haling provided me with indispensable suggestions regarding the book's structure and format and was a voice of constant encouragement in my initial conceptualization of this book. And of course, the thoughtful comments, advice, and support of Emily Spangler at Teachers College Press were invaluable as I navigated the writing process. She aided me during every step of the process, from elements of writing as mundane as book length and securing permissions to substantial aspects of my writing, such as conceptual and discursive cohesiveness. Thanks also to John Bylander at Teachers College Press, whose ability to attend to the finest details of text and the big picture simultaneously is frankly amazing.

I am endlessly grateful to my family—my global positioning system. When I am with my husband, Craig Lundstrom, and my children, Evan and Nate Lundstrom, I know who and where I am. Craig has been as patient as they come, providing me with endless love and encouragement from this book's initial conception through the publication process. All the while, Evan and Nate provided boundless wit, humor, and inspiration, which surely found their way into the pages that follow.

But perhaps above all, I am grateful to this book's readers. Just as theory is meaningless without practice, a book may as well not exist without its readers—people willing to pick it up and make something out of it; to put it to use. So ultimately, I am thankful to this book's readers, whose voices breathe life into my words.

CHAPTER 1

Introduction

I would like this book to be read as an homage to classroom practice—the messy, difficult, artful, and concrete work of teachers. This is no simple task, however, given that the notion of theory in the popular imagination, and particularly in the educational community, rarely evokes images of real everyday practice. On the contrary, theories are more often viewed as things akin to museum artifacts—on display and decontextualized from the everyday practices and phenomena from which they were derived. In her poem *To Be of Use*, Marge Piercy (1982) writes in a similar way about cultural artifacts such as Hopi vases and Greek amphoras. While they may sit on display in museums, "you know they were made to be used" (p. 106). Indeed, theories are also made to be used. They may be used to inform or understand practice, but they are also meant to be practiced themselves and oftentimes reshaped in the process to better suit the contingencies of real students, real classrooms, and everyday classroom life.

The purpose of this book is to introduce readers to an array of salient, influential, and potentially influential theories of reading and literacy and to illuminate and invite connections between these theories and classroom practices. In the process, I hope to resituate theory as a part of everyday practice. Like teaching, theory is made to be used and is worth doing well. This is particularly relevant for today's political context, which is largely demarcated by standardizing curricular policies and increasing scrutiny over teachers' expertise. While this is not a simple problem, the practice of theory and the theorization of practice create frameworks for communicating why students and teachers do what they do in the classroom, how they might do things differently, and how teachers might adjust their theories along the way.

CONCEPTUALIZING THEORY

The term *theory* is operationalized in myriad ways, which complicates adherence to any one definition. Most people, for example, are familiar with the theory of evolution or have heard of theoretical physics. These uses of the term invoke particular scientific theories, which represent the most

likely explanations for natural phenomena and become the subjects of experiments designed to test for falsification. Yet, in our everyday lives, we
often use the term *theory* to refer to abstractions or ideal (rather than practical) circumstances or situations rather than how things actually are. For
example, a friend of mine who is a teacher once remarked in frustration, "In
theory I'm a professional, but I rarely get to decide what or how I teach!"

In education, theory evades easy definition. Its uses range from the
colloquial, as in my friend's comment, to explicit references to theories of
teaching and learning, such as when a teacher states that she uses "a constructivist approach to teaching math, grounding instruction in inquiry and
the use of manipulatives." And sometimes teachers use theory to articulate
their thinking regarding why students behave in particular ways and what
they might do about it. Consider the following conversation in the staff
room at an elementary school:

> *Amy*: I heard Bryson got in trouble earlier this morning. What
>   happened?
> *Collette*: You know, this has been happening during independent
>   reading. He reads, or maybe just looks at his books for a little
>   while, but then he's flicking his pencil around, poking another kid,
>   or getting up and talking to his friends. It's wearing me down.
> *Amy*: Why do you think it's happening?
> *Collette*: I don't know, but I'm thinking it might be because he's not
>   finding books that are engaging and easy enough for him to read
>   by himself. I know he's nuts about NASCAR, so maybe tomorrow
>   I'll bring in some of my son's NASCAR books. He has some that
>   are at different levels. We'll see.
> *Amy*: Well, let me know what happens. I have a couple of kids doing
>   the same thing.

This is a process of inquiry in which two teachers identify a problem,
theorize about its cause, and articulate a plan for testing the theory. Teachers engage in this kind of inquiry multiple times a day as they come to know
their students and craft instruction based on their students' strengths and
needs.

In addition to variations in everyday applications of theory in education, its use among literacy researchers has changed over the past several decades. Dressman (2007), for example, explains how uses of theory in literacy
research reports have shifted from specific propositions about phenomena
to be tested empirically and quantifiably (e.g., experimental studies testing
Kintsch's 2013 construction–integration model of reading comprehension),
to framings, or sets of assumptions, to inform research and practice (e.g.,
using transactional/reader response theory as a framework for designing
a study about an afterschool book club for young adolescents). This shift

means that scholars who frame their research according to different theories may talk about and use theory quite differently from one another.

My own understanding of theory, and the one operationalized in this book, is similar to that of Unrau and Alvermann (2013): "Theories are propositional networks commonly used to help members of a community of researchers and practitioners understand, explain, and make predictions about key concepts and processes in a particular field of study" (p. 49). From this angle, theories have both explanatory and predictive value for phenomena and practice. This definition is also broad enough to include the different uses of the term identified above. Importantly, however, theories are not neutral or devoid of ideology. Rather, they involve "pragmatic commitments" that ground our approaches to everyday problems and events (Kamberelis & Dimitriadis, 2005, p. 15). These pragmatic commitments include assumptions regarding what counts as learning and what counts as "literacy"; where learning and literacy occur (e.g., in the head or in dialogue with others); how we determine whether progress in learning is occurring and how learning and literacy are measured; and where to look when we believe learning is not occurring to a desired degree.

[margin note: Authors def. of theory]

And yet, we do not always make our theoretical grounding explicit. Collette's ideas regarding her student's behavior reveal tacit assumptions about the interrelationship between engagement, reading development, social behavior, and the teacher's role in that relationship—assumptions that are not shared by all. And these assumptions matter not just for the sake of knowledge (knowing the foundations of our practices or how our practices invigorate or animate particular theories) but also because considering the assumptions that anchor our practices can support efforts to map out new practices for the benefit of our students.

Moreover, how we understand what is happening in any given instance of practice (how a reader makes sense of a given text) or set of practices (how a teacher guides middle school students in selecting books for independent reading) also depends on what we consider to be the phenomena of interest within those practices. In the case of how a reader makes sense of text, the phenomenon of interest could be how the student draws on her first language as she decodes text in her second or third language. Alternatively, it could be how she positions herself as a particular kind of reader among her peers when she argues for her interpretations of a text. What we deem to be important, indeed what we are even *able* to see, can depend on our theoretical lens. If you view reading as a process of decoding, then you will likely attend to students' strategies for identifying unknown words in a text, but you may be less likely to notice how students use their peer-group status to get their opinions heard during read-aloud time.

With these understandings in mind, to talk about theory without considering practice would not make sense. Like many museum artifacts—everyday objects such as cooking pots and arrowheads that have been exhumed from the earth—theory does not exist for itself or solely for the admiration of those who generate it. Theories are made to be used. To be sure, theory is not only practiced but *requires* practice to live and thrive. Similarly, practice does not exist in a vacuum, and so it is never devoid of theory. My practice of asking students to engage in conversations about texts to generate interpretations animates my theoretical assumption that meaning is socially mediated and constructed. The texts and assessments we use, the tasks we ask students to complete, and the kinds of questions we ask all privilege, negate, reflect, and animate different theories of literacy, teaching, and learning. And because different theories and practices attend in different ways to the strengths and needs of diverse students, our pedagogical choices are tied up with issues of power and equity, including whose ideas are heard, whose languages are valued, and so on.

always applying theory

Some literacy educators refer to the connection between theory and practice as *praxis*, a reciprocal relationship between practice and reflection (Freire, 1970; Morrell, 2008). Likewise, theory undergirds policies that impact literacy instruction, although, as with practice and theory, the theoretical assumptions guiding policy are seldom made explicit. Such policies may include national or statewide initiatives or legislation, such as the Common Core State Standards (CCSS) or Reading First, or more locally generated policies (e.g., a district's decision to block particular websites in schools). While I do not focus on policy, it surely impacts the curricula and instructional practices highlighted in this book, and so I remark on policy where relevant.

praxis

Despite the interdependence of theory and practice, popular discourse in education often sets theory apart from practice. What is more, theories themselves may be viewed in isolation from one another. Why is this? Perhaps there is some value in distilling an idea or a theory into something self-contained, tidy, and conceptually manageable. For people relatively new to thinking about theory, constructing such conceptual boundaries may ease the learning process, facilitating differentiation between multiple ways of understanding the practice and teaching of reading and literacy. And the false dichotomy between theory and practice likely makes ideas about teaching and learning easier to package and market to a broad audience in the form of professional texts or curricula. Here we might point toward the "methods fetish" in education—the valuing and privileging of practice over reflection and analysis, or praxis.

Despite the conceptual, political, and economic benefits of compartmentalizing theory and practice, it is not all that helpful for moving the field forward. Sociologist Pierre Bourdieu (Bourdieu & Wacquant, 1992) criticized the tendency of researchers to adhere to particular theories because of their eloquence and tidiness, but abstracting them from the processes they were meant to explain. He called this the "scholastic point of view," which is unresponsive to the messiness of everyday practice. To treat theory as separate from practice is to objectify it and place it on a shelf, where it exists to be admired but never touched. In this book I try to dismantle this artificial theory–practice divide. I invite readers to *touch* and *play with* theory.

SITUATING PRAXIS WITHIN A CONCEPTUAL CONTINUUM

In framing different theoretical influences on methods of literacy research, Kamberelis and Dimitriadis (2005) distinguish between strategies, models, theories, and epistemologies. Here I adapt their continuum to map out relationships between theories of reading and literacy and classroom practices. At the most concrete level are *instructional strategies*—pedagogical techniques to engage students, develop key understandings, initiate thoughtful discussions about texts, create and maintain classroom order, assess students' progress, and so forth. Instructional strategies are often of primary concern to teachers seeking specific ideas for classroom engagements (Kamberelis & Dimitriadis, 2005) and imply or call forth material tools and resources. For example, shared writing may require a Smartboard or an easel with chart paper and pens. Teachers may feel constrained by the tools and resources available to them and therefore may shy away from particular strategies or adjust them accordingly (e.g., rearrange furniture or work in small groups instead of independently because only eight laptops have been fully charged).

Curricular models are less specific than strategies. While the terms *theory* and *model* are often used interchangeably, they indicate different levels of abstraction, with models referring to more concrete representations of processes or practices (Alvermann, Unrau, & Ruddell, 2013). In general, models can be understood as social or scientific representations of phenomena that reflect theories, or that inform how practices might be carried out, and often appear as visual representations (e.g., a drawing or a 3-D model of a solar system). However, it can be helpful to distinguish between theoretical models (representations of theories, such as a diagram representing the storage of short- and long-term memory in the brain) and curricular models (e.g., reading workshop, which may include various instructional configurations). While the former is meant to represent a phenomenon as explained by a theory, curricular models represent potential practices as informed by a theory. Curricular models are often presented as steps or guidelines, or even as rigid templates for teaching, and are often the focal point of specific policies and initiatives. However, in everyday practice, educators typically adapt curricular models and their associated instructional strategies to suit their professional context and students. In this sense, they can be thought of more as guides or tools than tidy representations of reality (Kamberelis & Dimitriadis, 2005).

A *theory* is more abstract than a model and attempts to explain or predict phenomena in the world. Some readers may be familiar with well-known and influential theories of reading and literacy, such as schema theory, transactional/reader response theory, or critical literacy theory. Terms such as constructivism and poststructuralism may also be used to refer to theories. However, many would consider these to be epistemologies (see below) rather than theories. Morphologically speaking, the -ism suffix may indicate a broader philosophical frame that is characteristic of epistemology, although this is by no means a steadfast rule.

Epistemology is a branch of philosophy focused on the nature of knowing and how people come to have knowledge. According to Cunningham and Fitzgerald (1996), epistemology's concern with what knowledge is valued, where it is located, and how it is acquired makes it relevant to educators because strategies, models, and theories are intimately tied to epistemologies. While I do not spend significant time describing the epistemological underpinnings of the theories and practices in this book, I do offer inset epistemological discussions in Part I for readers interested in the more philosophical aspects of praxis.

Theories, then, can be understood as nested within a continuum from broad epistemologies to specific and contextualized instructional strategies. Figure 1.1 illustrates how different epistemologies, theories, curricular models, and instructional strategies may be mapped out in relation to one another. Keep in mind, however, that such relationships are tentative at best because they may shift in practice. For example, readers' theater may be implemented by providing students with scripts to read and asking them to practice reading the scripts aloud and with inflection to the point of mastery. Alternatively, students may be asked to read and reread a portion of a book with a significant amount of dialogue to make the characters' words come alive and then discuss how they interpreted characters through their voices. In both cases, repeated readings would occur, and students' fluency development would be supported. However, these two instantiations of readers' theater map onto very different theories and epistemologies of reading. That said, the purpose of such a continuum is not to chart definitive relationships between epistemologies, theories, models, and strategies. Rather, it is to orient readers as they consider how elements along the continuum may connect to one another in everyday practice.

Another risk of such a continuum is that it suggests concrete boundaries between different theories, between epistemologies and theories, and between curricular models and instructional strategies. Humans have a natural tendency to impose borders on their perceptions and conceptions of the world, even when those borders are not really there to begin with (something that optical illusions make clear to us). As Davis (2004) explains, such conceptual distinctions are "vital for our processes of self-definition and collective identification—to our having a reality" (p. 7). That said, the continuum I have presented should be viewed as a fluid tool for conceptualizing praxis rather than as a metric for delineating steadfast distinctions between these concepts. And to be clear, the continuum also reflects my own theoretical orientation toward literacy and teaching and has influenced how I wrote this book.

Figure 1.1. Continuum of Epistemologies, Theories, Models/Approaches, and Strategies*

	Examples
Epistemologies	Radical empiricism, cognitive constructivism, social constructivism, critical social science, poststructuralism
Theories	Grain size theory, stage theories, schema theory, transactional/reader response theory, new literacy studies, critical sociocultural theory, critical race theory
Curricular models	Heggerty's Phonemic Awareness Curriculum, transactional strategies instruction, *Units of Study for Primary Writing* (Writing Workshop), participatory action research
Instructional strategies	Daily Oral Language, repeated reading, directed reading-thinking activity, miscue analysis, readers' theater, process drama

*Continuum adapted from Kamberelis and Dimitriadis (2005), with examples.

CONTENT AND ORGANIZATION OF THIS BOOK

My own theoretical inclinations lean toward social constructionism (see Chapter 5). Rather than viewing knowledge as simply out there to be discovered, I view it as socially constructed in the context of day-to-day interactions and practices. I understand teaching and learning as socially and historically situated practices that cannot be separated from relations of power. Accordingly, teachers and students negotiate relations of power via their everyday practices in the classroom. My theoretical commitments prompt me to ask particular questions in my own research, particularly as related to literacy instruction in multilingual classrooms. They also impacted my choices about what theories and practices to include and exclude from this book and how to organize the chapters that follow.

Inclusions and Exclusions

I attempt to present a wide range of theories and practices and to illustrate how practices can be explained in multiple ways from different theoretical lenses. That said, readers will likely find theories in this book that are absent in other books on the topic, as well as some theories that are presented in detail elsewhere but are absent in these pages. Ultimately, my goal is to cover a breadth of theories and practices while also honoring the rapidly changing nature of 21st-century classrooms. For example, while grain size theory (Ziegler & Goswami, 2005) has not yet been taken up widely in reading research, I include it in Chapter 2 because it addresses phenomena (specifically, reading processes in different languages) that other information-processing theories do not. Thus, my decisions regarding which theories to include are partially driven by my own ideological commitment to understanding and supporting the academic success of an increasingly multilingual student population. While there are moments in the ensuing chapters where my ideological commitments may not appear front and center, there are others where they serve as more obvious filters for my discussion of theories and practices.

In addition, I include some theories that are considered less relevant to current reading and literacy research (e.g., Gough's information processing model of reading, and behaviorism) and that have been shown to be inadequate over the past few decades. My decision to include them is based not on their current explanatory power or their potential to inform quality instruction but rather on their historical significance and their enduring saliency in classrooms.

I also exclude topics identified by other researchers as theories of reading and literacy but which I view as phenomena. For example, Tracey and Morrow (2012) include family literacy and metacognition as examples of theories. These topics are undoubtedly of high importance to readers, and they merit discussion. However, because I understand them as phenomena that occur in contexts and processes of literacy development (and that could be theorized in a variety of ways), I include them within my discussion of theories rather than as theories in themselves.

Finally, I cluster some theories together in ways that may be considered unconventional. My own understanding of theory and practice as intertwined guided these decisions. While behaviorism and information processing have traditionally been considered distinct theoretical families, when we use curricula and everyday instructional practices as points of departure for theorizing, we see them sitting together quite comfortably (Davis, Sumara, & Luce-Kapler, 2008; Reynolds & Sinatra, 2005). Accordingly, I have placed them together in Chapter 2.

Introduction to the Chapters

I have organized this book differently from other books about theory, which are typically arranged solely according to historical periods or epistemological foundations. Instead, I have tried to structure this book in a way that foregrounds instructional strategies and curricular models and uses them as entryways into thinking about theories and epistemologies. In this way, I invoke all four elements of the continuum shown in Figure 1.1.

Each chapter in Part I (Chapters 2–5) includes a detailed description of a curricular model and then offers an overview of individual theories clustered around shared epistemological foundations that relate to the model. My inclusion of these grounding curricular models is not meant as an endorsement of those approaches but rather as practically grounded examples on which to base my introduction to the particular theories. In addition to these grounding curricular models, I follow descriptions of each theory with connections to additional curricular models and instructional strategies. Drawing in part on the work of Davis et al. (2008) and Hruby (2001), I differentiate between correspondence theories (Chapter 2), cognitive constructivist coherence theories (Chapter 3), social constructivist coherence theories (Chapter 4), and social constructionist theories (Chapter 5). I describe correspondence, coherence, and social constructionism in detail at the beginning of these respective chapters. Throughout the chapters in Part I are inset discussions that elaborate on specific topics. Some of these describe debates and confusions regarding common terms while some address epistemological matters and are targeted to readers who wish to delve more deeply into the philosophical and historical issues surrounding the theories presented. Still others highlight concepts connected to the theories and their potential impact on practice. At the end of each chapter, I include questions for praxis and suggested readings and resources. Table 1.1 offers an overview of Part I's organizational structure and content.

I have organized Part II according to areas of literacy instruction that teachers undertake in their classrooms. Chapters 6 through 10 each include two or three detailed vignettes that spotlight specific literacy practices and instructional strategies. I then analyze and critique each vignette from two to four theoretical angles, drawing connections back to the theories introduced in Part I. I conclude the book in Chapter 11 with a vignette illustrating how one teacher's theoretical and pedagogical understandings have shifted over a 10-year period. I then use this vignette as a springboard into discussions of teacher inquiry, including literacy coaching and classroom research. My purpose in this final chapter is to support readers in thinking about how they might inquire with colleagues as they adapt and refine their own practice and considering how they might put theory to use in the inquiry process.

Some of the vignettes in Part II are taken from my own research and teaching experiences while others are fictional amalgams of real instructional events and teachers I have worked with. Still others were solicited directly from practicing teachers and researchers. I have tried to include vignettes of literacy instruction and practice across the Pre-K–12 grade span. In presenting these vignettes, I assume that readers have a general familiarity with reading and literacy instruction. Although my intention is not to introduce readers to new practices or to advocate for particular practices over others, readers may likely encounter new ideas or become inspired to design new instructional engagements. It is my hope that the vignettes and theoretical discussions will prompt readers to view literacy practices and instruction in new and diverse ways, and spark critical conversations regarding their own practice and development as teachers. As in Part I, at the end of each chapter, I offer questions for praxis and suggested readings and resources.

Readers may choose to read this book in a linear fashion, and indeed, the sequence of chapters was determined in part with the cover-to-cover reader in mind. However, readers may decide to read chapters in any order, cross-referencing theoretical and practical discussions along the way. To this end, in the sidebar I cross-reference specific theories in Part I with practical vignettes and theoretical discussions in Part II. That said, reading the chapters in Part II prior to those in Part I may prove difficult for readers who are completely new to the theories presented. However you approach the book, it is my intention that you will take it up as a space of engagement in which the semantically separate things we call theory and practice animate one another in praxis. In the end, I hope that you will put this book to use.

Table 1.1. Theories Included in Part I of the Book

Chapter	Grounding Curricular Model	Theories Included, with Key References

2: Correspondence Theories	Heggerty's Phonemic Awareness Curriculum (www.literacyresourcesinc.com/what/about)	• Behaviorism (Watson, 1913; Skinner, 1954)
		• Information-processing theories
		  » Information processing model and the simple view (Gough, 1972; Hoover & Gough, 1990)
		  » Automatic information processing (LaBerge & Samuels, 1974)
		  » Interactive model (Rumelhart, 1994)
		  » Grain size theory (Ziegler & Goswami, 2005)
		  » Dual route cascaded model (Coltheart, 2005)
		  » Parallel distributed processing (Rumelhart & McClelland, 1986)
		• Stage theories of reading and writing (Ehri & McCormick, 2013; Gentry, 2000)

3: Coherence Theories, Take 1: Cognitive Constructivism	Transactional strategies instruction (Brown, Pressley, Van Meter, & Schuder, 1996; Pressley et al., 1992)	• Schema theory (Anderson & Pearson, 1984) • Psycholinguistic theory (Y. M. Goodman & K. S. Goodman, 2013; Smith, 1971) • The construction–integration model (Kintsch, 1988, 1998) • Transactional/reader response theory (Iser, 1978; Rosenblatt, 2004)
4: Coherence Theories, Take 2: Social Constructivism	*Units of Study for Primary Writing* (Calkins, 2003) and *Units of Study in Opinion, Information, and Narrative Writing* (Calkins, 2014)	• Sociocultural-historical theory (Rogoff, 2003; Wertsch, 1991) • Sociolinguistic theory (Gumperz, 1982; Heath, 1983) • Emergent literacy theory (Clay, 1972; Teale & Sulzby, 1986)
5: Coherence to Incoherence: Social Constructionist Theories	Youth Participatory Action Research (Y-PAR; Bautista, Bertrand, Morrell, Scorza, & Matthews, 2013; Kinloch, 2009; Morrell, 2008)	• Critical literacy theory (Freire, 1970) • New literacy studies (Street, 1984) • Multiliteracies/new literacies (Lankshear & Knobel, 2003; New London Group, 1996) • Critical sociocultural theory (Lewis, Enciso, & Moje, 2007) • Critical race theory (Ladson-Billings & Tate, 1995)

PART I

INTRODUCTION TO THEORETICAL FRAMES OF READING AND LITERACY

My goal in Part I is to provide an overview of theories that explain and inform literacy instruction. As these theories are brought to life in Part II, readers can refer back to Part I and explore additional readings and resources as desired. I begin each chapter with a brief introduction to the family of theories presented, followed by a description of a grounding curricular model anchored in those theories.

These grounding curricular models can be helpful for readers who are immersed in school contexts on a daily basis because they provide familiar frames of reference with which to consider specific theories. However, curricular models are by definition abstracted from real, everyday classroom life. They are thus only *idealized* representations—*potential* enactments or translations of theories. Borrowing from the words of the film character Captain Barbossa (played by Geoffrey Rush) in *Pirates of the Caribbean: The Curse of the Black Pearl* as he describes the pirate's manual, curricular models are not so much steadfast rules to abide by, but rather general "guidelines" that are best adapted to suit the contingencies of actual children, teachers, and professional contexts.

CHAPTER 2

Correspondence Theories

One of the most persistent assumptions in teaching and learning is that ideas that are learned are internalized; that is, that learning is a process of taking knowledge from outside the body (objective knowledge) and bringing it into the body, specifically into the brain (subjective knowledge). Of course, concepts do not actually move into the brain during learning in any sort of concrete way (Davis et al., 2008). Rather, we mimic, enact, or process information to create internal representations of the external world. However, one complicating factor challenging this assumption is that research in neuroscience has yet to identify specific models or structures in the human brain that represent knowledge from the external world (Davis et al., 2008). This is not to say that we do not generate mental representations of the world. However, we have no evidence that these representations are actual models that can be pinpointed or identified in our cerebral anatomy. Nevertheless, the metaphor of internalization is a powerful one, persisting in both academic circles and the popular imagination, and it underlies correspondence theories of learning and literacy.

Correspondence theories presume a direct correspondence, or match, between subjective knowledge, or how people understand the world around them, and objective reality (Davis et al., 2008). They are also grounded in empiricism—the idea that knowledge is based on sense data, or what observers can see, hear, touch, and so forth. Learning occurs when an individual's representation of a new concept (a mental representation of it or an observable action demonstrating it) corresponds to the real world (Hruby, 2001; Sumara & Davis, 2006). Some direct instruction approaches to teaching beginning readers, for example, rest on the assumption that phonics has been learned when students verbally reproduce sounds that correspond to specific letters as presented by the curriculum guide or the teacher. Similarly, successful comprehension would be thought to occur when a reader's understanding accurately matches, or corresponds to, the printed text.

Correspondence theories gained prominence within the burgeoning field of psychology beginning in the early 20th century (Kliebard, 1995). They construe learning as a psychological phenomenon, occurring in the head, although different correspondence theories hold different conceptions of how learning is evidenced in the classroom and in scientific studies of teaching and learning. Correspondence theories privilege the individual, view learning as a linear process of accumulating skills supported by highly controlled and structured engagements, and typically do not attend to broader social and cultural contexts. These characteristics are evident in Heggerty's Phonemic Awareness Curriculum.

GROUNDING CURRICULAR MODEL:
HEGGERTY'S PHONEMIC AWARENESS CURRICULUM

Michael Heggerty's Phonemic Awareness Curriculum is designed for kindergarten, 1st grade, and 2nd grade and is produced by Literacy Resources, Inc. (LRI; 2013). LRI is based in Illinois and may not be familiar to readers beyond the U.S. Midwest. Nevertheless, teachers who work with beginning readers will likely recognize its central features. The purpose of Heggerty's curriculum is to explicitly and directly teach phonemic awareness and the alphabetic structure of language in a whole-class setting. It is not intended to be a comprehensive instructional program. Rather, it is meant to comprise a small portion of daily literacy instruction in K–2 classrooms (approximately 12–15 minutes a day) and is organized into a delineated scope and sequence across 37 to 38 weeks. As stated on LRI's website, "The kindergarten curriculum covers all consonants, short vowels, digraphs, blends, and rime patterns. By comparison, the yellow book also goes into long vowels, R-controlled, special vowel sounds, and multisyllabic words" (www.literacyresourcesinc.com/what/about/). A stated goal of the curriculum is to make phonemic awareness instruction engaging and fun.

Citing research by literacy scholars who have examined word reading, dyslexia, and the neuroscience of reading (for example, Marilyn Adams, Keith Stanovich, and Sally Shaywitz), LRI maintains that phonemic awareness predicts later reading success, that phonological processing in the brain should be activated and developed to support such skills, and that all students will benefit from explicit phonemic awareness instruction (www.literacyresourcesinc.com/research/). As such, Heggerty's recommendation is that it be taught in whole-class contexts, with reinforcement or follow-up as needed in small groups. A typical lesson proceeds at a quick pace, with specified teacher prompts and student repetition. This is evident in a sample 1st-grade weekly plan available on the curriculum website, which includes an emphasis on "training" students to hear and manipulate sounds.

Key elements of the curriculum include highly controlled interactions with explicit teacher input and student response, and a tight, predetermined scope and sequence. The assumption underlying this design is that students will undergo incremental progression in which they experience success or mastery of one skill before moving on to subsequent skills. Phonemes are taught explicitly and as isolated components of language, decontextualized from everyday contexts of language use. These elements align with three different sets of correspondence theories: behaviorism, information processing, and stage theories of word recognition and word writing.

BEHAVIORISM

While behaviorism is no longer sufficient for explaining reading development and literacy practices, behaviorist principles still influence K–12 literacy instruction. If we are interested in understanding the impact of different theories on literacy instruction over time, then we should neither ignore behaviorism nor dismiss its influence in many classrooms. Perhaps the most recognizable feature of behaviorism is the concept of stimulus and response: the idea that human behavior is a response to environmental stimuli. This constructs learning as a passive, rather than intentional, process. Three behaviorist theories have impacted teaching and literacy instruction: connectionism, classical conditioning, and operant conditioning.

Connectionism, developed in the early 1900s by Edward Thorndike, proposes that learning is an automatic and incremental process of associating sense impressions (what we see, hear, feel, etc.) and impulses to action (behavior) (Hilgard, 1948; Thorndike, 1903). These connections are strengthened or weakened through patterns of stimulus and response. Thorndike also proposed the law of readiness, which states that connections and responses will vary in quality based on the learner's readiness to act. Readiness is the idea that connections and responses are supported when more simple tasks are presented incrementally prior to more difficult ones (Hiebert & Raphael, 1996). This is the same principle that underlies reading readiness programs. Thorndike was also influential in the development of intelligence and achievement testing (Kliebard, 1995; Thorndike, 1912), which persists more than a century later as standardized assessments of discrete skills permeate instructional policies and practices, such as No Child Left Behind (2001), Race to the Top, and the Partnership for Assessment for Readiness for College and Careers assessments of the CCSS.

Classical conditioning is typically associated with Pavlov's research in which he conditioned dogs to salivate at the ringing of a bell by associating the sound with the presentation of their food. Classical conditioning includes a focus on involuntary responses and association, such as the substitution of stimuli (e.g., a bell for food) to elicit responses (e.g., salivation). American psychologist John B. Watson advocated an approach to psychology using stimulus–response relationships to explain and predict human behavior. According to Walberg and Haertel (1992), he believed in the correspondence between the subjective and objective worlds and maintained that psychology should be the study of *behavior*, not the mind. Alongside Thorndike's connectionism, Watson's work moved empiricism to center stage in the fields of psychology and teaching.

Operant conditioning centers on the modification of deliberate (rather than involuntary) behavior by changing stimuli, that is, by *operating on* the environment. B. F. Skinner showed how behaviors can be *shaped* by reinforcing increasingly accurate responses (Walberg & Haertel, 1992). This involves controlling the environment through stimulus control and schedules of reinforcement. Reinforcement refers to a consequence that causes behaviors to increase in frequency while punishment causes a behavior to decrease. Extinction, the cessation of behavior, occurs when a particular response is no longer reinforced. For example, a student's undesired behavior would eventually stop if the teacher increasingly ignores the behavior instead of reinforcing it by providing the attention that the student seeks (e.g., when a teacher ignores a student who is talking out of turn).

Connecting Behaviorist Theories to Curricular Models and Instructional Strategies

Behaviorist teaching approaches were well received in the mid 20th century with their emphasis on observable and testable outcomes (Reynolds & Sinatra, 2005). Guided by the view that learning is the result of "repeated and controlled stimulation from the environment" (Alexander & Fox, 2013, p. 6) to prompt predictable student responses, reading came to be understood as a set of conditioned behaviors. Elements of behaviorist instruction include the parsing out of content into manageable chunks and basic sub-skills, requests for observable responses by students, repetition and drill to achieve mastery, and teachers' immediate feedback to students. According to Reynolds and Sinatra (2005), "The translation of the behaviorist ideal to reading instruction may have reached its pinnacle with the development of reading programs such as DISTAR [Direct Instruction System for Teaching And Remediation] and Reading Mastery" (p. 27) in the 1960s. DISTAR was designed as a basic skills program based on Bereiter and Engelmann's (1966) research with disadvantaged preschool children and was grounded on principles of operant conditioning. (Bereiter

> Elements of behaviorism are brought to life in the vignette "Put It on the Train!" (p. 104).

& Engelmann's study has been widely critiqued and disproven by socio-linguists [see, e.g., Labov, 1972] for using a methodology that was not attuned to the cultural and linguistic context of the community.) DISTAR included explicit and scripted instruction, ability grouping, quick-paced and efficient instruction, and frequent assessment. As with other direct instruction approaches, the teacher's role included clear oral prompting and providing immediate feedback to student responses.

As noted above, Thorndike's law of readiness has also influenced reading instruction, particularly the notion of reading readiness and the assumption that children must be taught specific sub-skills (e.g., phonemic awareness and letter–sound relationships) as prerequisites for learning to read. This approach has been criticized, however, by advocates of emergent literacy theory (see Chapter 4). An example of physical readiness might be a teacher who prompts his 1st-graders to get their mouths "ready to say the word" during reading instruction.

Several literacy curricula currently on the market apply behaviorist principles. Returning to Heggerty's Phonemic Awareness Curriculum, we note an emphasis on efficiency of instructional delivery with its quick pace and delineated and linear scope and sequence. These elements contribute to a highly controlled environment to support the transfer of knowledge from the external world (initiated with teacher-directed stimulus) to students' internal representations (evidenced through oral or physical response). There is also an emphasis on "training," which implies conditioning of specified behaviors reflective of operant conditioning. Finally, the curriculum stresses observable behaviors, or responses, rather than mental processes.

Many primary grades teachers in the United States will also be familiar with The Daily Five (Boushey & Moser, 2006), designed to help students participate in literacy activities in self-directed ways. Daily Five is a management system meant to accompany the authors' literacy curriculum, C.A.F.E. (Comprehension, Accuracy, Fluency, and Expanding vocabulary; Boushey & Moser, 2009). Activities students may choose from during Daily Five include read to self, read to someone, listening to reading, word work, and working on writing. One focus of Daily Five is increasing students' stamina to work independently by beginning with only 3 minutes and over several weeks building up to larger chunks of time. While also informed by information-processing and constructivist theories, Daily Five's behaviorist influences are not difficult to identify: The program emphasizes short intervals of practice and repetition, with an emphasis on incremental growth and stamina. Consistent with Thorndike's law of readiness and elements of operant conditioning, the goal of Daily Five is to sharpen, or condition, observable behaviors. Although the influence of behaviorism is still widespread, it became the object of intense criticism with the development of information-processing theories of reading.

EPISTEMOLOGICAL DISTINCTIONS AND CONNECTIONS WITHIN CORRESPONDENCE THEORIES

Behaviorism is grounded in the empiricism of John Locke and the assumption that only *sense data*, what can be perceived through the human senses, can spawn knowledge. Many American behaviorists, such as Thorndike, Watson, and Skinner, were radical empiricists, understanding learning as a mechanistic series of bodily responses. However, other philosophers and psychologists took exception to the reduction of human behavior to glandular functions and viewed mental activity as intentional, values-driven, and beyond observation. In 1920, a critic of Watson's wrote the following: "We can not believe that thought is 'highly integrated bodily activity *and nothing more*.' It seems rather that Watson has, either arbitrarily or blindly, cut the heart out of thought and asked us to be satisfied with objective, post-mortem observations upon its cold carcass" (Weber, 1920, p. 666).

Despite such concerns, behaviorism dominated psychology for decades, its radical empiricism carrying the banner of objective science. It was not until the mid-20th century that information-processing theories gained purchase, ushering in what has been termed the "cognitive revolution." However, the cognitive theories of the 1960s and 1970s represented a range of epistemological influences and perspectives on cognition, rather than a unified set of understandings. While they moved away from some aspects of behaviorism, early information-processing theories were not as "revolutionary" as cognitive constructivist theories (see Chapter 3; Reynolds & Sinatra, 2005). Early information-processing theories did not stray far from the assumption that learning involved stimulus and response. Rather, they sought to explain and model the cognitive processes *involved* in responses to stimuli (Cobb, 1990).

One assumption of information-processing theories that is shared with behaviorism is that learning (whether construed as behavior or cognitive processing) is universal—that it is essentially the same for all "normal" individuals. In other words, information processing and relationships between stimulus and response are understood as independent from culturally and historically grounded experiences and social contexts. This is consistent with the assumption that learners' subjective responses (whether overt behavior or mental models) correspond to input from the external objective world.

INFORMATION-PROCESSING THEORIES

While behaviorist theories in education saw their heyday in the 1950s, many psychologists turned their attention to trying to understand the unobservable processes occurring inside the head, and in the 1960s and 1970s, information processing gained purchase (Alexander & Fox, 2013). The distinction between observable behaviors and unobservable mental operations or representations as evidence of learning is the primary distinction between behaviorism and information-processing theories. Behaviorism centers on what individuals *do*, whereas information-processing theories attempt to explain how knowledge is represented *in the head* (Rumelhart, 1980). In other words, information-processing theorists focus on learning as a cognitive process. Although they were unable to directly observe how cognition works, psychologists began proposing detailed models to explain and represent these hidden processes. Research informed by information-processing theories turned to questions of attention, perception, memory, and how knowledge is stored and accessed during activities like reading. Importantly, not all cognitive theories are correspondence theories. For example, Bartlett (1932) and Piaget (1950) viewed the processing of information as experience driven, active, individualized, and dependent on learners' prior experiences (see Chapter 3).

Information-processing theories share with behaviorism the assumption that learning is a correspondence between the external world and internal representations (Davis et al., 2008) and that knowledge originates in the senses rather than the mind (Reynolds & Sinatra, 2005). For this reason, information-processing theorists address the processing of stimuli. They are also influenced by work in artificial intelligence. Indeed, the computer became the predominant metaphor for thinking and learning within these theories (Cobb, 1990).

Information-processing theories can be divided into three categories: bottom-up theories, top-down theories, and interactive theories. Bottom-up theories emphasize building up toward meaning as information passes through discrete stages from visual processing up toward meaning-making (Samuels, 2007). Top-down theories are informed by cognitive constructivist theories, discussed in Chapter 3, and view reading as guided by readers' experiences and prior knowledge. These understandings are then cross-checked with graphophonic and syntactic patterns. Interactive theories identify both bottom-up and top-down processes that occur simultaneously and that may compensate for one another during reading. Table 2.1 provides an overview of the three categories of information-processing theories.

The theories presented in this section include Gough's information processing model, automatic information processing, the interactive model, the dual route cascaded model, parallel distributed processing, and grain size theory.

Table 2.1. Types of Information-Processing Theories

Type of Theory	Theories and Theorists	General View of Reading
Bottom-up	• Information processing model and "the simple view" (Gough, 1972; Hoover & Gough, 1990) • Automatic information processing (LaBerge & Samuels, 1974)	Reading begins with the processing of letters and words and moves through discrete stages "up" toward higher-level processes and meaning.
Top-down (cognitive constructivist; see Chapter 3)	Psycholinguistic theory (Y. M. Goodman & K. S. Goodman, 2013; Smith, 1971)	Reading is a hypothesis-driven process in which meaning begins with readers' experiences and prior knowledge and then moves "down" to inform the processing of small-scale components of print and syntactic patterns.
Interactive	• Interactive model (Rumelhart, 1994) • Grain size theory (Ziegler & Goswami, 2005) • Dual route cascaded model (Coltheart, 2005) • Parallel distributed processing (Rumelhart & McClelland, 1986)	Reading occurs through both bottom-up and top-down processes simultaneously. These processes may compensate for one another in the processing of text.

Gough's Information Processing Model and The Simple View

Gough (1972) attempted to explain what occurs behind the eyeballs in the first second of reading. He identified the letter as the unit of recognition, arguing that word recognition is a "letter-by-letter process" (Samuels, 2006, p. 339). In the original model, the decoding process passes through discrete stages, beginning with visual perception and the conversion of visual stimuli into letter recognition (see Figure 2.1). From there, phonemic (sound) representations are attached to letter representations. These connected representations are stored in the "code book" and then recoded in the "phonemic tape," akin to a cognitive recording of the sounds corresponding to specific letters. Processing then proceeds to the search for word meanings stored in the lexicon. The "librarian" attaches the appropriate word meaning before the information is sent to the "primary memory," where words are ordered

Figure 2.1. Gough's Model of Information Processing

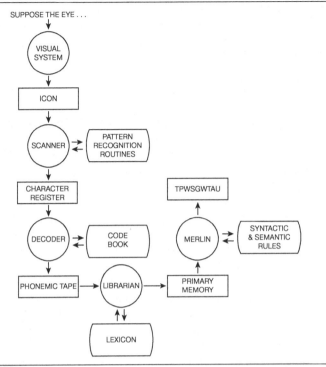

Note. Originally appeared in James F. Kavanagh and Ignatius G. Mattingly (Eds.), *Language By Ear And By Eye* (p. 345). Copyright © 1972 Massachusetts Institute of Technology. Used by permission of The MIT Press.

into sentences. Semantic and syntactic rules are then accessed to make sense of these sentences in the "Merlin," a reference to the unknown and presumably magical process of comprehension (Hoover & Gough, 1990). These sentences are then stored in "The Place Where Sentences Go When They Are Understood," or "TPWSGWTAU" (Gough, 1972), at which point reading has successfully occurred.

The labels "Merlin" and "TPWSGWTAU" are indicators of reading scholars' uncertainty regarding the processes involved in comprehension. These processes were construed as unknowable, even magical, because unlike perception and decoding, reading comprehension could not be easily explained with sense data. However, while the model does not elucidate comprehension beyond vaguely naming the process "Merlin," Gough and his colleagues argued that it accurately *predicts* reading comprehension (Hoover & Gough, 1990).

Gough later revised the model to account for the recognition of high-frequency words. In this revised and more interactive model, referred to as "the simple view" (Hoover & Gough, 1990), reading consists of two distinct components: decoding and linguistic comprehension (the comprehension of oral language). This theory maintains that while both components are necessary for successful reading, neither is by itself sufficient (Hoover & Gough, 1990).

Automatic Information Processing

LaBerge and Samuels's (1974) automatic information processing model uses the concept of automaticity to explain why experienced readers can successfully decode and comprehend while novice readers have difficulty (Samuels, 1994). The model outlines specific components through which information passes during reading. A central element of this model is attention—both external (indicated with orienting behavior toward tasks, such as looking at a teacher as he or she demonstrates an activity) and internal (directing cognitive attention to a task; Samuels, 1994). Automaticity is the ability to complete a task with minimal attention. The model also includes memory components: visual memory, which processes visual input from the text; phonological memory, where visual codes are processed as auditory representations; episodic memory, in which contextual details of specific events (e.g., who, where, and when) are processed; and semantic memory, where additional reader knowledge, or prior knowledge, is stored. Attention is thought to be particularly crucial for beginning readers learning a perceptual code, such as a letter or its corresponding sound, because it supports visual and phonological memory.

The model, then, is grounded in two assumptions. First, the brain can process only a limited amount of information at one time. As Samuels (2006) explains, "If all of the reader's attention is focused on decoding, comprehension cannot occur at the same time" (p. 336). Second, readers must both decode and comprehend the decoded text. While less proficient readers may be able to slowly decode, this process impedes comprehension because of the limited amount of time that previously decoded text remains in the reader's short-term memory.

In its original form, the automatic information processing model reflected a bottom-up sequence, starting with letters and words and then flowing "up" toward meaning, without considering how prior knowledge influences decoding (LaBerge & Samuels, 1974). The model was later revised to include a "top-down" route whereby a reader recognizes a word as a whole unit and sends the recognized word directly to semantic memory (Samuels, 1994), making the model more interactive.

Interactive Model

Rumelhart (1994) proposed a nonlinear interactive model that conceptualized text processing as involving multiple sources and routes. He was concerned that linear models, which assumed that information is processed in a unidirectional, step-by-step process, could not account for how syntax (sentence structure) and semantics (meaning) mediate the reading process. Instead, he argued that how readers perceive words depends in part on the syntactic and semantic contexts in which they are encountered. He suggested that four processors, or knowledge sources, work simultaneously during successful reading: syntactic knowledge, lexical knowledge, semantic knowledge, and orthographic knowledge (see Figure 2.2). Reading begins with perception, as graphemic input (print) enters into the visual information store. A "feature extraction device" then selects relevant information, which is sent to the "pattern synthesizer," where four processors converge in parallel to generate the most probable representation. Hypotheses regarding meaning can be initiated in any one of these processors or in multiple ones simultaneously.

According to Rumelhart (1994), "All that is interesting in the model takes place in the box labeled *Pattern Synthesizer*" (p. 733). He connects the complex parallel operations occurring in this part of the process to computer programs for speech recognition, one indication of the influence of artificial intelligence on information-processing theories (see inset).

Dual Route Cascaded Model

Like other models discussed so far, dual route models aim to identify the specific components involved in processing print and the routes through which information passes within and between those components. The dual route cascaded (DRC) model (Coltheart, 2005) is a computational model meant to simulate how humans process print into speech. The model computes

Figure 2.2. The Interactive Model

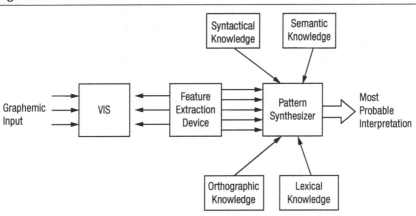

Note: Adapted from Rumelhart, 1994.

ARTIFICIAL INTELLIGENCE AND COMPUTER MODELS

At the time of the cognitive revolution, the principal metaphor for cognition was the computer (Cobb, 1990). As Reynolds and Sinatra (2005) explain, "The computer provided a model from which to study how sensory data passed through a cycle of mechanical processing and emerged as higher-level ideas" (p. 25). The notion of specific mechanisms, or mechanical devices being activated during reading is reflected in Rumelhart's (1994) interactive model through the use of terms like "pattern synthesizer" and "visual information store (VIS)." As Handsfield and Jiménez (2009) argue, "The agent of reading within such models is not a person but rather a device, organ, or machine (or, alternatively, the reader functions as a machine). Following this logic, teachers would be technicians, providing input in order to maximize output or output quality" (p. 162). The dominance of the computer metaphor was also consistent with the standardizing and normative discourses of the time regarding "normal" intelligence and cognitive functioning (Kliebard, 1995). From this view, reading problems are often viewed as "processing" problems that exist within the reader, sort of like a hardware glitch.

---

pronunciation from print through one of two paths: a lexical route (involving recognizable words and word parts) and a nonlexical route (involving letter–sound correspondences; Coltheart, 2005). As shown in Figure 2.3, the model appears to suggest three routes rather than two (the lexical semantic route, the lexical nonsemantic route, and the graphophonemic rule system route). However, the lexical semantic and lexical nonsemantic routes feed back into each other, forming one route.

The DRC model is referred to as "cascaded" because input cascades, like a waterfall, from one component to another. However, unlike a waterfall, these routes are not unidirectional. Instead, interactions occur between different layers and components of the model. Information can move forward from the orthographic lexicon to the phonological lexicon as well as back in the other direction (Roberts et al., 2011). This feedback process allows the computer to more quickly and accurately recognize common letter–sound patterns.

The lexical route involves accessing a representation of the orthographic lexicon of real words (e.g., familiar combinations of letters such as -ish or un-). The model's phonological lexicon is then activated, connecting the orthographic lexicon and phonological output lexicon (sounds associated with those letter sequences), subsequently activating the pronunciation of the word (Coltheart, 2005). After the orthographic lexicon, the word or word parts may be recognized in the semantic system and then fed into the phonological output lexicon. However, like other dual route models, the DRC model does

Figure 2.3. Dual Route Cascaded Model

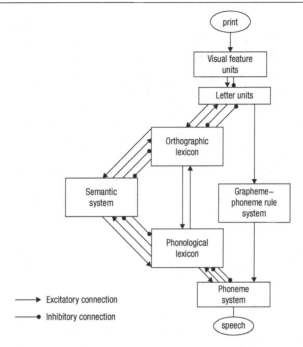

Note: Adapted from Margaret J. Snowling & Charles Hulme (Eds.), *The Science of Reading: A Handbook* (p. 12). Copyright © 2005 Blackwell Publishing. Used by permission of Wiley and Sons.

not include a route whereby words or word parts are directly recognized in a semantic processor (Roberts et al., 2011). The nonlexical route "applies grapheme–phoneme correspondence rules to the input string to convert letters to phonemes" (Coltheart, 2005, p. 13) and is the primary route for reading pseudowords. However, some pseudowords share orthographic characteristics with real words (e.g., "vose," "flane"). Thus, even though such nonwords are thought to be computed via the nonlexical route, the lexical route supports the process. Indeed, the word reading time for nonwords that share orthographic characteristics with real words ("ruke") is shorter than for nonwords that are less orthographically familiar (e.g., "rukt").

Research testing the DRC model suggests that it is a powerful predictor of both "normal" reading and "impaired" reading (dyslexia, in particular). However, the model is not meant to explain comprehension, and it has not yet shown applicability to multisyllabic words or multisyllabic nonwords (Coltheart, 2005). Such limitations lead critics to question whether computational models such as the DRC model can sufficiently represent natural cognitive processes.

Parallel Distributed Processing

In dual route models, one route must be selected and followed, although the processing of text may be influenced by components of other routes, as in the DRC model. Connectionist dual process models, on the other hand, explain text processing without rigid adherence to one route (Roberts et al., 2011). Building on Rumelhart's (1994) interactive model, theorists began to articulate not only the interactive qualities of text processing but also the compensatory capabilities of multiple processors when individuals face difficulties in reading. Influenced by computer-based models of speech recognition, Rumelhart and McClelland (1986) detailed a parallel distributed processing (PDP) model. In this model, input (e.g., printed text) is represented in four different processors through connections that are strengthened through repeated experience. These processors, which work interactively, include the orthographic processor, phonological processor, meaning processor, and context processor (see Figure 2.4).

The frequency with which connections are activated through repeated experiences with text contributes to automaticity, or fluent reading. As Adams (2013) explains,

> For the skillful reader, as the letters of a word in fixation are recognized, they activate the spelling patterns, pronunciations, and meanings with which they are compatible. At the same time, using its larger knowledge of the text, the context processor swings its own bias among rival candidates so as to maintain the coherence of the message. Meanwhile, as each processor homes in on the word's identity, it relays its progress back to the others such that wherever hypotheses agree among processors, their resolution is speeded and strengthened. (p. 789)

One important aspect of the model is the phonological processor's "back-up" capacity for the orthographic processor. While the orthographic processor receives basic perceptual data from print word recognition, the phonological processor serves as a support, particularly for words that sound familiar but have not yet been encountered in print. Word identification is facilitated as connections between letters and sounds are activated and interact with information from other processors. In this sense, the phonological processor, in concert with the orthographic and other processors, supports both fluent reading and comprehension.

Grain Size Theory

Like in the DRC model, the relative reliance on lexical and nonlexical routes, as well as syntax and semantics, is addressed by psycholinguistic grain size theory (Goswami, Ziegler, Dalton, & Schneider, 2003; Ziegler & Goswami, 2006). Grain size theory focuses on the size of phonological and

Figure 2.4. Visual Representation of the Parallel Distributed Processing Model

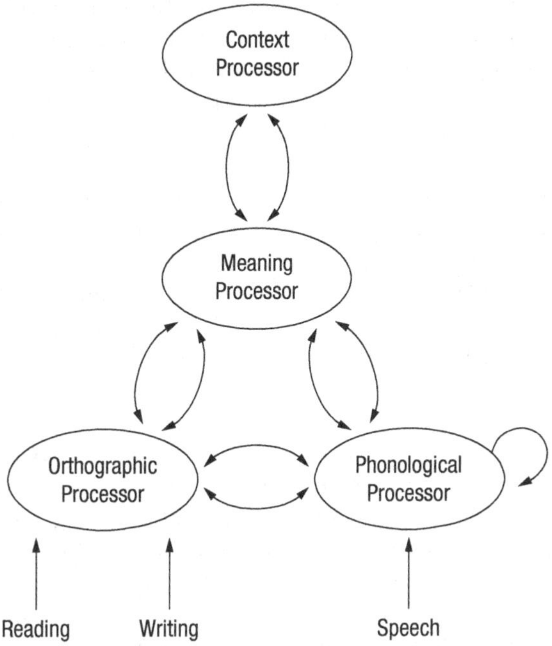

Note: Adapted from M. J. Adams, "Modeling the Connections Between Word Recognition and Reading," in D. A. Alvermann, N. J. Unrau, & R. B. Rudell (Eds.), *Theoretical Models and Processes of Reading* (5th ed., p. 1225). Copyright © 2004 International Reading Association. Used by permission.

orthographic units, such as syllables, onsets and rimes, and phonemes, and has been used to explain variations in word recognition across different languages (Roberts et al., 2011). For example, some languages (e.g., Spanish, Italian) are orthographically consistent. In Spanish, the phoneme /au/ (pronounced as -ow in English) can only be represented with the grapheme –au, as in the words *autor* ("author") and *miau* ("meow"). In other languages, such as English, smaller grain sizes of phonological units are less consistent and may be represented with more than one spelling pattern (Ziegler & Goswami, 2006). The phoneme /ow/ can be represented in English with -ow or -ou, and each of these may also be pronounced differently ("glow," "ghoul"). And consider the words "right," "write," and "rite." Not only are these homophones spelled differently, but these different spellings include two different representations of the words' endings, or rime units (-ight, -ite), and three different combinations of silent letters (-gh, wr-, -te).

Ziegler and Goswami (2006) argue that the DRC model is not sufficiently sensitive to the grain size of rime units and that "the prominent dual route architecture (i.e., two separate routes to pronunciation in the skilled reading system) may in fact only develop for English" (p. 434), which is less orthographically consistent than many other languages. Because of differences in grapheme–phoneme consistency at different grain sizes, beginning readers of different languages will use different sources to recognize words. As Ziegler and Goswami (2006) explain,

> Children who are learning to read more orthographically consistent languages, such as Greek, German, Spanish or Italian, rely heavily on grapheme–phoneme recoding strategies because grapheme–phoneme correspondences are relatively consistent. Children who are learning to read less orthographically consistent languages, like English, cannot use smaller grain sizes as easily, because inconsistency is much higher for smaller grapheme units than for larger units like rimes. (p. 431)

One pedagogical implication is that teaching approaches centered on small grain size, such as matching letters and sounds, may work fine for novice readers of languages with consistent phoneme–grapheme correspondences, like Spanish. However, the same method will be insufficient for beginning readers in less orthographically consistent languages like English. Recent research bears this out. Goldenberg et al. (2014) compared the relationships between phonemic awareness and Spanish reading skills in Mexican and U.S. students and found that phonemic awareness instruction was negligible in supporting children's reading development in Spanish. A child who already reads in Spanish and relies heavily on small grain size information, such as matching letters and sounds, may need to be taught how to draw on information available in larger grain sizes, such as letter patterns and whole word recognition, when reading in English.

Connecting Information-Processing Theories to Curricular Models and Instructional Strategies

There are many approaches to instruction and assessment grounded in information-processing theories. The emphasis in Heggerty's Phonemic Awareness Curriculum, for instance, is on phonological processing, and is grounded in part on connectionist principles and repetition to build up automaticity. Indeed, there is wide recognition that phonemic awareness is critical for reading development.

Information-processing theories are brought to life in two vignettes: "Put It on the Train!" (p. 104) and Using VoiceThread and Inquiry to Boost Vocabulary and Fluency (p. 124).

Information-processing theories also support an array of approaches to assessment and the identification of reading difficulties. Diagnostic Indicators

NEUROLOGICAL THEORIES OF LITERACY

GEORGE G. HRUBY, PhD, UNIVERSITY OF KENTUCKY

Three distinct camps use neuroscience research to explain literacy. The first is one that can be dismissed as entertaining gibberish but that neuroscientists politely call "neuro-myth" (Dekker, Lee, Howard-Jones, & Jolles, 2012). This is a grab bag of popular but false or nonsensical nostrums repeated in the media. Examples include "Some people are left-brained and other people are right-brained," "You only use 10% of your brain," "Brains are hard-wired" (presumably through genetic "blueprints"), "Male and female brains are different" (and that is why men and women are different), and "The brain lights up when you [fill in the verb] . . ." (suggesting that brain scans are photographs of someone's brain in action, rather than what they really are: well-tidied-up statistical charts based on multiple measures averaged across multiple subjects) (Helmuth, 2011). Given the complexity of the neurosciences, it is not surprising that simplistic claims about the brain abound (Weisberg, Keil, Goodstein, Rawson, & Gray, 2008). Nonetheless, insights-on-the-cheap are not well recommended.

The second approach to informing literacy theory with neuroscience findings is known as "brain-based," or "brain-compatible" education (e.g., Sousa, 2006; Wolfe & Nevills, 2009). This view makes rhetorical reference to brain research suggesting scientific evidence for instructional recommendations. Well intended, the allusions to research are usually vague, yet often employed to make sweeping claims about learning. The emphasis on the *brain* (rather than the nervous system) implies that reading is an interior ("in-the-head"), cognitive process.

This is not a new view of reading. The idea that literacy is cognitive in nature—and that the mind has a deep structure like a computer software program—was a productive view that dominated reading research in the 1970s and 1980s (Alexander & Fox, 2013) and continues to inform diagnoses of specific reading delays or difficulties in emerging readers (e.g., American Psychiatric Association, 2013, pp. 66–74). It is reductive, however, in that it does not sufficiently acknowledge the importance of social and cultural factors in children's language, literacy, and intellectual development (Gee, 1991), nor does it offer an adequate causative account of why literacy skills change over time in response to effective instruction (Hruby & Hynd, 2006).

Moreover, cognitive theories of reading were established well in advance of current neuroscience research, so the suggestion that they are the result of neuroscience is anachronistic, more a 21st-century rebrand of older theoretical idioms. Journalists may eagerly echo the cognitive metaphor that the brain is an information processor, but as it turns out, most neuroscientists are agnostic about nonbiological analogs of the nervous system, and the current research does not support hard claims for representational computation in neural architecture (see Fitch, 2014, and comments, especially Bowling, 2014; Bornkessel-Schlesewsky, Schlesewsky, & Small, 2014).

The third approach to research from the neurosciences to better understand literacy is found in formal reviews of the neuroscience research base. These reviews can be found both in the peer-reviewed neuroscience research journals, as well as, on occasion, those of literacy and linguistics (e.g., Hruby & Goswami, 2011). The technical sophistication of these journals can make for difficult reading, so this genre is less familiar to teachers and administrators.

These reviews caution that neuroscience on literacy and language processes, although impressive, is still quite formative, a point too often ignored in journalistic reporting. Neuroscience findings are correlational (and in multiple ways) rather than causal (Bennett & Miller, 2010). Subject sets (n) are small (Barch & Yarkoni, 2013; Button et al., 2013). Data are often analyzed in ways that have given neuroscientists pause (Vul, Harris, Winkielman, & Pashler, 2009). Typically, the neuroscience studies that have generated the most media attention have yet to be replicated or have failed to replicate in similar research designs (Fedorenko, Nieto-Castañón, & Kanwisher, 2013). There have been vigorous debates on neuroscience theory and method. And models of typical brain function and development in average people or within subgroups of interest to educators are only starting to emerge (most brain research has been done at selective research universities on right-handed, young adult, White male graduate student volunteers of above average intellect).

Still, the potential for a living systems theory of literacy is profound. Such a theory would emphasize that neurons are not wires but cells, living systems in their own right, growing in functional response to their cytological environment. Similarly, the nervous and endocrine systems are biological systems, and as such have evolved in species-specific ways to allow organisms to respond functionally to environmental conditions (Fitch, 2014). In the case of humans, these are uniquely social, symbolic, and linguistic environments, and they are historically situated in particular cultural and material conditions. Scholars have already identified the need for a nested model of development to connect social and cognitive literacy research findings (Purcell-Gates, 2012). Inspired by bioecological models of development (Bronfenbrenner & Morris, 2006), they lack only a realistic account of the neurobiological substrata that makes responsive development possible, clarifying how children as living entities come to be agents in their own socialization.

of Basic Early Literacy Skills (DIBELS), for instance, includes several diagnostic components, including one minute of oral reading and pseudoword reading. The merits of these approaches have been heavily debated (Riedel, 2007; Samuels, 2007). Nevertheless, theories such as Gough's information processing model and the DRC model would provide theoretical support for pseudoword reading in order to isolate issues that may arise in nonlexical components of text processing.

Repeated reading is an approach to supporting fluency that is supported by the automatic information processing model (LaBerge & Samuels, 1974). Repeated reading generally includes selecting a short passage or authentic text at a student's approximate instructional level and inviting the student to read and reread the text until he or she reads at a suitable rate and with appropriate inflection, emphasis, juncture, and so on. Limiting fluency assessments to one minute should be discouraged, as such a short period of time may prevent readers from building contextual understanding of the text, which could then be used to predict words while reading to support meaningful reading, including fluency (Rasinski, 2010).

Explicit instruction in grammar and morphology, including skills worksheets meant for repeated practice, are also consistent with information-processing theories because they reflect an assumption that learning to read is an accumulation of sub-skills and need not be taught using whole texts. However, these approaches are widely considered to be deficient because they do not engage meaning-making and higher-order thinking, and are often repetitive and tedious.

STAGE THEORIES OF WORD RECOGNITION
AND SPELLING DEVELOPMENT

While information-processing theories seek to explain the specific components involved in text processing, stage theories are meant to explain the *developmental* stages of alphabetic knowledge that beginning readers and writers move through (Baer, Invernizzi, Templeton, & Johnston, 2011; Chall, 1983; Ehri & McCormick, 2013; Gentry, 1982, 2000). Stage theories emphasize alphabetic knowledge, phonemic segmentation, and letter–sound correspondences.

Word Recognition

Stage theories of word recognition include the pre-alphabetic phase, the partial-alphabetic phase, the full-alphabetic phase, the consolidated-alphabetic phase, and finally the automatic-alphabetic stage (Ehri & McCormick, 2013). In the pre-alphabetic phase, word identification occurs not through alphabetic knowledge but rather through sight word reading from memory or by relying on context. Readers may also rely on logo-graphic elements of words, such as their shape or their length or visual cues in the environment (e.g., a logo associated with a company name; Mason, 1980). This is a typical stage for children in prekindergarten and kindergarten. As children move into the partial-alphabetic stage, they can begin using some alphabetic cues, such as the initial or final letter in a word, combined with context. Readers at this stage will begin to notice and identify some letters in words. However, they are not yet able to use letter–sound correspondences to decode unknown words (Ehri & McCormick, 2013).

As the name implies, in the full-alphabetic stage (characterizing readers between kindergarten and 2nd grade), readers have full knowledge of the alphabetic system, which they can apply to word reading. At this stage, readers rely heavily on their newfound alphabetic knowledge and may appear to be glued to the print while reading, progressing from slow to more rapid decoding (Chall, 1983). Readers may also be able to use analogy to read unfamiliar words (e.g., "bear" and "pear") and are also rapidly increasing their sight vocabulary.

In the consolidated-alphabetic stage, readers can combine larger units of letter–sound correspondences by recognizing spelling patterns. This has led some to call this stage the "orthographic phase" (Ehri & McCormick, 2013). Finally, in the automatic-alphabetic phase, readers will integrate orthographic and sight word knowledge and decoding to achieve high automaticity, appropriate rate, and accuracy in identifying words (Chall, 1983; Ehri & McCormick, 2013).

Spelling Development

Stage theories of word writing elucidate qualitative differences in children's spelling across a continuum of development and represent how children at each stage think about spelling. Gentry's (2000) model includes five stages. In the first, the precommunicative stage, children realize that spelling involves stringing letters together, but they do not match letters and sounds. In the semiphonetic stage, children understand that letters represent sounds. They can represent some sounds accurately, but word writing often includes one or two letters that accurately represent sounds and omits others. In the phonetic stage, matching letters to sounds takes on increased importance, and children begin representing most, if not all, sounds with letters. The transitional stage is characterized by the addition of morphological and visual strategies rather than invented spelling based on matching letters and sounds. Finally, the conventional stage involves consistent increases in children's repertoires of words they can spell, and their spelling becomes largely conventional. (See Baer et al., 2011, for additional perspectives on stages of spelling development.)

Rubin and Carlan (2005) built on Gentry's work to illustrate how monolingual Spanish children's and bilingual Spanish–English children's spelling stages may differ. Because Spanish is more regular than English in terms of letter–sound correspondence, there is no corollary to the transitional stage for monolingual Spanish-speaking children. Rather, they move directly from the phonetic stage to the conventional stage. For bilingual Spanish–English children, the stages are similar but also include unconventional spellings based on differences in letter-sound representations between the two languages. In the semi-phonetic stage, bilingual children may represent words the same in English and Spanish but read them differently.

Gentry (2000) characterizes his model as constructivist, grounded in the work of Piaget (1954). However, its focus on precise skills rather than the construction of meaning across whole texts, along with its close relationship to stage theories of word reading, also warrant its placement among correspondence theories.

Connecting Stage Theories to Curricular Models and Instructional Strategies

Repeated reading is a practice for developing automatic word recognition that is well supported by stage theories (Ehri & McCormick, 2013). Readers may also be familiar with Baer et al.'s (2011) *Words Their Way* approach, which emphasizes the need for children to gain repeated exposure to new words within meaningful contexts or texts rather than through memorization and isolated skill and drill activities. They also highlight the benefits of focusing on individual words and manipulating words and word features.

In addition, teachers informed by stage theories of word reading will often gear their instruction to the specific stages students are in. For example, teachers may remind students in the full-alphabetic stage of particular strategies that extend beyond letter–sound correspondence, such as looking for parts of a word that they might know or using spelling analogies (e.g., "nose," "rose," "hose"). These strategies may not be as necessary for students reading in Spanish, as their oral attempts to match letters and sounds may be more likely to produce recognizable and meaningful words. That said, monolingual Spanish-speaking children can still benefit from an analogy approach and building automatic word recognition.

> These vignettes bring stage theories to life: "Put It on the Train!" (p. 104), Using VoiceThread and Inquiry to Boost Vocabulary and Fluency (p. 124), and Small Moments Writing: Adaptation and Experimentation (p. 161).

Gentry's (2000) model is consistent with the recognition of invented spelling as a normal developmental phenomenon as children write in the classroom. That is, it supports arguments against correcting young children's approximations of conventional spelling (also see emergent literacy theory in Chapter 4). Gentry (2000) likened invented spelling to reading miscues in that they offer "'windows into the mind' (Goodman, 1979, p. 3) that allow the observer to assess and teach not only spelling, but also important aspects of phonemic awareness, phonics, writing, and other essential elements of literacy" (p. 318). As such, Gentry's model can be used to understand children's development with respect to phonics and spelling over time and to tailor instruction to meet students' developmental needs. For example, his model lends support to the practice of prompting young students in the semi-phonetic and phonetic stages to stretch out the sounds they hear as they attempt to spell unfamiliar words.

Instruction grounded in correspondence theories (behaviorism, information-processing theories, and stage theories) has been criticized on several grounds. Those working from social constructivist or social constructionist theories (Chapters 4 and 5) argue that the emphasis on sub-skills isolated from meaningful texts or contexts offers a limited framework that is insufficient for developing real world and higher-level literacy skills. Moreover, many teachers worry about undifferentiated or "cookie cutter" approaches. Coupled with the absence of active problem solving, and minimal use of high-quality children's literature, such approaches are no longer considered sufficient for fully supporting students' literacy development.

criticism of correspondence theories

CONCLUDING THOUGHTS

Information-processing theories are often considered part of the "cognitive revolution." But while that label may be embraced by cognitive scientists investigating unobservable mental processes, the view from the classroom prompts many to question how revolutionary such theories really are (Reynolds & Sinatra, 2005). In addition to the lack of neurological evidence, such theories fail to account for phenomena such as imagination and creativity (Davis, Sumara, & Luce-Kapler, 2008). Also, important differences between behaviorist and information-processing theories notwithstanding, their shared underlying assumptions explain why they may provide support to some similar instructional approaches and practices. As Davis et al. (2008) argue, they are "two sides of the same coin" and "both lines of thought seem to co-exist comfortably in most textbooks, curriculum guides, and classrooms" (p. 97). Indeed, the real revolution was arguably ushered in by the development of cognitive constructivist theories, which comprise Chapter 3.

QUESTIONS FOR PRAXIS

1. Think about children or students you know who have been diagnosed with a reading disability, such as dyslexia. How might some of the theories in this chapter explain the students' difficulties? In what ways might these theories be insufficient?
2. What kinds of skills instruction do you engage in in your own classroom? How do these animate or reflect correspondence theories of reading and literacy?

RESOURCES AND ADDITIONAL READINGS

Goodman, K. S. (2006). *The truth about DIBELS: What it is, what it does*. Portsmouth, NH: Heinemann.

Hruby, G. (2011). Commentary: Minding the brain. *Journal of Adolescent and Adult Literacy, 54*(5), 316–321.

Reading Rockets. (2014). Timed repeated readings. Retrieved from www .readingrockets.org/strategies/timed_repeated_readings

> This Reading Rockets site explains how to use repeated readings to support students' automatic word recognition, fluency, and comprehension.

Prior, J. "A is for apple": Building letter-recognition fluency. Retrieved from www.readwritethink.org/classroom-resources/lesson-plans/apple-building-letter -recognition-132.html

> This lesson uses the KiddoNet Alphabet website to support young children's automaticity in letter identification through repeated practice.

Reutzel, R. (2015). Early reading research: Findings primary-grade teachers will want to know. *The Reading Teacher, 69*(1), 14–24. doi:10.1002/trtr.1387

CHAPTER 3

Coherence Theories, Take 1
Cognitive Constructivism

Coherence theories differ from correspondence theories in that they reject the expectation that subjective, or internal, knowledge will bear a direct correspondence to objective, or external, reality. While correspondence theories assume a division between knowers and knowledge, coherence theories view knowledge and truth as inseparable from the knower (Davis et al., 2008). That is, objects, phenomena, events, and texts do not have inherent meaning; rather, their meanings depend on knowers and their interpretations of them.

Language may be understood in similar ways. According to linguist Ferdinand de Saussure (1959), the words, or "signifiers," we use to describe objects, phenomena, and events in our world are not independent of the ideas we harbor about those things. Saussure referred to those ideas about things as the "signified." In other words, a word is a sign for something rather than a direct representation of it. For Saussure, language was viewed as a "set of relations rather than as a set of world-referencing units" (Sumara & Davis, 2006, p. 39). This means that the relationship between words and their ideas is arbitrary. There is nothing inherent in a chair, for example, that requires it to be called "chair." Indeed the object is signaled in other languages with different words (e.g., *silla* in Spanish, *uija* in Korean, *Stuhl* in German) or characters (e.g., 椅 in standard written Chinese). There is no inherent reason that an object with four legs made for a person to sit on could not be called a "potato" or a "blunk." What is more, in a different context, the word "chair" can refer to the head of a committee or a position of authority.

Nevertheless, while the relationship between words and the objects or phenomena they reference may be arbitrary, their social uses and understandings do not arise out of nowhere. Imagine that you have been invited to dinner at the house of an acquaintance. The table is set, and it is time to sit down for dinner. Most guests will likely understand that the chairs are for sitting in (regardless of what they are called—"chairs," *sillas*, *Stuhle*, "potatoes," or "blunks"). However, *where* and *when* to sit may not be so obvious. Do you choose your own seat? If it's a buffet, you might, but if it's a formal dinner, you might wait to be told where to sit and sit down only after the host is already seated. And if this dinner is in a different country or cultural context, you may feel completely lost as to when and where to sit. This highlights how the meanings we attribute to signifiers are tied to context, experience, history, and culture. We only come to understand objects, phenomena, ideas, and the words we use to reference them by examining how they are *used* and how people make sense of them. This principle lies at the heart of coherence theories.

Literacy researchers and teachers operating from coherence theories are interested in how people make sense of and with texts. From this view, reading and writing processes do not involve the replication or transfer of text into corresponding or matching mental representations or behaviors. Rather, they involve the construction of meaning through interactions between teachers, texts, and students' own understandings and experiences. Coherence theories suggest that different elements within a system (whether it be a society's laws, species in an ecosystem, or relationships between a reader's experiences and events that occur in a novel she is reading) *cohere*; that is, they make sense, or *work*. Davis et al. (2008) argue that

> The major point of departure of these coherence theories from earlier theories of learning is that they are organized around the assumption that what really matters is internal coherence. For a system to be viable, its parts must be compatible with one another—and it really doesn't matter if they match, reflect, represent, model, or otherwise correspond to a realm beyond the system. (p. 99)

Emphasis is placed on whether or not each individual reader has *constructed* meaning from the text, not whether each reader's understanding matches the text exactly. This view underlies constructivism—and specifically, cognitive constructivism.

FOUNDATIONS OF COGNITIVE CONSTRUCTIVIST THEORIES

One of the thinkers most commonly associated with cognitive constructivist theories is Jean Piaget. A primary tenet of Piaget's (1954) work is that learning is experiential. Through experience, people internalize new knowledge, a process that involves accommodating and assimilating knowledge into mental structures, or schemata. For Piaget, "learning was the continuous process of adjusting interpretations in order to keep them coherent with one another" (Sumara & Davis, 2006, pp. 39–40). Cognitive constructivism is also consistent with the work of the American philosopher John Dewey. Like Piaget, Dewey emphasized experiential learning and inquiry. He is considered a constructivist because his pragmatist philosophy embraces the idea of internal coherence. From a pragmatic view, the primary criterion for whether interpretations of the world are viable is if they cohere within a given system (Hruby, 2001).

Although cognitive constructivist coherence theories do not recognize direct correspondence between subjective understandings and objective phenomena, they continue to situate learning as an individual cognitive phenomenon—occurring behind the eyeballs—albeit connected to lived experience. One characteristic that sets cognitive constructivist theories apart from information-processing theories is attention to the mind and *intentional* cognitive activity. These ideas are brought to life through a variety of classroom approaches. A common thread among these approaches is an emphasis on individuals' cognitive processes as they bring their own experiences and understandings of the world to bear on texts. This is evident in transactional strategies instruction.

GROUNDING CURRICULAR MODEL: TRANSACTIONAL STRATEGIES INSTRUCTION

metacognition

What often passed as comprehension instruction was actually a process of assigning texts and assessing students' understanding of them (Durkin, 1978–1979). However, research in the 1960s and 1970s began mapping out strategies readers use to successfully understand texts, such as predicting, making connections, summarizing and paraphrasing, analyzing text structure, visualizing, clarifying meanings, generating questions about texts, and for bilingual readers, identifying cognates (Jiménez, García, & Pearson, 1996) and translating (Jiménez, David, Fagan, Risko, Pacheco, Pray, & Gonzales, 2015; Orellana, Reynolds, Dorner, & Meza, 2003). Researchers have also identified strategies relevant to online text comprehension, including synthesizing and critically evaluating information, identifying important questions, and locating and communicating information (Leu, Kinzer, Coiro, Castek, & Henry, 2013). Transactional strategies instruction (TSI; Brown, 2008; Brown et al., 1996; Pressley et al., 1992) is one approach to teaching reading comprehension.

In TSI, teachers explicitly model the use of strategies to demonstrate how and when students may use those strategies in their own reading, particularly when comprehension breaks down. Such modeling typically occurs in the context of a read-aloud of an authentic text. Meaningful discussion around text is an important element of TSI. During such discussions, students are invited and encouraged to talk about their own strategy use and interpretations of texts. Another characteristic of TSI is flexible strategy use. Rather than requiring all students to stop reading at a particular moment to use a strategy, teachers prompt students to pay attention to when meaning breaks down and to apply strategies as needed. A central goal is for students to ultimately use comprehension strategies automatically as they read, without prompting or consciously selecting strategies to apply (Afflerbach, Pearson, & Paris, 2008). However, when readers notice that what they are reading does not make sense, they will consciously apply strategies to render the text meaningful. Thus, self-monitoring and active problem solving, key elements of metacognition, are fundamental to TSI. Many teachers will integrate TSI into structures such as guided reading or literature discussion groups and will also engage students in conversations regarding strategy use during individual reading conferences. (See Table 3.1 for a summary of TSI.) TSI emphasizes individuals' unique interactions with texts in which they draw on their experiences and prior knowledge of both content and text features to construct meaning. TSI is consistent with several cognitive constructivist coherence theories: schema theory (Anderson, 2013), psycholinguistic theory (Y. M. Goodman & K. S. Goodman, 2013; Smith, 1971), the construction–integration model (Kintsch, 2013), and transactional/reader response theory (Iser, 1978; Rosenblatt, 1978, 2004).

Table 3.1. Implementing Transactional Strategies Instruction

Focus	Teaching Structure	Materials/Texts	Description of Teacher Practices
Teacher modeling and class discussion	Whole-class read-aloud	• Authentic children's literature or other text (e.g., website, film, audio, visual text) • Chart paper and easel with sticky notes or Smartboard	• Teacher preselects moments in text to stop and apply new strategy • Meaningful discussion of text content and response to the text • Discussion of student strategy use
Supported practice	Small-group instruction (e.g., guided reading, comprehension focus groups, or teacher-led literature groups)	• Authentic children's literature or other text (e.g., website, film, audio, visual text) • Sticky notes or reading notebooks	• Teacher prompts students to read strategically (using the modeled strategy as needed) • Additional modeling if necessary
Independent practice	Self-selected or independent reading, partner reading, or student-led literature discussion	• Authentic children's literature or other text (e.g., website, film, visual text) • Sticky notes or reading notebooks	• Meaningful discussion of text content and response to text • Discussion of strategy use

SCHEMA THEORY

Schema theory attempts to explain processes of learning and memory. Schema theorists maintain that as children learn, they build schemata— flexible and individualized cognitive structures or representations. Anderson (2013) characterized schemata as structures that organize knowledge of the world (p. 476), and according to Spivey (1987), "A schema (the plural is schemata) is conceived to be a global, generic structure in memory that has been abstracted by induction from experience" (p. 171). Although the concept of schema can be traced back to the philosopher Immanuel Kant, modern use of the term was initiated by Bartlett (1932) to describe a hypothetical cognitive structure (Spivey, 1987), and broad uptake of the term did not occur until the cognitive revolution in the 1960s. However, as McVee, Dunsmore, and Gavelek (2005) explain, cognitive psychologists often glossed over the complexities of social and cultural influences on learning, instead emphasizing individual experience and prior knowledge.

According to schema theory, readers construct interpretations of a text's meaning using both analysis of the print and their hypotheses about the text based on experiences and cultural understandings. As Anderson (2013) explains,

> Comprehension is a matter of activating or constructing a schema that provides a coherent explanation of objects and events mentioned in a discourse. In sharp contrast is the conventional view that comprehension consists of aggregating the meanings of words to form the meanings of clauses, aggregating the meanings of clauses to form the meanings of sentences, and aggregating the meanings of sentences to form the meanings of paragraphs, and so on. (p. 479)

Anderson's emphasis on "coherent explanations" reveals schema theory as a coherence theory. During reading, these schemata are activated, enabling the reader to find a mental "home" for new textual material (Anderson & Pearson, 1984).

Anderson (2013) also outlines six functions of schemata, or ways in which they are activated during reading. Schemata function as follows:

1. provide "ideational scaffolding," or "slots," for assimilating information from the text;
2. facilitate readers' selective allocation of attention, or a determination of important aspects of the text, as they read;
3. enable inferential elaboration, or a "basis for making inferences that go beyond the literal";
4. allow orderly searches for information to be recalled from memory;

5. facilitate editing and summarizing of important information, such that less important information is filtered out;

6. and permit inferential reconstruction, or the generation of hypotheses to fill in gaps in information within the text and a reader's schemata. (p. 480)

These functions highlight the cognitive constructivist notion that reading is an experience-based, hypothesis-driven cognitive process of generating coherent meanings.

Schema theory is typically taken up in ways that privilege the less politically laden concept of prior experience over cultural factors that impact schemata. Quoting McCormick (1994), Aukerman (2007) explains,

> Many cognitive psychologists have tried to harness and tame the unruly heterogeneity of readers' schemata, aiming to "reproduce traditional roles in students who must passively accept from their teachers the 'appropriate' background knowledge so that they can understand texts 'correctly'" (McCormick, 1994, pp. 21–22). (p. 60)

The emphasis on "appropriate" background knowledge and "correct" understandings of text is not all that different from correspondence theories—specifically, the idea that a reader's understanding will match, or correspond to, the printed text or preferred interpretations that may not cohere with students' own prior knowledge or experiences. McVee et al. (2005) offer a different understanding of schema theory, emphasizing Bartlett (1932) and his contemporaries' (e.g., Louise Rosenblatt, John Dewey) view of schemata as existing and developing in a reciprocal relationship between memory and culture:

> If we think of schema as embodied and not just in the head, then it becomes clear that patterns of enactment, ways of engaging the world, both shape our interpretation of cultural activity and are shaped by cultural activity. This requires very different ways of thinking about teaching and learning. Not only must teachers scaffold and model for students, but they must also be cognizant of the role of schemas as embodied social and cultural constructs that mediate students' learning. (p. 550)

This reconceptualization of schemata as socially and culturally situated is more closely aligned with the theories discussed in Chapter 4.

Connecting Schema Theory to Curricular Models and Instructional Strategies

Comprehension strategy instruction (CSI), including TSI as described earlier, aims to teach students to monitor their own understanding and to use a variety of strategies while reading. These include making connections to prior knowledge, identifying important information in the text, examining text features, making inferences, summarizing, and predicting, and these strategies can be mapped onto the six functions of schema theory identified by Anderson (2013; see p. 42). Similarly, reciprocal teaching (Palincsar & Brown, 1984), in which students work together to summarize, generate questions, clarify meanings, and predict, is based in part on schema theory.

Schema theory also supports the practice of building students' background knowledge on a topic prior to reading. This may be done through explicit instruction but is often accomplished through read-alouds and experiential learning, including hands-on activities, fieldtrips, and other engagements. Fingeret (2008), for example, describes a teacher's use of the documentary film *March of the Penguins* (2005) to support her kindergartners' development of content knowledge and to prompt them to access prior knowledge regarding penguins. She used the film much like she would use a piece of literature for a read-aloud, pausing to pose questions and discuss details as they watched.

Anderson (2013) also describes the Directed Reading-Thinking Activity (DR-TA) as a practice aligned with schema theory. In a DR-TA, the teacher guides students in asking questions and making predictions about a text, revisiting their predictions as they read, and then evaluating their predictions upon completing the text. Anderson (2013) explains that strategies such as DR-TA "appear to cause readers to search their store of background knowledge and integrate what they already know with what is stated [in the text]" (p. 486). In addition, DR-TA supports students in monitoring their comprehension, emphasizing reading as an active and metacognitive problem-solving process—key characteristics of coherence theories.

The use of advance graphic organizers and text previewing activities is also meant to help readers activate their prior knowledge regarding text structures and features. Such practices can help students connect prior knowledge to new concepts and support several of the functions of schemata outlined by Anderson (2013), such as allocating attention, inferential reconstruction, and editing and summarizing important information.

> Schema theory is brought to life in these two vignettes: "It's Not a Appropriate Word" (p. 129) and "We're Not Going to Talk About That Stuff Right Now": (Re)presenting Racial Injustice During Reader Response (p. 141).

At the word level, semantic mapping can help students connect to their schemata for words (specifically, building on morphological schemata) to support vocabulary development and the development of prior knowledge regarding a text or topic (Baumann, Edwards, Boland, Olejnik, & Kame'enui, 2003).

PSYCHOLINGUISTIC THEORY

Like schema theory, psycholinguistic theory conceptualizes reading as a hypothesis-driven and active process. Its emphasis on language distinguishes psycholinguistic theory from other cognitive constructivist coherence theories. Psycholinguistic theory posits that reading involves the use of four language cueing systems: graphophonics (letter–sound correspondences), syntactics (a system of grammar rules guiding how words are combined in different languages, as well as word parts, or morphemes), semantics (the meaning conferred upon language), and pragmatics (social and cultural contexts of language use). Successful reading involves the integration and coordination of these four cueing systems (Y. M. Goodman & K. S. Goodman, 2013) to make meaning. Psycholinguistic theory also maintains that language consists of two levels: surface structure, including sounds and written representations of language, and deep structure, or meaning. Psycholinguistic research indicates that language is processed at the deep level rather than at surface levels.

Miscues and Miscue Analysis

Miscues are unexpected responses to text that are prompted by readers' linguistic and conceptual understandings. Miscues are not negative indicators of a reader's ability but rather windows into a reader's cognitive textual processing—specifically, the strategies he or she uses to make sense of texts (Y. M. Goodman & K. S. Goodman, 2013). Consider three readers' renderings of an excerpt from Kate DiCamillo's *The Miraculous Journey of Edward Tulane* (2006). Edward is a self-centered china rabbit who becomes lost at sea and then passes through the lives of several unexpected companions, his outlook on life and love shifting along with his circumstances. In this excerpt, a fisherman pulls Edward from the sea and presents him to his wife:

> An old woman stepped out of the kitchen, wiping her hands on an apron. When she saw Edward, she dropped the apron and clapped her hands together and said, "Oh, Lawrence, you brung me a rabbit." (p. 63)

Readers' miscues are shown in **bold**.

A. An old woman stepped out of the kitchen, wiping her hands on an apron. When she saw Edward, she dropped the apron, **clasped** her hands together and said, "Oh, Lawrence, you **brought-** brung me a rabbit."

B. An old woman **walked** out of the kitchen, wiping her hands on an apron. When she saw Edward, she dropped the apron and clapped

> her hands together and said, "Oh, Lawrence, you **brought** me a rabbit."
>
> C. An old woman stepped out of the **ki-kitchen**, wiping her hands on an **apple- ap- apen.** When she saw Edward, she dropped the **apen** and **claped** her hands together and said, "Oh, Lawrence, you **brushed** me a rabbit."

You will notice that Readers A and B both made sense of the text although neither of their readings were free of miscues. While Reader A's "clasped" is graphophonically similar to "clapped," Reader B's "walked" bears only a syntactic similarity to "stepped." In addition, both examples are semantically and syntactically consistent with the text. While this example is admittedly limited, we can say that Reader A has likely drawn on semantic, graphophonic, and syntactic cueing systems in an integrated way. Reader B, on the other hand, appears to have privileged the semantic and syntactic cueing systems. It's important to remember, however, that we do not simply draw meaning from the semantic cueing system, from whole words that bear some social meaning for us. Indeed, when something "sounds right," or sounds syntactically acceptable to us, it is thus more meaningful. In this sense, and as psycholinguistic theory would suggest, it can be difficult to separate out the cueing systems in meaningful reading.

Reader C, however, has struggled to make sense of the text. Her rendering of the passage includes nonwords ("apen" and "claped") as well as a word that does not make sense in the context of the text ("brushed"). This does not mean that Reader C's attempt is devoid of strategies. She appears to apply initial letter–sound correspondences (graphophonics) well, using them to successfully identify the word "kitchen." Indeed, this can be a useful strategy at times. When attempting the word "apron," she uses this strategy to read "apple" but then reconsiders, presumably because it does not make sense in the context of the story. However, she does not arrive at a semantically acceptable word, instead opting for the nonword "apen," reusing it in the next sentence, and substituting a nonword for "clapped" ("claped"). We can argue that she has not fully integrated the cueing systems to render the text meaningful.

According to K. S. Goodman and Burke (1973), more proficient readers will make a greater proportion of semantically acceptable miscues (non–meaning changing miscues) and self-correct semantically unacceptable miscues. Less proficient readers, on the other hand, over-rely on graphophonics while relying less on semantics (like Reader C), and are less likely to self-correct unacceptable miscues. This can lead to monotonous word calling, or what Samuels (2007) referred to as "barking at print" (p. 563), with little indication that the reader knows the text is supposed to make sense.

Connecting Psycholinguistic Theory to Curricular Models and Instructional Strategies

As noted above, miscue analysis is an assessment approach that is consistent with psycholinguistic theory, as teachers try to ascertain the cueing systems that developing readers recruit as they read. As with other cognitive constructivist theories, readers' self-monitoring is also emphasized. One approach to supporting students' self-assessment and monitoring of their strategy use is retrospective miscue analysis (RMA; Y. M. Goodman, 1996). In RMA, the teacher reviews an audio recording of the student reading and selects self-corrections and miscues to reflect on. The idea is to illustrate to readers places in which they acted strategically to make sense of the text and to prompt them to articulate their thinking regarding their reading processes and how they may recruit different cueing systems to support meaning-making.

Because psycholinguistic theory emphasizes top-down processes of reading, it is consistent with approaches that utilize whole texts and authentic literature. This does not mean that phonics is ignored. Rather, analytic and embedded approaches to phonics instruction will likely be used. In analytic phonics teachers will prompt students to analyze phonics patterns within words, such as onset and rime (e.g., "rack," "back," "sack"). In embedded phonics, a teacher may read a piece of authentic children's literature aloud and engage students in conversation about the text, drawing students' attention to graphophonic patterns (National Reading Panel, 2000). In both of these approaches, students may then brainstorm additional words with the same sound and spelling pattern (e.g., "hack," "stack," "tack"). They will then be encouraged to look for and use the pattern when reading and writing new texts. This contrasts

> Psycholinguistic theory is brought to life in two vignettes: "It's Not a Appropriate Word" (p. 129) and "My Tomatoes Don't Like Soda": Experimenting with Plant Foods (p. 176).

with synthetic phonics instruction, a bottom-up approach in which students are taught to convert letters into sounds and to blend sounds to form words (National Reading Panel, 2000). Analytic phonics is consistent with whole language, which gained favor in the 1980s and 1990s (Stahl, 1999).

Whole language views learning to read as a natural process. Just as learning oral language occurs through exposure to and engagement with natural, authentic speech, learning to read and write will occur naturally when children engage with authentic texts in print-rich environments (K. S. Goodman & Y. M. Goodman, 1979). While parts of language (e.g., phonics and phonemic awareness) are not taught for their own sake, they are taught in the context of whole texts. Thus, as Stahl, Duffy-Hester, and Stahl (1998) contend, the phonics/whole language divide (the "reading wars") is a false dichotomy. Some refer to whole language as a curricular approach, and others label it a philosophy (Stahl et al., 1998) or a set of instructional principles (Moorman, Blanton, & McLaughlin, 1994). However, it is not a set of materials or a predefined curriculum. While whole language is consistent with psycholinguistic theory, Smith and Goodman (2011) have strongly argued against converting psycholinguistic theory into a method.

Psycholinguistic theory has not been without criticism. Researchers and teachers who subscribe to information-processing theories may express concern that psycholinguistic theory does not place enough emphasis on bottom-up decoding. They would argue that top-down processes are insufficient for some novice readers learning how to decode, particularly readers with identified learning disabilities, such as dyslexia. On the flip side, from the perspective of social constructivist and constructionist theories (Chapters 4 and 5), there is concern that psycholinguistic theory's view of reading as an individual cognitive process does not sufficiently account for how social interaction and social contexts impact the construction of meaning.

CONSTRUCTION–INTEGRATION MODEL

Chances are, if you picked up a relatively simple children's book—Margaret Wise Brown's *Goodnight Moon*, say, or Faith Ringgold's *Tar Beach*—you could read it fluently without working too hard or explicitly deploying comprehension strategies to understand it. The same is certainly true for road signs, most Facebook posts, and other everyday texts. According to Kintsch (2013), these kinds of reading experiences constitute "normal reading": reading that is fairly automatic and that can be carried out without explicit planning and problem-solving efforts. But what happens when you attempt to read something more difficult? Something like Paolo Freire's *Pedagogy of the Oppressed*? Or a novel like Toni Morrison's *Beloved*? If you are anything like me, these texts pose challenges that make reading more effortful. At times like this, when normal reading processes break down and readers are unable to render a text meaningful, they will employ problem-solving measures, devoting more energy to comprehension (Kintsch, 1998, 2013). This is the focus of the construction–integration model, a theory of text comprehension that "leaves room for problem solving and planning when that becomes necessary to complement normal reading" (Kintsch, 2013, p. 808). This is particularly significant in K–12 classrooms, where developing readers are pushed to engage with texts beyond what they can read without support.

Key to the construction–integration model is the notion of propositions, idea units that contain multiple words in a schematic form (Kintsch, 2013). Kintsch (2013) offers the example, "The hiker watches the elk with his binoculars," which includes several propositions: watches, an agent (or subject), and object (elk), and an instrument (binoculars). Identifying propositions in a text enables theorists "to represent the meaning of sentences independent of their syntactic structure. . . . Furthermore, propositions can be combined to form representations of whole texts" (p. 809). The model suggests a propositional level of representation, which comprises an idea in a given text. While identifying the propositions may be straightforward for short, simple sentences, it can be quite tedious with more complex texts. Importantly, it is not just the length of a text or whether a reader recognizes the words that determines text complexity but also the number of idea units or propositions in a text and how they are structured with respect to one another (Kintsch, 2013).

Texts are also made up of micro- and macrostructures. While the microstructure consists of a network of propositions that represent the meaning of the text, the macrostructure refers to the larger organization of a text—for instance, the setting, problem, and resolution for some narratives. The microstructure and macrostructure together make up what is called the textbase, or the "semantic underpinning of a text" (Kintsch, 2013, p. 811). Stated otherwise, the textbase is the meaning construed by the reader from the text itself—recognizing what the text says. However, constructing the textbase is not sufficient for text comprehension, which occurs when the textbase is *integrated* with prior knowledge, experiences, and reader goals to construct a situation model. The construction of the situation model is thus dependent on a wider set of factors than the words on the page or screen and how they are organized. Integration involves using additional contextual information to select the proposition in the text to construct the most *coherent* situation model. In other words, the integration process involves constraining the propositions constructed from the textbase. Because readers construct different situation models that cohere with their own understandings, purposes, and experiences, the construction–integration model is reflective of cognitive constructivist coherence theories.

Connecting Construction–Integration to Curricular Models and Instructional Strategies

A key pedagogical implication of the construction–integration model is that assessment must address both students' surface-level understandings of text (how they construct the textbase) and deeper-level understandings (how they construct situation models). Moreover, how we evaluate students' construction of their situation models (their comprehension) must take into account the integration of prior knowledge and reader goals with the textbase, ruling out approaches that limit assessment to basic recall or standardized approaches.

As with TSI, the construction–integration model is also consistent with efforts to support students in self-monitoring comprehension and actively applying strategies when meaning breaks down. And because inferring is thought to underlie the integration of the textbase with prior knowledge, purposes, and experiences to form the situation model, teaching students the concept of inferring and explicitly drawing inferences as they encounter challenging texts would also be advised. Finally, engaging in prereading activities to draw students' attention to text features can facilitate students' navigation of complex texts.

infer!

> The construction-integration model is brought to life in two vignettes: "It's Not a Appropriate Word" (p. 129) and "I Know the Words, but I Don't Get How They're Used": Reading Historical Documents in a WebQuest (p. 184).

One limitation of the construction-integration model is that, like other cognitive constructivist theories, it focuses attention on internal cognitive processes and thus may not sufficiently account for contexts in which meaning is coconstructed or debated, such as classroom literature discussions. As Kintsch (2013) argues, the field needs both studies of basic cognitive processes as well as further research on instructional practices to support comprehension.

TRANSACTIONAL/READER RESPONSE THEORY

Transactional/reader response theory builds on schema theory to argue that readers bring their own schemata to bear on the meaning they construct from texts (Rosenblatt, 2004). Because individuals' schemata differ, the meaning readers construct and their responses to texts will also differ. Below I focus on Rosenblatt's explanation of reading as a transaction, aesthetic and efferent stances from which readers approach texts, response to reading transactions, and writing as a transactional process. I then describe alternative views of stance and reader response.

Transaction, Stance, and Response

Rosenblatt (1978) drew on Dewey and Bentley's (1949) use of the term *transaction* to suggest reciprocity between subject and object (or knower and knowledge). That is, the knower and the outside world come together to mutually construct meaning. Rosenblatt (2004) explains that upon beginning to engage with a text, the reader forms expectations or tentative ideas that further guide the selection, synthesis, and organization of information from the text and his or her cultural, social, and personal histories (Rosenblatt, 2004). A transactional view of reading reflects its emphasis on coherence rather than correspondence: "From a to-and-fro interplay between reader, text, and context emerges a synthesis or organization, more or less coherent and complete" (Rosenblatt, 2004, p. 1371).

Readers will also approach texts from different stances. Stance refers to a "selective attitude whereby readers focus their attention on certain aspects of the text and their experiences, while de-emphasizing others. In this sense, a reader's stance reflects their purpose" (Rosenblatt, 2004, p. 1372). Rosenblatt argued that a reader's stance will fall somewhere along a continuum between the efferent and aesthetic. Efferent stance refers to reading in which attention is devoted predominantly to what is to be learned or remembered, while an aesthetic stance refers to attention devoted to sense, feelings, and intuitions, including the sounds or rhythms of language within a text. A reader may take a predominantly efferent stance when reading a news article regarding global warming, instructions on tax forms, or a warranty for a new piece of furniture. When reading plays, stories, poems, and other forms of fiction, a reader may take a mostly aesthetic stance. However, Rosenblatt (1978) cautioned against labeling texts or genres as efferent or aesthetic, as any given text may evoke both efferent and aesthetic responses.

In addition to stance, response is a key element of transactional/reader response theory. As Fecho and Meacham (2007) explain,

> when we are in transaction with text, response is evoked and we position ourselves in terms of our response. As such we are enmeshed in an ongoing cycle of transactions, each one being colored by the ones that came before and each projecting a response on which future response will be built. (p. 167)

As readers construct meaning, they respond in several ways. Second stream responses are made during reading and may include acceptance or confirmation of ideas or reflection on instances in which interpretations run contrary to prior understandings. Expressed responses typically occur postreading although the groundwork for them is laid during reading. These include reflecting on the meaning of a text and may recapture and express second stream responses, recalling specific aspects of the reading. Finally, there are expressed interpretations, or continued efforts to clarify meaning. These typically occur postreading and involve "arriving at a sense of the whole" (Rosenblatt, 2004, p. 1377). Reading is considered to be a communication, or even a contract, between the author and the reader. Rosenblatt argues that when the author's and the reader's linguistic and cultural experiences resemble one another, "the more likely the reader's interpretation will fulfill the writer's intention" (2004, p. 1383).

Writing can also be viewed as a transactional process. As Rosenblatt (2004) explains, "For the writer, too, the residue of past experiences of language in particular situations provides the material from which the text will be constructed" (p. 1378). The context in which writing occurs will guide the writer's selection of language and textual elements. Along with the motives of the writer, this includes the social purposes for writing and the potential audience for the text.

According to Rosenblatt (2004), this context also relates to the writer's stance, which, like in reading, will fall along an aesthetic–efferent continuum. Stance impacts the ideas a writer chooses to convey and how. For example, when writing a political blog, a writer will likely select syntax and vocabulary that both convey facts and support elements of argumentation. But if the same writer is composing a poem, he or she will likely choose words and structures to elicit more aesthetic responses, such as sensory images and other descriptive language. However, teachers and researchers may need to consider stances that extend beyond the efferent and aesthetic continuum. This brings us to additional perspectives on reader response.

Additional Views on Stance and Reader Response

Going beyond efferent and aesthetic responses, Sipe (1999) describes a stance of resistance, in which children may question authors' word choices or texts that do not mirror their own cultural realities, ideologies, or experiences with injustice. He also raises the question of whether readers bring different individual response styles based on personality and cultural experiences to their reading transactions. Finally, he addresses children's varied kinds of responses to texts, which may also be characterized by pleasure. McLaughlin and DeVoogd (2004) suggest that a critical stance might be construed as an additional stance along the aesthetic–efferent continuum. Within a critical stance, readers move beyond meaning-making to engage as text critics (see also Luke & Freebody, 1999). In addition, Langer (1998) conceptualized meaning-making as envisionments, "meanings that contain questions as well as already-formed ideas that will change over time (p. 17). She also articulated four stances that readers may adopt during reading transactions: being out and stepping into an envisionment, being in and moving through an envisionment, stepping back and rethinking what one knows, and stepping out and objectifying the experience (Langer, 1990).

   In addition to theorizing different kinds of stances that readers and writers assume, Paulson and Armstrong (2010) suggest that there is a multidimensionality to the stances taken up by readers. They suggest a stance of reading-for-the-writer, whereby readers read specifically to offer feedback to an author. These additional perspectives on stance may prompt teachers to consider a wider array of possibilities for how students may respond to texts in classrooms.

Connecting Transactional/Reader Response Theory to Curricular Models and Instructional Strategies

As noted at the beginning of the chapter, TSI recognizes the transaction that takes place between the reader and the text, and the strategies that are taught within this approach are meant to facilitate this transaction. The emphasis on self-monitoring within TSI is also consistent with transactional/reader response theory, as students become aware of the stances they take before, during, and after reading.

Reader response theorists are skeptical of new critical and formalist approaches to literary interpretation as carried out in secondary English classrooms. These approaches emphasize interpretation as a process of arriving at the author's true meaning or a correct interpretation, and are associated with the close reading called for by the CCSS. Transactional/reader response theorists, however, argue that interactions with text should not center on what the text *is* but rather what the text *does* (Fish, 1980) to and for readers, and how readers fill in the gaps in texts by using their own understandings, experiences, and frames of references in the process of interpretation (Iser, 1978; Rosenblatt, 2004). Not surprisingly,

> Transactional/reader response theory is brought to life in three vignettes: "Dude, I Don't Know": Combining Sentences with To Kill a Mockingbird (p. 114), "There Won't Be No Cure Till White Folk Start Dyin'" (p. 146), and Being Melody: Stepping into Role Through Social Media (p. 151).

then, transactional/reader response theory is associated with reader response activities in classrooms. One common example is reader response journals, in which students write about their interpretations of a text. In some cases, these are framed as letters to the author or to their teacher, although teachers may ask students to respond online using blogs, wikis, or chat rooms to provide students with broader audiences for their responses (Handsfield, Dean, & Cielocha, 2009). Other activities may include conversations regarding literature within approaches such as literature circles (Daniels, 1994). In this approach, students assume responsibility for different roles, such as discussion director, illustrator, connector, and so forth to structure conversations. Other approaches to literature discussion may be more loosely structured with all group members expected to sustain conversation in a variety of ways.

Establishing purposes for reading is also emphasized by teachers influenced by transactional/reader response theory. Teachers may prompt students prior to and/or during reading to articulate their stance toward the text and to establish specific purposes for reading. Teachers' roles in this regard relate to the importance that Rosenblatt (2004) places on collaborative dialogue to "foster growth and cross-fertilization in both reading and writing processes" (p. 1390). This attention to collaborative dialogue speaks to the importance of social context and language use, which are addressed more explicitly by the theories presented in Chapters 4 and 5 (also see the inset discussion on drama and imagination in responding to fictional texts).

DRAMA AND THE ROLE OF IMAGINATION IN RESPONDING TO FICTIONAL TEXTS

Tom Crumpler, Illinois State University

In an 8th-grade classroom in a small Midwestern school district, the students read a staple of the literary canon, Harper Lee's (1960) *To Kill a Mockingbird*. The teacher engages her students in process drama as a pedagogical practice to enrich and extend their understanding of the novel. Process drama uses dramatic structures such as teacher and students in role, and tableau to invite learners to use their imaginations to facilitate deeper understandings of texts (Edmiston, 2013; O'Neill, 1995). Through interactions with a skilled teacher, learners draw upon the fictional world of the text, their own experiences, and the imaginative drama world they create to explore possible meanings and examine issues that arise. Process drama focuses on what students generate in these interactions, which requires teachers to think on their feet, choose potentially rich responses, and improvise to keep participants engaged in the dramatic work.

I had the opportunity to observe this teacher leading a discussion around racism and desire for freedom as manifested in the characters of Scout (the protagonist) and Boo Radley. To help the students understand the historical feel of the 1930s, the teacher stepped into the role of a proper Southern lady from this time period. She read to the students from an imaginary "book of manners" that described how to sit, speak, and dress if you were really a lady (Crumpler & Wedwick, 2011, p. 70). Then, she stepped back into her teacher identity and asked students to write down an example of an emblem or symbol that could represent how girls Scout's age were expected to behave during that time period. The teacher used her work in role to invite students to draw upon what they knew about Scout, their interactions with their teacher as someone other than herself, and their own imaginations to construct representations of Southern gentility. While sharing their emblems or symbols, she asked them to agree on one term that captured their understanding of the novel's time period. The students chose *curtseying*. The teacher then employed tableau to facilitate the students' engagement in collaborative imaginative play.

Tableau refers to silent frozen moments in which participants configure their bodies to represent an idea or theme. The teacher split the students into two groups and asked the groups to face each other in the center of the classroom. When she counted to three, they all curtsied and froze in their positions. The tableau was a text, composed as part of the process drama sequence; participants drew upon multiple meaning systems (textual, personal, dramatic) to design it. She then asked one group to relax, view, and interpret the poses of the other group, which remained frozen. The teacher moved students in the frozen group behind one another, asked them to drop their arms to the side, step away from the group, and perform other gestures that shifted the configuration. These small revisions to the living text changed the student observers' interpretations, and a new narrative emerged about how some of the figures in the tableau were constraining the freedom of others. This strategy invites participants to reflect on how small changes in a tableau text (facial expression, standing, or sitting) reframe meaning. Reframing allows the teacher to follow up and talk with students about how small changes to a linguistic text (word choice, sentence structure) can also shift meaning. Next, they return to the novel to examine Harper Lee's literary style.

Closure is an important aspect of process drama. To end this sequence of drama, the teacher wonders aloud with her students about creating a second tableau that signals the opposite of curtseying. Since freedom and its relationship to the novel emerged in this process drama work, the students compose a second tableau that portrays freedom by creating a mosh pit—something that can happen at a punk or heavy metal music concert in which listeners push and body slam into one another to enjoy the music in an active fashion. All 18 students froze into a silent response to music they enjoyed. Students wrapped their bodies loosely together, lay beside one another, and raised one leg off the floor with arms stretched to simulate flying through the air. This moment of silent bedlam was an imaginative act that brought these 45 minutes of process drama to an exhilarating close (Crumpler & Wedwick, 2011).

As a teaching practice, process drama activates imagination to help learners gain a deeper understanding of fictional texts. Iser (1993) theorized the role of imagination in understanding fictional texts by arguing that, as readers, we engage in boundary crossings to construct meaning. Dramatic engagement with a novel like *To Kill a Mockingbird* (Lee, 1960) opened spaces for these 8th-graders to crisscross boundaries among the textual, the personal, and the coconstructed drama world. Their understanding of the novel was strengthened in the process.

CONCLUDING THOUGHTS

Practices designed to enhance student engagement have drawn on a variety of cognitive constructivist theories. John Dewey's inquiry learning approach involves a child-centered curriculum, in which students make choices regarding specific problems to solve. Student-centered approaches are also consistent with psycholinguistic theory and a whole language philosophy, which emphasize student choice of authentic texts and writing topics, as well as thematic units of interest to students. According to Guthrie and

Wigfield (2000), students should play a central role in text selection in order to boost motivation and engagement. Similarly, relating texts to students' prior knowledge and experiences can boost engagement.

Although individuals' experiences are necessarily grounded in social contexts and cultural worlds, critics argue that these aspects of experience are not sufficiently conceptualized within cognitive constructivist coherence theories. And as noted above, recent reframings of schema theory also challenge this trend (McVee et al., 2005). The recognition of social and cultural contexts, and how student learning is mediated, is central to social constructivist coherence theories, which are presented in the next chapter.

QUESTIONS FOR PRAXIS

1. The Common Core State Standards emphasize the need for students to engage with complex texts. How do cognitive constructivist theories inform approaches to supporting students' understanding of complex texts at different grade levels?
2. Imagine a literacy instructional activity in your classroom or school that is taught in undifferentiated ways. How might that activity be reimagined to reflect cognitive constructivist theories?

RESOURCES AND ADDITIONAL READINGS

Assaf, L., & Garza, R. (2007). Making magazine covers that visually count: Learning to summarize with technology. *The Reading Teacher, 60*(7), 678–680.

Dewitz, P., Jones, J., & Leahy, S. (2009). Comprehension strategy instruction in core reading programs. *Reading Research Quarterly, 44*(2), 102–126.

Kalemba, C. Lesson Plan: Let's Read It Again: Comprehension Strategies for English-Language Learners. ReadWriteThink.org. International Reading Association and the National Council of Teachers of English. Retrieved from www.readwritethink .org/classroom-resources/lesson-plans/read-again-comprehension-strategies -1045.html

Reading Rockets. Directed Reading Thinking Activity (DRTA). Retrieved from www.readingrockets.org/strategies/drta

Serafini, F. (2011). When bad things happen to good books. *The Reading Teacher, 65*(4), 238–241.

CHAPTER 4

Coherence Theories, Take 2

Social Constructivism

Coherence theories reject the notion that subjective, internal knowledge will bear a direct correspondence to objective, external reality. Instead, they consider meaning to be dependent on knowers and their interpretations of reality (Davis et al., 2008). What matters for coherence theories is how people make sense of their world—how they make the different elements, phenomena, events, and so on *cohere*. However, not all coherence theories are alike when it comes to understanding teaching and learning, and literacy more specifically. While cognitive constructivism focuses attention on how learning occurs cognitively and metacognitively, social constructivism attends to how knowledge is internalized via social engagement in the world (Davis, 2004; Hruby, 2001; Spivey, 1997). I begin this chapter by discussing the work of Lev Vygotsky, perhaps the most central thinker associated with social constructivism.

VYGOTSKY'S IMPACT ON TEACHING AND LEARNING

Vygotsky (1978) was concerned that psychological frameworks of his time (the early 20th century) failed to account for complex behaviors and higher-order psychological processes. He argued that parsing out different components of human behavior without considering the social contexts in which they occur does not do justice to the complexity of human behavior and learning. He attempted to develop a comprehensive framework of human psychological development, which included several elements:

> It included identification of the brain mechanisms underlying a particular function; it included a detailed explication of their developmental history to establish the relation between simple and complex forms of what appeared to be the same behavior; and, importantly, it included specification of the societal context in which the behavior developed. (Cole & Scribner, 1978, pp. 5–6; see also Smagorinsky, 2009)

Vygotsky maintained that social contexts impact learning through a process of semiotic mediation. That is, development is mediated by culturally produced tools and signs. For Vygotsky, language was the principal means of mediation. As Smagorinsky (2009) explains,

> Listening to and engaging in speech with cultural elders and veterans is what provides a person with a worldview and the specific language through which to characterize it, allows for new ideas to emerge through the process of expression and articulation, enables the development of signs that embody concepts, and provides the means through which people communicate with others and act upon their worlds. (p. 89)

It is through this process of semiotic mediation in cultural communities that knowledge becomes internalized.

Vygotsky is widely known for his concept of zone of proximal development (ZPD). In his words, ZPD refers to "the distance between the actual development level as determined by independent problem solving and the level of potential development as determined through problem solving under adult guidance or in collaboration with more capable peers" (1978, p. 86). Vygotsky proposed the concept in part as a critical response to the use of IQ tests to measure individuals' learning ability or potential (Dixon-Krauss, 1996). He argued that using the ZPD, psychologists and educators can account not only for learning that has already taken place but also for *processes* of learning that are currently in a state of development. He articulates how this relates to internalization:

> Learning awakens a variety of internal developmental processes that are able to operate only when the child is interacting with people in his environment and in cooperation with his peers. Once these processes are internalized, they become part of the child's independent developmental achievement. (1978, p. 90)

Social activity and interaction, including play, are central to the ZPD (Moll, 2014). Because social activity and ways of interacting are culturally grounded, the concepts of semiotic mediation and ZPD explain how "children grow into the intellectual life of those around them" (Vygotsky, 1978, p. 88). As such, Vygotsky's theory of development was *genetic*, not in the sense of microbiology but rather in the historical sense, emphasizing change over time. He argued that human development should be studied as "processes in motion and in change" (p. 7).

Vygotsky's emphasis on change and the influence of cultural and social worlds on development is evidence of the Marxist foundation of his thinking. According to Cole and Scribner (1978), Karl Marx maintained that "historical changes in society and material life produce changes in 'human nature' (consciousness and behavior)" (p. 7). Vygotsky worked in the Soviet Union when it was very much grounded in Marxist philosophy (Smagorinsky, 2009). However, as his ideas were taken up in the West, the

TERM CONFUSION AND EPISTEMOLOGICAL DIVERGENCES
WITHIN RUSSIAN SOCIAL THEORY

A confusing aspect of social constructivist theories is the plethora of terms used to refer to them. Literacy researchers and teachers may use terms such as *social-cognitive, socio-cognitive, sociocultural, cultural-historical,* and *sociocultural-historical* somewhat synonymously. Moreover, some use the word *sociocultural* broadly, as an umbrella term to describe many of the theories in this chapter and in Chapter 5. However, these terms have their own histories. The terms *social-cognitive* and *socio-cognitive* are likely derived from Bandura's (2001) social cognitive theory, which suggests that learning occurs through observation—a clear connection to teacher modeling. However, the other terms likely come out of Russian social theory. As Roth and Lee (2007) explain, "scholars basing their work in Vygotskian philosophy generally term their approach 'sociocultural,' whereas those walking in the footsteps of Leontiev prefer their research to be known as 'cultural-historical'" (p. 190). While Vygotsky emphasized language mediation, Leontiev (1981) focused on mediation through tool use and collective action. Finnish psychologist Engeström (1987) has built on Leontiev's understandings, foregrounding collective activity in social contexts.

I use the term *sociocultural-historical* to attend to both individual development and collective activity, drawing largely on the work of Barbara Rogoff. Indeed, questions about terminology extend to the concept of activity, which is central to cultural-historical activity theory (CHAT; Leontiev, 1978). Again, as Roth and Lee (2007) explain,

> The term *activity* is related to work, trade, and professions. . . . The activity concept therefore differs from the kind of events educators usually denote by activity, which are structures that allow children to become engaged, involved, and busy and that one might better refer to as tasks. (p. 201)

Leontiev's emphasis on collective activity aligns more closely with Marxism. While Vygotsky explicitly connected his ideas on human development to Marxist theory, his emphasis on individuals' development opened his work to harsh criticism in the Soviet Union (Smagorinsky, 2009; Van der Veer, 2007).

At the end of the day, whether we use the term *sociocultural, cultural-historical, sociocultural-historical, constructivist,* or *social constructivist* to situate teaching or research may be less important than simply clearly stating what we mean by those terms.

Marxist aspects of his psychology, such as social labor, were de-emphasized, with more focus placed on elements of his theory that were more consistent with philosophies of individualism. This translated into an emphasis on the individualized psychological aspects of Vygotsky's work (Davis, 2004; Smagorinsky, 2009) such as linguistic scaffolding and connecting to prior knowledge.

Along these same lines, scholars have articulated concerns regarding "drive-by" applications of Vygotsky's work. This includes, for example, references to the ZPD in which the social context is limited to the space and time of the moment and construed as an individual's "level" rather than nested in previous interactions and cultural histories (Smagorinsky, 2009). Stated differently, historically and culturally grounded forms of mediation are neglected. For example, the ZPD is often used to validate practices such as assigning particular book levels to students or providing them with seatwork or tasks presumed to be within their ZPD. In short, Vygotsky's work has been applied in ways that more closely resemble cognitive constructivist coherence theories. However, as Smagorinsky (2009) asserts, "For a Vygotskian analysis to have any relevance, the culture of the setting needs to be taken into account, including the ways in which the mediational tools emphasized in the interaction have a cultural value in the traditions and conventions that govern the setting" (p. 90). This is particularly important when teaching students from historically marginalized communities.

Vygotsky's ideas are reflective of social constructivist coherence theories because as individuals interact with others and use various tools, they construct meanings about their world or about texts that *cohere* with their culturally grounded understandings and ways of viewing the world. The emphasis on semiotic mediation and historically and socially contextualized activity distinguishes social constructivist coherence theories from cognitive constructivist coherence theories. Many of the elements of social constructivism are evident in Lucy Calkins's *Units of Study* for teaching writing.

GROUNDING CURRICULAR MODEL: LUCY CALKINS'S UNITS OF STUDY FOR WRITING

Units of Study for Primary Writing (Calkins, 2003) is a year-long curriculum including seven month-long units for teaching writing in K–2 classrooms. Calkins's newer series, *Units of Study in Opinion, Information, and Narrative Writing* (2014), builds on the original curriculum but is aligned to the CCSS and covers the K–5 grade span. Each grade level includes four 6-week units, each of which are divided into three to four "bends," or foci, that take writers through the writing process. The newer series includes increased emphasis on informational texts, and essays and persuasive writing, relative to narrative.

Units of Study is grounded in process writing and other tenets of writing workshop, principally, the goal of children becoming lifelong writers by engaging in writerly practices in the classroom (Calkins, 1994; Graves, 1983). The approach includes the following features: (1) transference of skills and strategies from one content area and one school year to another; (2) gradual release of responsibility that moves from demonstration and explicit teaching to guided practice and then to independent work; (3) examples of structured feedback as students progress to focus instruction on students' specific strengths and needs; and (4) high-level expectations, with teaching that aims to build students' higher-order thinking across the curriculum (Calkins, 2014). The series suggests specific language to use with students to build interest, find out what they already know, and scaffold learning through modeling and targeted feedback. Another essential characteristic of the curriculum is the use of authentic texts, such as high-quality children's literature, websites, videos, and students' own writing.

On a given day, sessions may include five components: The *prelude* explains the rationale for the session and how it relates to the larger unit. In *minilessons*, teachers spend 10 to 20 minutes introducing points of instruction and modeling specific writing strategies or concepts. *Conferring and small-group work* support the teaching of specific tips and ideas for individual students or small groups of writers. If you were to walk into a classroom during this time, you would likely find some students reading each others' drafts; others working independently; a student conferring with a teacher about his or her writing or, possibly, a teacher conducting a small-group writing lesson; and students engaged in prewriting. During student and teacher conferencing, you would hear interactions designed to further students' understandings and writing practices. *Mid-workshop* teaching is a time to extend students' thinking or strategy use, or to address any problems the teacher notices during independent or small-group work. This may take the form of another minilesson. Finally, in the *share*, teachers bring students back into a large group to close the lesson and to offer students a time to share and celebrate their writing. Calkins explains that while some teachers follow the curriculum fairly tightly, others adapt it to suit the specifics of their students and classroom situations.

Several features of *Units of Study* reflect social constructivist coherence theories. These include attention to dialogue and interaction to mediate students' learning. The teacher, acting as the more knowledgeable other, models for students how writers engage in their craft. And because students write alongside each other, they also serve as peer models. Vygotsky's emphasis on the importance of contextualized social and cultural activity is also clear in *Units of Study*. As Calkins (1994) explains, "In mini-lessons, we teach into our students' intentions. Our students are first deeply engaged in their self-sponsored work, and then we bring them together to learn what they need to know in order to do that work" (pp. 193–194).

In a workshop approach, students' writing practices come to *cohere* with the kinds of writing practices that more experienced writers participate in, even though students' writing processes may be more individualized. This lies in stark contrast to correspondence theories, in which students are expected to map their writing processes and products onto universal expectations of what they should look like (particularly with respect to conventions). When influenced by correspondence theories, we see more rigid and one-size-fits-all implementation in which everyone is expected to prewrite on Monday, write a draft on Tuesday, revise on Wednesday, and so forth, and use the same strategies (for instance, the same graphic organizer) within each of these stages. Workshop approaches, such as *Units of Study*, reflect several social constructivist coherence theories, including sociocultural-historical theory, sociolinguistic theory, and emergent literacy theory.

SOCIOCULTURAL-HISTORICAL THEORY

Vygotsky's ideas have been taken up by theorists and researchers interested in how individuals learn to participate in communities and cultural activities (Lave & Wenger, 1991; Rogoff, 1995, 2003; Wertsch, 1991). As noted in the inset discussion on p. 59, Vygotsky's work has been taken up in different ways. Many language and literacy scholars distinguish between sociocultural theory and cultural-historical activity theory (CHAT). However, while sociocultural theory and CHAT may support different analytical approaches in research, their instructional implications are fairly similar. Therefore, following in the footsteps of other researchers and practitioners (e.g., Larson & Marsh, 2005), I bring them together under the term *sociocultural-historical theory*.

Sociocultural-historical theory builds directly on Vygotsky's ideas about the social basis of human development. Unlike schema theory, in which an individual's schemata are thought to scaffold the assimilation of information from text (see Chapter 3), sociocultural-historical theory emphasizes social interaction as a scaffold, or mediator, for generating meaning with texts. A key aspect of social interaction includes teacher and peer modeling, whereby individuals more experienced at a particular activity or task scaffold participation for novices.

Collective Activity, Apprenticeship, and Learning

Sociocultural-historical theory emphasizes collaborative learning and the notion that learning is intimately tied to social and historical contexts of practice. Social interaction is considered to be the primary means by which students are apprenticed into culturally and historically grounded literate activities. *Units of Study* is one example of this. Other activities may include the bedtime story routine, or translating for family members, texting, book club conversations, writing thank you notes, online social networking (e.g., Twitter, Instagram), and so on.

Rogoff (1995) highlights the relationships between individual learning, collective activity, and cultural practices, offering three concepts to explain these relationships: apprenticeship, guided participation, and participatory appropriation. *Apprenticeship* refers to individuals actively participating together in culturally grounded social activities in which one purpose of the participation is the development of less experienced members of the community. *Guided participation* refers to how people communicate and work together as they participate in a culturally grounded social activity. Guidance is provided to more novice participants by those more experienced at the activity. For Rogoff, participation and guidance may be face-to-face, side-by-side, or asynchronous via materials or previous instruction. This represents a departure from Vygotsky's ideas of mediation and ZPD, which he envisioned as face-to-face encounters involving speech interactions.

Participatory appropriation refers to the process of change that individuals undergo as a result of their participation in cultural activities. This is a personal process of development, which prepares people for later independent success in the community. Rogoff (1995) views this not as a process of acquisition but rather one of becoming. The focus on appropriation marks a further development of Vygotsky's notion of internalization, emphasizing the social and identity aspects of development alongside the cognitive. Thus, learning can be thought of as changes in individuals' participation in cultural activities.

Funds of Knowledge

The connection to culturally and historically grounded social activity has influenced educators seeking to improve instruction for linguistically and culturally diverse students. Central to this work is the concept of funds of knowledge. Scholars Norma González, Luis Moll, and Cathy Amanti (2005) have built on the work of anthropologists who studied Mexican American households' social and work histories, as well as knowledge and resources that they accumulated over time (Vélez-Ibáñez, 1988). Moll, Amanti, Neff, and González (1992) define funds of knowledge as "historically and culturally developed knowledge and skills essential for household or individual functioning and well being" (p. 133). This may include language abilities and practices (e.g., translating), folk medicine, household economics, cooking, auto repair, ranching, construction, religious knowledge, and so on.

Funds of knowledge are not simply "prior knowledge" abstracted from historical and cultural contexts. Rather, they are tied to individuals' and families' cultural histories. For example, Mexican American immigrant families who work in agriculture and ranching will often have funds of knowledge about things like horseback riding, animal husbandry, soil systems, irrigation, plant life cycles, and herbal remedies (Moll et al., 1992). These funds of knowledge are directly tied to cultural experiences of rural life in Mexico and the economic necessities of immigration. Interactions (including specific vocabulary and ways of using language) and tool use in cultural activities mediate people's participation and learning within these communities (Valencia, 2010).

The concept of funds of knowledge has been recruited by educators to counter deficit assumptions about students from historically marginalized communities. Deficit assumptions claim that ways of talking and other social practices of marginalized communities are evidence of cultural deprivation that translates into school failure. Ruby Payne's (2013) writings and consulting work are known for this view, constructing students and families of poverty as having a cultural deficit. Indeed, her work has been called out and debunked by several educational scholars (e.g., Bomer, Dworin, May, & Semingson, 2008; Valencia, 2010).

Many teachers mistakenly believe that only students from marginalized racial, cultural, or linguistic backgrounds have funds of knowledge—that funds of knowledge do not pertain to mainstream, White, middle-class people. However, everyone has funds of knowledge that are culturally and historically accumulated. It is just that the funds of knowledge of people from mainstream cultural and economic groups are recruited in school *by default*, and so they often go unnoticed. For example, in mainstream middle-class households, the bedtime routine of storybook reading and the practice of leisure reading are common (Heath, 1983). Because most teachers come from mainstream communities, the value of such practices in schools is assumed. However, students from other social, economic, and cultural groups may be less familiar with mainstream literacy practices. Further, the academic and social value of their culturally grounded home or community literacy practices may not appear obvious to teachers, and in some cases, such practices may be outright frowned upon.

Connecting Sociocultural-Historical Theory to Curricular Models and Instructional Strategies

As noted at the beginning of this chapter, a significant part of *Units of Study* is writing workshop, in which students compose texts within a community of writers. Through conferencing, small-group work, and teacher-led minilessons, students are apprenticed into the kinds of practices that writers engage in. Within *Units of Study* and other approaches influenced by sociocultural-historical theory, opportunities for student–student and teacher–student interaction around reading and writing are highly valued.

Sociocultural-historical theory is also consistent with the use of authentic literature. Mentor texts serve as models for writing craft (Ray, 1999), and teachers will also read high-quality children's literature to their students to model reading strategies and promote literate conversations. Consistent with Vygotsky's ideas regarding social mediation, conversation is key during these kinds of instructional engagements. During whole-group instruction, teachers may pose questions and ask students to talk with one another as a way to mediate learning. Classroom interactions also allow teachers to model vocabulary and academic language to apprentice students into different language and academic communities. Indeed, thoughtful language use and interaction is a core principle behind cooperative grouping, including group writing projects, response to literature, literature discussion groups, and the production of multimedia or other texts across the content areas.

Collaborative Reasoning (CR; Chinn, Anderson, & Waggoner, 2001) is an approach to small-group discussion in which students are apprenticed into high-level conversations about texts. CR discussions are peer led and centered around a question regarding a broad theme in the text, such as friendship, belonging, equity, love and loss, environmental sustainability, and so forth. Students take up and argue a position on the issue, supporting their assertions with warrants from the text and actively listening to and evaluating others' contributions. As Zhang and Stahl (2011) explain, "The goal of CR is not to reach a consensus or win a debate. The purpose is for students to cooperatively search for resolutions and develop thoughtful opinions about the topic" (p. 257). The teacher's role is to participate "from the side" and to enter the conversation only occasionally and as needed. CR has

> Sociocultural-historical theory is brought to life in three vignettes: "Dude, I Don't Know": Combining Sentences with *To Kill a Mockingbird* (p. 114), *Using VoiceThread and Inquiry to Boost Vocabulary and Fluency* (p. 124), and "We're Not Going to Talk About That Stuff Right Now": (Re)presenting Racial Injustice During Reader Response (p. 141).

been shown to positively impact students' social skills and thinking about texts and to increase students' language use during discussions (Chinn et al., 2001; Jadallah et al., 2010). Research also indicates that CR has a positive impact on students' writing (Reznitskaya et al., 2001).

Extensive research has documented the value of building on students' and communities' linguistic and cultural funds of knowledge to support classroom literacy learning. For example, Kamberelis and de la Luna (1996) illustrated how a teacher supported her African American students in critiquing their basal reader via the culturally grounded language practice of signifying. Similarly, Morrell and Duncan-Andrade (2002) and Lee (2007) argue for integrating hip-hop texts alongside novels written by African American authors, as well as canonical texts, to promote academic literacies in the secondary English classroom. While some have framed these understandings as community funds of knowledge (González et al., 2005), others refer to them as "cultural models" (Lee, 2007; Martínez, Orellana, Pacheco, & Carbone, 2008; Orellana et al., 2003). Either way, teachers are encouraged to learn about students' specific and culturally grounded knowledge. González et al. (2005) recommend conducting in-depth home visits to learn about students' and families' funds of knowledge.

Sociocultural-historical theory has also been taken up in ways that many would argue veer away from, or oversimplify, key principles such as social interaction and apprenticeship, as well as meaning- and activity-based learning. For example, the practice of matching readers to texts at a particular level, using systems such as Lexile or Fountas and Pinnell benchmarks, has been connected to the concept of ZPD. This is problematic because limiting students' reading selections to particular levels risks stripping students of the ability to self-select texts. Nevertheless, sociocultural-historical theory is widely influential in literacy instruction and research. Its emphasis on social interaction is shared by sociolinguistic theory.

SOCIOLINGUISTIC THEORY

Sociolinguistic theory also recognizes the centrality of language as mediation. However, sociolinguistic theory focuses more on how people *use* language. A key understanding among sociolinguists is that language mediates socialization into different social and cultural groups. This prompts sociolinguists to focus their analyses on language-in-use. Unlike traditional linguistics, which focuses on structures of language, such as syntactic or phonological systems, abstracted from contexts of interaction, sociolinguistic theory seeks to explain language learning as it occurs within social contexts (Cazden, 2001; Hymes, 1996).

Language Variation and Participation Structures

A primary focus within sociolinguistics is language variation, along with the understanding that such variations develop as individuals become capable participants in their communities. A central concept in sociolinguistics is *register*. Register refers to a variety of language with specific lexical and grammatical features used within a particular context or for a particular purpose (Cazden, 2001). A scientific–academic register, for instance, is more formal than everyday conversation, and includes more nominalizations (when verbs are used as nouns), discipline-specific vocabulary, and passive voice. In a scientific report, a geologist would likely write, "The deposition of sediments at the bottom of the Grand Canyon is known to have occurred 300 million years ago." However, when conveying the same idea to a nonscientist, perhaps at a visitor center at a national park, he or she might write, "Geologists know that the sediments at the bottom of the Grand Canyon were deposited 300 million years ago." While both sentences communicate the same information, they assume different things of their audiences.

Sociolinguists have also argued for the value of linguistic diversity and against language policies favoring monolingualism (Blommaert & Rampton, 2011), emphasizing different communicative patterns in varying social contexts. Sociolinguists refer to the array of linguistic and discursive forms that people employ in a given community during meaningful interaction as linguistic or communicative repertoires (Blommaert, 2005; Blommaert & Rampton, 2011; Gumperz, 1982; Rymes, 2014). Repertoires may be distinguished by variations in vocabulary, syntax, intonation, phonology, gesture, gaze, and other elements of discourse that are considered useful and appropriate in different social contexts. This explains why a 14-year-old may be able to interact fluidly and confidently about car repair when working the counter at his uncle's auto shop using both Spanish and English but have difficulty engaging fluidly in monolingual conversations regarding novels in school, even if his understanding of those texts is fairly sophisticated. Such academic registers may not be part of his communicative repertoire.

In addition, language variation may entail different relationships between speakers and listeners and norms for participating in interaction within different social contexts. These sets of norms, which are not always made explicit, are referred to as participation structures (Cazden, 2001; Philips, 1972). When one or more participants in a given interactional context are unfamiliar with the participation structure, miscommunication will likely occur. In schools, the predominant participation structure has been recitation scripts, often referred to as Initiation-Response-Evaluation (IRE), in which a teacher *initiates* an interaction, typically in the form of a question or directive, a student *responds*, and the teacher then *evaluates* the response. This may also be referred to as I-R-F, in which the teacher provides *feedback* in addition to or instead of evaluation. Other kinds of participation structures include call and response (Moss, 2001), which is common within some African American sermons, and "talk-story," a collaborative form of storytelling in native Hawaiian communities (Au & Jordan, 1981).

Language and Literacy Learning in Diverse Communities

Register differs from *dialect*, which refers to a variety of language with its own phonological, syntactic, and lexical features that is used by members of a specific speech community, often distinguished along geographic, cultural, or economic boundaries. Many sociolinguists steer clear of the term *dialect*, which is often associated with nonstandard varieties or varieties of language that carry less social capital, arguing that it reinforces deficit views of many community languages. Indeed, early sociolinguistic research was central in showing that complex understandings and relationships can be understood and articulated in a variety of registers or dialects. Labov (1972), for example, studied the linguistic features of African American Vernacular English (AAVE) and showed that it has its own grammatical logic that made its speakers just as capable as speakers of standardized varieties of English of communicating complex ideas. This finding countered the work of those who developed the Direct Instruction for Teaching Arithmetic and Reading (DISTAR) curriculum (also described in Chapter 2; Bereiter & Engelmann, 1966). DISTAR was a behaviorist curriculum based on the faulty assumption that AAVE was not sufficient for students' success in learning to read, and was designed to remediate the language of poor African American preschool students.

Shirley Brice Heath's work is seminal in the field of sociolinguistics and literacy education. In her 1983 book *Ways with Words*, Heath documented how questioning and other language and literacy practices were used differently in a middle-class White and Black community ("Maintown"), a working-class White community ("Roadville"), and a working-class Black community ("Trackton") in the Carolina Piedmont. Although children from Trackton and Roadville tended to succeed less at school, Heath found that families in both areas engaged in rich language and literacy practices that supported children in becoming productive members of their communities. However, the language and literacy practices in Maintown more closely matched those at school. Heath suggested that teachers take the time to learn about their students' home language and literacy practices, build on language and participation structures familiar to students to support them in expanding their linguistic repertoires, and work with children to analyze differing language and literacy practices. This is consistent with the notion of funds of knowledge. In short, Heath found that cultural differences are not reflections of ability or parenting skill but rather are reflections of specific community norms for how language and literacy practices are used by people as they become successful participants in different communities.

Connecting Sociolinguistic Theory to Curricular Models and Instructional Strategies

Educators grounding their work in sociolinguistic theory advocate classroom practices that challenge deficit assumptions about families and children from marginalized communities (Valencia, 2010). Because of this, sociolinguistic theory has been influential in bilingual education. Basic instructional principles include grounding instruction in authentic texts and meaningful activities that offer opportunities for peer interaction. In literacy instruction, this would include literature discussion groups and activity-based learning. For example, a bilingual kindergarten class may take a fieldtrip to a pumpkin patch. Upon returning to school the next day, they may participate in read-alouds and shared reading in both Spanish and English of texts about pumpkins and the fall season. In the afternoon they could plant their own pumpkin seeds, using discipline-specific language in authentic ways. These sorts of activities offer rich contextualization for language learning and literacy development, as well as ample opportunities to build social and academic communicative repertoires across content areas.

Educators may also teach students the specific linguistic or discursive features of different registers within the content areas. That is, they not only will teach the content of the discipline but also will teach the communicative expectations of the discipline. The recognition that distinct academic disciplines have their own language features and literacy practices is referred to as disciplinary literacy, which is also discussed in Chapters 5 and 10. Disciplinary literacy may be taught explicitly, by teaching elements of academic language specific to particular disciplines (Draper & Siebert,

> Sociolinguistic theory is brought to life in two vignettes: "Put It on the Train!" (p. 104) and "My Tomatoes Don't Like Soda": Experimenting with Plant Foods (p. 176).

2010), or implicitly, by modeling the target language or register and recasting students' utterances into the academic register of the discipline (Cazden, 2001). For example, in a writing conference, a student who is still learning English might say, "I write about people in my story. I use describing word." The teacher could respond, "Yes, I noticed that you used adjectives to describe the characters in your story. You wrote 'frightening' and 'slimy.'" Such linguistic scaffolding is consistent with Vygotsky's ideas regarding language as mediation. In this case, the teacher acts as a more knowledgeable other with respect to the target language variety (standard English) and/or register (conventions of written narratives), as well as the academic content (descriptive writing and parts of speech).

Codeswitching (Wheeler & Swords, 2004), which uses contrastive grammar analysis to teach students to distinguish between and become proficient in multiple varieties of English, is another curricular approach consistent with sociolinguistic theory. Rather than correcting students' non-standardized grammars (e.g., "I ain't got no money") and insisting that they rephrase in standardized form (e.g., "I don't have any money"), teachers ask students to analyze the grammars of both informal and formal registers and consider which language varieties are most appropriate for different social contexts, purposes, and audiences.

The instruction highlighted here and key features of sociolinguistic theory reflect social constructivist coherence theories because they focus on language mediation and the social and contextualized nature of learning. Particular varieties of language, and their uses in different contexts and purposes, will differentially support the construction of coherent meanings.

The social and linguistic mediation of literacy learning is also a feature of emergent literacy theory.

EMERGENT LITERACY THEORY

In his book *Thought and Language*, Vygotsky (2012) wrote that "gestures are writing in air" (p. 107) and characterized writing, or written signs, as "gestures that have been fixed" (p. 107). Emergent literacy theory suggests that literacy development, like language learning, is natural and shaped as individuals engage in their social worlds. Specifically, emergent literacy theory proposes that literacy development is ongoing from birth as children develop conventional reading and writing.

Approximating Conventional Literacy Practices

Marie Clay coined the term *emergent literacy* in her research on the early literacy behaviors of young children (Clay, 1966). She found that there were significant continuities between these behaviors and conventional reading and writing. These early literacy behaviors might include making writing-like marks, drawing pictures to convey meaning (see Figure 4.1), telling a story based on the pictures in a book, or reciting a book by memory while turning the pages. These emergent literacy behaviors can be thought of as approximations (Holdaway, 1979) of conventional literacy practices.

The concept of approximation is akin to Vygotskyan understandings of development, in which novices develop within social contexts of practice, and interaction mediates learning. In this sense, emergent literacy theory marks a significant departure from "readiness" perspectives (see the discussion of Thorndike's law of readiness in Chapter 2), which assume that literacy development is a linear and in-the-head phenomenon (Razfar & Gutiérrez, 2003) and that it should be taught when children reach a particular age or developmental stage. Central to emergent literacy theory are student–teacher relationships, and communication forms the bedrock of such relationships. Conversations between teachers and emergent readers and writers are cooperative endeavors, in which both speakers and listeners draw on their prior understandings and language to achieve understanding.

Emergent literacy theory is also grounded in the notion that different aspects of language and language use (listening, speaking, reading, writing, viewing, and visually representing) are interrelated in the process of development. Because of the relationships between oral and written language and other semiotic modes, experiences such as talking with children, engaging in dramatic play, creating and responding to visual texts,

Figure 4.1. A Kindergartner's Emergent Writing, Including the Use of Pictures to Convey Meaning

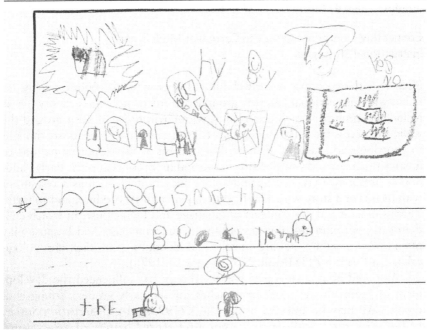

and oral language development are all considered key components of a child's literacy development.

Developing Concepts About Literacy

Through social interaction with adults, exposure to print materials and tools, and participation in everyday literacy activities, children develop specific behaviors and concepts about language and literacy, including social uses of texts (Dyson & Genishi, 2013). During the preschool years, as children are exposed to print and engage alongside others in activities involving print, they develop concepts about how text works. These include concepts about print (CAP), such as book orientation and handling; directionality of print (left to right and top to bottom in English); the concept of a letter, a word, and punctuation; and the notion that written words convey particular meanings (see Clay, 2000). While CAP focuses on paper-and-pencil forms of print, educators have expanded the concept to include screen-based literacies. Turbill (2001), for example, developed a checklist for assessing children's developing concepts of screen, including clicking, dragging, scrolling, locating programs on a computer's desktop, and opening and closing programs. Educators must also consider how children acquire understandings regarding phenomena such as downloading, differences between Web 1.0 and Web 2.0 technologies, and concepts associated with touch screen technologies, such as tapping and swiping.

Connecting Emergent Literacy to Curricular Models and Instructional Strategies

Readers with experience in early childhood or primary classrooms may be familiar with instructional practices grounded in emergent literacy theory. These include creating print-rich classrooms, with environmental print around the walls and accessible children's literature. Print-rich environments are thought to contribute to students' literacy development as their approximations of literacy practices and skills become more and more conventional. Early childhood classrooms may also have dramatic play centers, such as a restaurant with menus or a store with a cash register, play money, produce, and so forth. These simulate real-life contexts of language and literacy use, in which children can approximate conventional forms and practices. And because play often involves children taking on roles and identities above their chronological age, it forms a ZPD (Moll, 2014; Vygotsky, 1978).

As noted above, emergent literacy theory has influenced the development of literacy assessment approaches for the early grades. Young children's CAP may be assessed using Clay's (1993a) *An Observation Survey of Early Literacy Achievement*, a norm-referenced battery of assessments. In addition to a CAP assessment, the Observation Survey includes assessments of letter recognition, word writing, dictation, and running records of children's oral reading. Observation, in which teachers pay close attention to what children know about text, is essential to assessing young children's literacy development. Through close observation, teachers can glimpse students' invented spelling and other approximations of conventional literacy practices. Clay (1993a) refers to this process as roaming around the known, spending time getting to know what young readers and writers know.

Shared reading is also consistent with emergent literacy theory. Grounded in the research of Don Holdaway (1979), shared reading is a classroom practice meant to mimic the home literacy practice of shared reading, in which a young child sits with a parent or caregiver and "shares" in the reading of a book. The purpose of this practice is not to explicitly teach reading skills but rather to enjoy a piece of children's literature together and scaffold children into the social practice of reading. In order to allow for multiple children to share a book with a teacher, the text must be visible to all of the students. Big books—large-sized books, often with dimensions as big as 18 to 24 inches in height—serve this purpose. Through shared reading, the more expert adult (or teacher) is able to apprentice emergent readers into storybook reading, modeling fluent reading and inviting student participation.

Perhaps the most widely recognized and acclaimed curriculum connected to emergent literacy theory is Reading Recovery, an intensive daily one-on-one intervention lasting 12 to 20 weeks for approximately 30 minutes per session. The program is designed to help 1st-graders accelerate their reading to reach grade level (Clay, 1993b). Reading Recovery teachers conduct assessments using the Observation Survey in order to understand young children's emerging understandings about reading and writing. Lessons ground skills instruction in the reading of actual texts and emphasize students' construction of meaning. Independent reviews of research on the implementation of Reading Recovery indicate its effectiveness in supporting many 1st-graders' reading development (T. Shanahan & Barr, 1995). The Spanish-language version of Reading Recovery, titled *Descubriendo la Lectura* [Discovering Reading], has also been shown to be effective in improving native Spanish-speaking 1st-graders' reading achievement (Escamilla, Loera, Ruiz, & Rodríguez, 1998).

> *Emergent literacy theory is brought to life in two vignettes: Dragging Valentines to the Trash (p. 110) and Small Moments Writing: Adaptation and Experimentation (p. 161).*

Emergent literacy theory is similar to other social constructivist coherence theories in its emphasis on social contextualization of learning, the role of more knowledgeable others in scaffolding learning, and the importance of social interaction. From this view, it is not crucial that students' writing or reading correspond directly to conventional models of language or texts. Rather, as students generate stories from pictures, or create invented spellings, they construct meanings that *cohere* with what they know and understand about how language and texts work. A kindergartner might spell "I found a giant sand dollar" as "I fnD a jIint snt Dolr" not because it corresponds directly to conventional English spellings but because it *coheres* with what he understands about letter–sound correspondences. To be clear, there is still an expectation of development toward conventional forms. However, the focus is on how students understand reading and writing processes and use them in meaningful and contextualized ways.

CONCLUDING THOUGHTS

Despite the appeal of social constructivist coherence theories to educators, they have also been critiqued by those who feel that they do not sufficiently account for issues of power and equity in the classroom. Also, some educators feel as if social interaction is valued only insofar as it impacts cognitive development, and they question the extent to which social constructivist theories can elucidate processes of identity development. In addition, some have critiqued social constructivist theories for contributing to the essentialization of cultural groups and languages (the assumption that all children from a specific cultural or linguistic group will speak in a particular way or engage in certain literacy practices). Issues of power, equity, and identity as related to language and literacy teaching and learning are addressed more explicitly by social constructionist theories, which are introduced in the next chapter.

QUESTIONS FOR PRAXIS

1. Vygotsky understood semiotic mediation as occurring in face-to-face encounters involving speech interactions and tool use. What might this mean for the use of digital literacies, in particular the use of online interactions and discussions, in the classroom?

2. Jot down some of your own or your family's funds of knowledge. Now do the same for a couple of your students. How do your own funds of knowledge support you in your daily life and in achieving economic or social well-being? How might you draw on your students' funds of knowledge to support their participation in learning activities?

RESOURCES AND ADDITIONAL READINGS

Goularte, R. (2015). Who's got mail? Using literature to promote authentic letter writing. Lesson plan retrieved from www.readwritethink.org/classroom-resources/lesson-plans/mail-using-literature-promote-85.html

Martínez, R. A., Orellana, M. F., Pacheco, M., & Carbone, P. (2008). Found in translation: Connecting translating experiences to academic writing. *Language Arts, 85,* 421–431.

Reading Recovery website: readingrecovery.org/reading-recovery

Teachers College Reading and Writing Project Vimeo channel: vimeo.com/tcrwp

Zucker, T. A., Ward, A. E., Justice, L. M. (2009). Print referencing during read-alouds: A technique for increasing emergent readers' print knowledge. *The Reading Teacher, 63*(1), 62–72.

CHAPTER 5

Coherence to Incoherence
Social Constructionist Theories

As described in Chapters 3 and 4, constructivists attend to students' prior learning and social contexts and posit that learning occurs best when it is connected to meaningful experiences and is socially mediated. Coherence theories are grounded in the assumption that people construct meanings that cohere within given contexts or systems and that knowledge cannot be separated from people's experientially and culturally based understandings of the world (Davis et al., 2008). Accordingly, they expect different people to interpret the same phenomena, events, or texts differently. The theories in this chapter also view knowledge as dependent on knowers and their experiences. However, they also seek to explain *why* some understandings are valued or deemed more coherent than others, and they attempt to make the familiar strange by challenging taken-for-granted understandings about the world. That is, they attempt to make the coherent seem *incoherent* in order to highlight the idea that there are alternative ways of understanding the world. These characteristics are consistent with social constructionist theories.

In what follows I spend more time than in previous chapters describing the epistemological underpinnings of the theories in this chapter prior to presenting a grounding curricular model. I do this for two reasons. First, social constructionist theories may be less familiar to readers because they are taken up less frequently in K–12 settings than the previous theories I have presented. Second, the language associated with these theories can be challenging and tedious. While many terms related to correspondence and coherence theories have entered everyday discourse in education (e.g., *language processing, schema, zone of proximal development, scaffolding*), this is not necessarily the case with social constructionist theories. Even instructional approaches that animate these theories may be less familiar to readers. My intention, then, is to introduce central concepts to support readers' understanding of the practice–theory nexus within this chapter.

SOCIAL CONSTRUCTIONISM

Constructionism can be understood in several ways (Hruby, 2001). Because it shares the same root and prefix as *constructivism*, its use contributes to a confusing mix of terminology in the social sciences (see the inset discussion on term confusion in Chapter 4). In fact, some social scientists use the term *social constructionism* to refer to the theories that I outline in Chapter 4, with an emphasis on social processes and mediation (Davis et al., 2008), and others may use the term *social constructivism* to refer to the theories in this chapter. However, I differentiate social construct*ionism* from social construct*ivism*. My view of social constructionism aligns with what Hruby (2001) characterizes as a discursive orientation—an orientation to how meaning is produced through communication and rhetoric within social contexts. It is influenced by both critical social science (J. Greene, 1990), which seeks to work against social structures and power relationships that privilege some and exclude others, and poststructuralism, which seeks to question and disrupt dominant power structures and ways of viewing the world. I discuss each of these influences below.

Critical Social Science

Just as with the terms constructivism and constructionism, people are not always sure what *critical* means. Many use the term to refer to thinking processes (e.g., critical thinking). While this questioning stance and scrutiny of texts and ideas is one element of critical social science, *critical* also refers to skepticism toward dominant social institutions. This aspect of critical social science can be traced in part to the philosophy of Karl Marx and the Frankfurt School (a group of philosophers, economists, and sociologists at Germany's Frankfurt University Institute for Social Research who collaborated during the early to mid 20th century). The Frankfurt School was oriented toward radical social change (Morrell, 2008) and argued that institutions such as schools are always ideological and cannot be divorced from historical and political contexts.

    The idea that schooling is inherently ideological prompts critical social scientists to take an action-oriented stance to their work to challenge social inequities and injustice (J. Greene, 1990). In other words, they explicitly work to transform social and economic realities for people who have been historically marginalized. For example, a literacy researcher might work with a group of teachers as they begin integrating culturally relevant pedagogy into their instruction. The researcher may take a role of colearner or facilitator to support the teachers in their efforts while documenting the challenges and successes that teachers face in modifying their pedagogy. Both the inquiry process and the teaching involve attempts to counter social inequities within the institution of schooling. Because this work is clearly ideological, critical social scientists will also make explicit and question their own biases. The recognition that schooling is ideological is also embraced by poststructuralists.

Poststructuralism

Poststructuralism is difficult to define because it does not refer to only one construct or way of thinking. However, a central element of poststructuralist thinking is a critique of humanism, which emerged out of the Enlightenment (Peters & Burbules, 2004). With the Enlightenment, scientific ways of knowing took hold, including (1) the assumption that there is a correspondence between objective reality and subjective knowing (consistent with correspondence theories) and (2) the view that through systematic scientific inquiry people can come to know what is true. Like constructivists, poststructuralists refute the notion that knowledge exists independent of peoples' experiences and social contexts. However, they also engage in inquiry to *deconstruct* how some sets of knowledge, ways of thinking, and practices become valued over others. That is, they interrogate and break down power relationships. They also may attempt to *reconstruct* meanings differently; that is, to propose alternative structures, relationships, or ways of knowing.

These features of poststructuralism are evident in what Pantaleo and Sipe (2008) call "postmodern picture books"—texts that challenge traditional or dominant story lines. In David Wiesner's retelling of *The Three Pigs* (2001), for instance, the pigs step outside the pages of the book and directly address the reader. Fairy tale characters from other stories appear in the three pigs' world, and the illustrations show the pages being pulled out, literally *deconstructing* the story. As this happens, dominant understandings of power are disrupted. The wolf becomes trapped within the original story line and is portrayed as both victim and criminal. Such blurring of lines is common in postmodern picture books and poststructuralist thinking in general.

Critical social science and poststructuralism's interest in exposing and breaking down the social processes in which power relationships are established and maintained come together in social constructionism. Social constructionism, then, seeks to explain how or why certain meanings or ways of understanding the world are deemed coherent (or incoherent) or valued (or worthless) and to work against these inequities. Social constructionists often focus on social practices because "practice" implies agency—people acting on their world. This differs from understanding learning as an active cognitive process, or even an active cognitive process mediated by social activity. As Luke and Freebody (1999) explain, "The notion of 'practices' suggests that they are actually *done*—performed, negotiated, and achieved in everyday classroom and community contexts, rather unlike psychological skills, schemata, competencies, and so forth" (para. 15). The social aspect of these practices underscores that they are "constrained, mediated, and shaped by relations of power—relations that may be asymmetrical, unequal, and ideological" (para. 7).

To summarize, social constructionism embraces tenets of coherence theories in that it considers knowledge as dependent on knowers and as contextual rather than universal. However, social constructionist theories also pose critical questions such as, "Whose understandings are valued here?" "Why are some meanings or understandings deemed *coherent* by those in power while others are deemed *incoherent*?" "How can those whose knowledge or ways of knowing are devalued or unrecognized still participate in this context?" To illustrate these points, and to set the stage for the theories presented later in this chapter, I describe Youth Participatory Action Research as a grounding curricular model.

GROUNDING CURRICULAR MODEL: YOUTH PARTICIPATORY ACTION RESEARCH

Youth Participatory Action Research (Y-PAR) is a classroom- and community-based approach to critical inquiry and literacy teaching. It is built largely on participatory action research (PAR), in which researchers investigate a topic relevant to the immediate community. It involves reliance on the knowledge and skills of researchers from within the community and a call to action to promote community change (McIntyre, 2000). A central feature of PAR is that community members become researchers and determine the focus of inquiry rather than researchers coming only from the university or other outside groups. In Y-PAR, youth and students become community researchers, participating in the design and conduct of critical inquiry in order to better their schools and/or communities. Y-PAR is typically implemented at the secondary or middle school level, but with additional teacher guidance and support, it can be implemented in the elementary grades.

As a curricular approach, Y-PAR capitalizes on youths' experiences and expertise rather than positioning them as passive learners waiting to receive knowledge from teachers. In this sense, it positions youth as critical sociologists (Bautista et al., 2013; Morrell, 2008) and as both consumers and producers of texts and knowledge. Within this context, critical textual production (Morrell, 2008) and the production of knowledge are part and parcel of literacy learning. Kinloch (2009), for example, documents how she and two high school students explored the issue of gentrification in Harlem, New York, using Y-PAR. They examined the history of the community and gentrification initiatives that radically changed the demographic landscape of Harlem. The students interviewed residents, both newcomers and those who had lived there for years, and generated video of their own experiences living and researching in Harlem. In doing so, they used a wide array of digital literacy tools and semiotic modes.

According to Morrell (2008), who facilitated a critical research seminar with high school youth using Y-PAR, dialogue is central to this approach. His seminar began with dialogue in which youth shared their perspectives, experiences, and emotions regarding the conditions of schooling in their community. This dialogue fed directly into writing about their experiences and, subsequently, into designing and conducting their research.

Importantly, skills instruction is not neglected in Y-PAR. Rather, the teaching of skills is embedded within the approach and connected to the specific goals of the inquiry. With support, the youth in Morrell's study generated data collection instruments, engaged with theory and relevant research studies, collected and analyzed data, and wrote research reports. They also wrote 1,500- to 2,000-word essays regarding their experiences of becoming researchers, and they presented their research findings to a wide array of audiences.

As a result of being taught specific skills pertinent to the research project, students build both academic and social skills while also engaging in civic life and working toward social change. Teachers attend to literacy skills, such as spelling, phonics, and grammar, but also recognize that conventions will shift based on social and cultural context and audience. For instance, composing research notes meant for their peers and coresearchers would merit different conventions and language choices than preparing a presentation for the local school board.

In short, Y-PAR focuses on meaningful literacy practices in the context of inquiry, whereby students take ownership of their learning and engage in transformative action. Dialogue and critical questioning are central components of this approach. Teachers recruit students' collective knowledge and understandings to support their critical consumption and production of texts within the context of their research. These elements align with social constructionism because Y-PAR engages students in critical inquiry about why things are the way they are and supports them in reading and writing for social change within their communities. These concerns are also voiced in the five theories I present in the remainder of this chapter: critical literacy theory, new literacy studies, multiliteracies/new literacies, critical sociocultural theory, and critical race theory. There are significant overlaps between these theories, which reflect the intellectual turn from coherence to incoherence and the blurring of conceptual boundaries. These theories also build on key aspects of theories presented in earlier chapters, particularly those in Chapter 4.

CRITICAL LITERACY THEORY

Critical literacy theory emphasizes individual and social transformation (Morrell, 2008). Also referred to as critical literacy pedagogy, it is most often associated with the work of Brazilian educator Paolo Freire, who argued that capitalism contributes to the dehumanization of oppressed people (1970). He maintained that schooling contributes to this dehumanization in part through the dominant "banking model" of teaching, which values knowledge transmission and rote learning. The positioning of learners as passive receivers of knowledge also aligns with the expectation that learners will uncritically accept dominant beliefs and inequitable social structures.

Reading the Word and the World

In his seminal work, *Pedagogy of the Oppressed*, Freire (1970) articulated the need for humanizing educational practices to promote both individual learning and a deep awareness of how social structures impact individuals' lives and how they can work to change those structures. He referred to this as *conscientização* (translated in English to conscientization). For Freire, this meant two things: a problem-posing approach and the grounding of learning in the lived experiences of everyday people, particularly those disadvantaged by dominant social structures. A problem-posing approach involves raising awareness of and reflecting on systems of oppression in learners' lives and lived experiences and moving from there to transformative action. As discussed in Chapter 1, this interaction between critical reflection and action is referred to as "praxis" (Freire & Macedo, 1987; Morrell, 2008). For literacy, this means reading both the "word" and the "world" (Freire, 1970).

Reading both the word and the world lay at the core of Freire's adult literacy programs for peasants in northeastern Brazil in the 1960s (Kamberelis & Dimitriadis, 2005). Freire worked with this community by engaging them in dialogue to identify how the local economic system marginalized them and how they had internalized dominant beliefs regarding their own abilities and socioeconomic situations (e.g., the assumption that they themselves were to blame for their poverty and illiteracy). His students' language became "generative words": As his students "read the world," Freire wrote down their words and then used them to teach his students literacy skills—"the word." They then put their words into action by using their literacy skills to work for social and political transformation in their communities.

While Freire's work in adult literacy with marginalized communities formed the groundwork for his framework of critical literacy, *conscientização* is equally important for the wealthy or dominant classes. This is because engaging in dialogue and critical readings to expose how the privileged benefit from (and are also oppressed by) inequitable social systems and policies is necessary for both individuals' transformation and social change (Davis et al., 2008). This is consistent with Freire's assertion that social change must be a collective effort rather than the sole responsibility of the oppressed or the privileged, and that dialogue is central to this process (Freire, 1970).

Key to critical literacy theory is embedding literacy skills instruction (whether it is comprehension, spelling, literary analysis, grammar, persuasive writing, etc.) within the larger project of social change. The idea is that in addition to becoming functionally literate, students should become critically literate. For Freire this meant acknowledging one's own humanity and the humanity of others and engaging in action for social change. Morrell (2008) states, "Although we would be remiss if we didn't place some value on improved academic literacy achievement, we would be negligent if achievement were our only goal" (p. 55).

Those building on critical literacy theory have applied it across the curriculum using a wide array of texts and activities. For example, Morrell and Duncan-Andrade (2002) explored the use of hip-hop literacies in English classrooms from a critical literacy perspective, and Hodson (2003) advocates approaches to science education to prepare a citizenry that is critically literate in science. Principles of critical literacy theory have been influential for other theoretical orientations, including sociocultural-historical theory; see the discussions of multiliteracies/new literacies theory (p. 86) and critical sociocultural theory (p. 89).

Connecting Critical Literacy Theory to Curricular Models and Instructional Strategies

Several approaches to classroom literacy instruction bring critical literacy theory to life. Importantly, instruction that animates critical literacy theory is not limited to the construct of critical thinking. While weighing evidence and taking a questioning stance toward texts and authors' purposes is certainly a vital part of critical literacy, instruction informed by critical literacy theory also moves toward action to effect real change in school communities and beyond. This is a core element of Y-PAR, as well as the four resources model, which is meant to guide instruction around a "family of practices," or four resources, that readers and writers engage with or draw from: code breaker, text participant, text user, and text critic (Freebody & Luke, 1990). The model advocates for teaching literacy skills, such as spelling, phonics, and grammar, but also recognizes that conventions will shift based on social and cultural context. The model also includes participating in meaning-making with texts, as well as supporting students in using texts and writing for multiple purposes and audiences. Finally, it recognizes that literacy practices and texts are mediated by power relationships, highlighting the need for supporting students in critically analyzing texts and the value systems they support or challenge. Within the four resources model, being literate means that people can draw on these resources as needed in different aspects of their lives.

Another example of literacy instruction consistent with critical literacy theory might include students writing letters to their local city council regarding the spraying of pesticides on farm fields adjacent to the school, or a group of 7th-graders doing research on voting restrictions in their state and creating a radio broadcast reporting their findings. In both of these examples, the students are engaging in literacy practices to effect change in their own communities. In the process, teachers support their literacy development through conferencing and minilessons geared to specific reading and writing skills.

While some teachers of young children shy away from engaging their students in critical literacy activities and conversations regarding oppression and inequity, critical literacy instruction has been taken up throughout the grade span. In an action research project in his own 1st-grade classroom, Bourke (2008) used the fairy tale genre to engage students in critical conversations about power and identity. He supported his students in questioning black-and-white constructs of good and evil as portrayed in fairy tales. His students then assumed authorial stances to rewrite stories such as "The Three Billy Goats Gruff" to alter power relationships within the dominant story lines. Bourke writes, "The moment I equipped my students with the power to create their own texts, and in doing so, insert their discourses into their renditions, a noticeable shift occurred in the way their stories depicted authority" (p. 310). The students then applied their skills of critique to other textual genres:

> As we read other genres, my students transferred their critical skills and began to discern the inequities present in various text types, deconstructing them in their conversations and writing. Fairy tales had been the medium through which critical literacy was introduced; however, in time, many genres would be made vulnerable to the critical gaze of my first-grade students. (Bourke, 2008, p. 311)

Similarly, Lotherington and Chow (2006) offer a detailed description of how Chow, a kindergarten teacher, engaged her students as text analysts by updating, or rewriting, the traditional "Goldilocks and the Three Bears" narrative. This included critiquing representations of characters and events, or "reading discourses of power" (Meacham & Buendia, 1999, p. 514). Students then reimagined Goldilocks as a member of a diverse cultural and linguistic community and rewrote the story line to more closely resemble the realities of the students' urban and 21st-century lives (Lotherington & Chow, 2006).

Critical literacy theory is not without its critics. Some scholars argue that its emancipatory agenda can take a paternalistic form—that it assumes that particular students or communities are "marginalized" and need to be liberated from oppression when perhaps they do not view themselves in that light. Critical literacy theory has also been criticized for overemphasizing economic forms of inequality while not paying sufficient attention to other vortices of power and difference, such as race and gender. Finally, while Freire's alternative to the banking model is widely embraced, critics point out that his model of dialogic teaching and learning could become yet another vehicle for imposing Western ideals and models of education on non-Western populations. The idea here is that if unchecked, critical literacy can be seen as simply replacing one form of colonial oppression with another. Critical literacy's supporters counter that when taken up reflexively and in partnership with communities, it can support

> *Critical literacy theory is brought to life in two vignettes:* Momentos de Cambio (*Moments of Change; p. 167) and* "I Know the Words, but I Don't Get How They're Used": Reading Historical Documents in a WebQuest (*p. 184*).

agency and transformation that is developed from *within* communities, rather than imposed upon them.

Critical literacy theory questions the coherence of taken-for-granted knowledge or ways of knowing. Within critical literacy theory, there is an overarching emphasis on how broad structures of power, in particular, social institutions, contribute to inequity, and teachers and students are prompted to use literacy to address social inequities in students' immediate or local communities. The next theory, new literacy studies, devotes closer attention to differences in local communities with respect to literacy practices and places less emphasis on taking social action.

NEW LITERACY STUDIES

New literacy studies (NLS) emerged largely out of educational and linguistic anthropology. Brian Street (1995), for example, whose anthropological research documented literacy practices in villages in Iran, illustrated the different literacy practices that occurred in these contexts. And Shirley Brice Heath's (1983) research on language and literacy practices in different socioeconomic communities in the Carolina Piedmont (described with respect to sociolinguistic theory in Chapter 4) is also considered seminal within NLS. Central to NLS is the assumption that literacy practices are situated in local contexts and are purposeful, tied to specific social goals, and that literacy practices change as contexts and tools change. Thus, within NLS, educators talk of *literacy practices* and *literacies* rather than *literacy* in the singular.

Like other social constructionist theories, NLS views all literacy practices as ideological. Street (1995) makes this point by differentiating between autonomous and ideological models of literacy. The autonomous model views literacy practices as independent from the contexts of practice in which they occur. From this perspective, literacy practices are thought to be universal and transposable from one context to another. The assumption is that if someone can decode, or recognize and spell words, and apply a predetermined set of strategies to understand a text, then that person should be able to read an article in their local newspaper, decipher a proposed referendum in the voting booth, enjoy a good novel, read the instructions on their federal income tax forms, and so forth. In other words, people are either literate or they are not, and therefore straightforward methods of teaching literacy ought to apply to all learners. As readers may have already noted, the autonomous model is aligned with correspondence theories (see Chapter 2).

In contrast, the ideological model views literacy practices as not only situated in social contexts but also tied to particular perspectives or values (Street, 1995). As Street (2003) explains, literacy "is always contested, both its meanings and its practices, hence particular versions of it are always 'ideological,' they are always rooted in a particular world-view and in a desire for that view of literacy to dominate and to marginalize others" (pp. 77–78). This means that being "literate" is not an either/or equation. Rather, people may engage in sophisticated literacy practices in one context but struggle to engage in literacy practices in another.

Scholars operating within NLS have explored relationships between home or community ("local") and dominant, normalized ("global") literacy practices, such as those valued in schools. Central to this work is the construct of discourses (Hull & Schultz, 2001). Gee (1996) differentiates between *discourses* written with a lower case *d* and *Discourses*, with an uppercase *D*. While *discourses* refers to social interactions, *Discourses* refers to "ways of behaving, interacting, valuing, thinking, believing, speaking, and often reading and writing that are accepted as instantiations of particular roles (or 'types of people') by specific groups of people" (Gee, 1996, p. viii). As such, Discourses are "products of social histories" and are connected to the distribution of power within social structures and contexts. Different discourses and literacy practices are tied to different Discourses. They are developed and practiced within different discourse communities, groups of people "who share common language norms, characteristics, patterns, or practices as a consequence of their ongoing communications and identification with each other" (Bazerman, 2009).

Understandings of d/Discourse and relationships between local and global contexts and practices help explain why a 9-year-old boy may be quite adept at playing Pokémon, and conversing with his friends regarding Pokémon characters and battles, but may be less participatory in classroom read-alouds and conversations about character and plot development in *Charlotte's Web* (White, 1952). To apply the language of NLS, he is proficient at "local" discourse practices but is less proficient in the discourse practices of literary interpretation and discussion (a "global" practice). The kicker is that the institution of schooling, and many of those who occupy positions of power relative to students (e.g., administrators, teachers, etc.), may not recognize Pokémon cards as valued texts, or playing Pokémon as a literate activity.

Connecting NLS to Curricular Models and Instructional Strategies

NLS prompts educators to consider a multitude of out-of-school literacy practices and how they may connect with academic literacy practices (Morrell, 2008). Using the example above, a teacher whose students play Pokémon might engage them in conversations regarding the game, asking them to identify the rules of the game and specific terminology and language conventions on the cards. Each creature has weaknesses and powers and can "evolve" into more powerful versions of themselves at different stages. This is represented numerically on the cards and through creatures' names and avatars. Nidorino, which looks like a baby dragon, evolves into Nidoking, which is more physically developed (pokebeach.com/tcg/base-set/scans). The ending –ino is similar to diminutive affixes in some languages (e.g., Italian), whereas –king indicates more power. Teachers might invite students to create their own cards and use these same morphological conventions. In Figure 5.1, for example, a student has made two creatures—Squidy Toad and Skormeleon—that evolve into Sea Kraken and Scorpioking.

Figure 5.1. A Student's Trading Cards Modeled After Pokémon Cards

Teachers may build on these activities to draw students' attention to how language conventions function within a novel and how characters change, or "evolve," as a result of specific experiences or events. Students may then create Pokémon-style cards depicting those characters and their evolution.

Instruction in the content areas to support students' disciplinary literacies is also consistent with NLS. Draper et al. (2010), for example, consider content literacies and each discipline as "local" contexts with their own discourse practices and conventions. Thus, different disciplines may be considered different discourse communities. Accordingly, teachers may pay

> NLS is brought to life in two vignettes: Momentos de Cambio (Moments of Change; p. 167) and "My Tomatoes Don't Like Soda": Experimenting with Plant Foods (p. 176).

particular attention to teaching students the language and literacy conventions of the discipline, including academic language. (Also see sociolinguistic theory, Chapter 4.)

Critics of NLS express concerns about "romanticizing the local" (Collins & Blot, 2003): embracing home and community language practices in instructional contexts without also teaching more "globally" valued forms of language and literacy practices. Along the same lines, some have argued that NLS does not sufficiently address issues of power, explain how power operates vis-à-vis literacy practices, or catalyze social action (Pennycook, 2001). The issue of power is addressed more explicitly within critical sociocultural theory and critical race theory, described later in this chapter.

MULTILITERACIES/NEW LITERACIES THEORY

While NLS and multiliteracies/new literacies are similar in name, they refer to two different social constructionist theories. NLS focuses not so much on the newness of literacy tools and practices but rather on the newness of ways of studying and understanding literacy. Thus, the studies are what is new, not literacy practices themselves. Of course, localized literacy practices, as understood from an NLS perspective, may indeed involve new forms of literacy tools and practices. However, with the term *multiliteracies/new literacies*, what is new is the proliferation and shift in tools and practices associated with rapidly changing communication technologies and globalization.

In 1996 a group of scholars called the New London Group (because they met in New London, Connecticut) developed a manifesto for literacy instruction: "A Pedagogy of Multiliteracies." Some of these scholars are also well-known in the areas of sociolinguistics (Courtney Cazden, Sarah Michaels), NLS (James Gee), and critical literacy (Allan Luke). However, in addition to sharing similar assumptions about the interface between global and local practices, social uses of language, and a critical framing, within a pedagogy of multiliteracies, attention is paid to multimodality—the idea that what counts as literacy should be broadened to encompass multiple semiotic modes (e.g., visual, movement, etc.; Kress & van Leeuwen, 2001).

The New London Group underscored how shifts in literacy technologies and the impact of the media in people's everyday lives come together to characterize what scholars have referred to as "new times." The principal argument here is that the rapidly shifting, or "deictic" nature of literacy technologies is radically different in speed and scope from earlier technological advances in literacy tools and practices, such as the development of the printing press or even the typewriter (Leu et al., 2013). In essence, we are educating students to be literate using tools that have not yet been invented. Proponents of this theoretical orientation argue that new times require corresponding shifts in how we think about teaching and learning (Lankshear & Knobel, 2003).

As the New London Group pointed out, Fordism (the name of which is derived from the Ford Motor Company) refers to production-based local economies, a model of efficient factory production, hierarchical organizational structures, and analog communication systems. In contrast, post-Fordism is characterized by a global information economy, collaborative and less hierarchical organizational structures, and proliferating literacy technologies. These economic changes and increases in mass communications technologies are accompanied by the flow of people and capital across geographic, linguistic, and cultural borders and the proliferation of language and literacy practices. The term *proliferation* is key because these demographic, economic, technological, and cultural changes do not necessarily mean the replacement of more antiquated language and literacy practices but rather a diversification of those practices.

Educational institutions and policies, however, have been slow to adapt to these changes. While the multilingual and multiliterate landscape of the new mainstream is incompatible with basic skills, one-size-fits-all instruction, neoliberal political forces have resulted in the widespread implementation of standardized, skills-based instruction that is more compatible with autonomous models of literacy. Those working from a multiliteracies/new literacies perspective argue that literacy instruction must help students negotiate the multitude of semiotic systems that permeate students' everyday lives. To accomplish this, teachers must function not as technicians but as curriculum designers (New London Group, 1996).

Connecting Multiliteracies/New Literacies Theory to Curricular Models and Instructional Strategies

Literacy instructional approaches consistent with multiliteracies/new literacies theory resemble those associated with other theories in this chapter.

The New London Group (1996) laid out a four-part pedagogical approach that includes four interrelated components. *Situated practice* refers to "immersion in meaningful practices within a community of learners who are capable of playing multiple and different roles based on their backgrounds and experiences" (p. 85). *Overt instruction* includes teaching skills to scaffold students' learning. While this does not mean rote skills practice or a transmission model of teaching, it does include the explicit teaching of skills and conventions that will help students participate in contextualized activities (like in Y-PAR). The goal of *critical framing* is to support students in understanding the historical, cultural, political, and ideological aspects of particular conventions, texts, and ways of making meaning. As the New London Group (1996) explains, "the teacher must help learners to denaturalize and make strange again what they have learned and mastered" (p. 86) through overt instruction. Finally, *transformed practice* suggests that teachers should support students in engaging in meaningful and reflective practice using what they have learned. These four interrelated components offer instructional spaces to engage in three processes of design: understanding and engaging with *available designs* (resources for making meaning and representations of meaning), *designing* (work that uses or focuses on available designs), and *the redesigned* (new resources and representations produced through designing).

Other instructional instantiations of multiliteracies/new literacies might include Internet-based inquiry projects such as WebQuests, inquiry-based learning engagements in which the majority of information sources are drawn from the World Wide Web (Dodge, 1995). When combined with explicit instruction in evaluating online sources and web navigation, opportunities for critical analysis of concepts and ideas found in the WebQuest, and generation of new texts such as multimedia presentations or new websites, students may engage in all four components of the New London Group's pedagogy. Teachers may also use geocaching, a digital treasure hunt, which involves finding or placing real or virtual caches around the world and then identifying their exact locations using the Global Positioning System (GPS; www.geocaching.com/). This process requires students to use an array of digital and print literacies (Jewett, 2011).

> Multiliteracies/new literacies theory is brought to life in two vignettes: Dragging Valentines to the Trash (p. 110) and Being Melody: Stepping into Role Through Social Media (p. 151).

A key principle of instruction anchored in multiliteracies/new literacies is that shifts in new media and technologies require concomitant shifts in teaching that go beyond basic skills and didactic interactions. This lies in contrast to the "old wine in new bottles" principle (Lankshear & Knobel, 2003), in which new technologies are used to simply teach basic skills or to position students as passive users or consumers of new technologies. This comes down not only to the specific digital tools used but to *how* they are used. iPads or

Smartboards can be used in innovative ways, or they can simply become very expensive worksheets.

CRITICAL SOCIOCULTURAL THEORY

As its name implies, critical sociocultural theory (CST) brings together elements of different theories, including sociocultural-historical theory, NLS, and critical literacy theory. CST was proposed by language and literacy researchers to extend sociocultural-historical theory to account for how learning and teaching both influence and are influenced by power relations (Lewis, Enciso, & Moje, 2007). CST embraces Vygotsky's (1978) concept of semiotic mediation: As learners engage in socially mediated activity with others, they appropriate new knowledge and ways of speaking relevant to the specific cultural activities or fields into which they are being apprenticed. Also, like NLS, CST views literacy practices as socially and historically situated. Additionally, CST shares critical literacy theory's interest in individual and social transformation. However, moreso than these other theories, CST emphasizes power, identity, and agency.

Power and Identity

CST developed in part as a response to criticisms of NLS and sociocultural-historical theory for not adequately attending to issues of power. CST pays special attention to how literacy practices occur in complex networks of power and how people take up different identities within contexts of teaching and learning (Lewis et al., 2007). There is attention devoted to understanding how language use, instructional practices, use of different texts in the classroom, interpretations of texts, and so forth convey subtle messages to teachers and students about who they are presumed to be and ought to be (Gee, 1996). This is referred to as social discursive positioning (Harré & Van Langenhove, 1999). The concept of social positioning via language use and other forms of discourse (e.g., body movements, attire, etc.) is a missing element of sociocultural-historical theory. The same semiotic mediation through which learners appropriate knowledge and language also involves the appropriation of ideologies of language and language learning (Handsfield, 2012).

CST embraces the work of Mikhail Bakhtin, a Russian literary theorist and contemporary of Vygotsky's. Bakhtin (1984) argued that people's words, whether written or spoken, do not exist in a vacuum and are never purely original or autonomous. Rather, they are dialogic, meaning that they are appropriated from others' words and from other contexts. An example of this might be a 2nd-grader's use of the phrase "Once upon a time . . ." to begin a story. The phrase is a common lead-in to fairy tales, which hold a privileged position in contemporary childhoods in Western industrial-ized countries. The student voices a discourse that carries with it particular expectations about the settings, characters, and plot elements that might be included. Bakhtin used these ideas to understand the development of characters within the novel, and these ideas align with CST's understand-ings about identity. For Bakhtin, people are positioned in certain ways and articulate particular identities through the course of an extended narrative. However, authors can diverge from expected story lines. What kind of story might the 2nd-grader tell? Will her story reinscribe dominant assumptions in fairy tales regarding who can be a hero? Or who is good and who is evil? Or might she dare to play around with the elements of her story to challenge those dominant narratives? This brings the issue of agency to the fore.

Agency and Negotiating Power Structures

As Moje and Lewis (2007) explain, "Agency might be thought of as the strategic making and remaking of selves, identities, activities, relationships, cultural tools and resources, and histories, as embedded within relations of power. At times, but not always, the relations of power are disrupted and remade" (p. 18). In the case of the 2nd-grader described above, diverging from dominant discourses or narratives is an example of agency. Another example might be a teacher who circumvents a literacy curriculum she dis-agrees with by using elements of it in unexpected ways in the classroom. In doing so, she can position herself as complying with district expectations while also being responsive to her students' strengths and needs.

Bakhtin also introduced the concept of chronotopes (literally, "space times") to describe sets of ideologies that endure over time and that struc-ture social practices (Morson & Emerson, 1990), such as literacy teaching and learning. For example, in a chronotope of self-selected reading, there is an assumption that students will select books from the library or a pot of books on their desks, read by themselves, and actually read the print text rather than just the illustrations. It is typically expected that students will not chat with one another, and oftentimes students are held accountable for their reading through the use of literature logs. In many classrooms students may select a comfortable spot on the floor or a classroom sofa. Some of the ideologies that structure this chronotope, then, include individualism and print text as more valuable than other media. Because these are dominant ideologies in schools, when different teachers talk about self-selected read-ing, they hold fairly consistent expectations for what will occur during that time, what it should look like, and how texts are used.

However, chronotopes are not completely stable. Because people can act with agency in practices like self-selected reading, the chronotopes that structure them are open to change, even if in small and subtle ways (Kam-berelis & Dimitriadis, 2005). Furthermore, literacy practices and instruction are complex, structured by multiple, overlapping, and sometimes conflicting chronotopes. A classroom may be shaped in part by a chronotope of standardization, manifested in scripted skills instruction and high-stakes tests. But the same classroom may also be molded by a chronotope of bilingual education, in which students' diverse funds of knowledge and opportunities for social interaction are valued (Handsfield, Crumpler, & Dean, 2010).

In a nutshell, CST recognizes that while power relationships and social structures may constrain language and literacy practices, as well as teaching practices, people may exercise agency to impact practices and identities, potentially shifting power relationships even if in small ways. Stated otherwise, CST views teachers and students as both consumers and agents of curriculum with the ability, or power, to creatively appropriate curricula and Discourses of language and literacy (Collins & Blot, 2003; de Certeau, 1984).

Connecting Critical Sociocultural Theory to Curricular Models and Instructional Strategies

Instructional practices that animate CST attend to issues of power, identity, and agency. Such approaches may include many of the same approaches discussed in previous chapters. However, teachers will likely also work to generate spaces and conversations in which dominant Discourses and social and discursive positioning are made explicit and challenged. Within TSI, for example, teachers may invite students to not only make connections to texts but also to articulate their disconnections (Jones, Clarke, & Enriquez, 2010).

Teachers may also support students in challenging dominant interpretations of both print texts and other media. For example, a 4th-grade teacher (Isabel; also featured in vignettes in Chapters 7 and 10) engaged her students in a conversation regarding character representation in graphic novels and comics (Handsfield, 2011). She asked her students to think about how authors of such texts would convey scary characters, and most of her students emphasized color, suggesting that authors or illustrators would use red, black, and white. She then asked, "So if I was wearing black and white, I would be scary? What if there was a horrible monster, but it was all pink and purple?" Her students decided that scariness would depend on a lot of other characteristics beyond just color, and they moved on to discussing how other character traits might be portrayed. Isabel drew students' attention to how different texts and authors position them as readers and how they may imagine and position their own readers when writing for different purposes. They recognized dominant meanings (e.g., that particular colors convey certain characteristics or emotions) but also questioned and critiqued those meanings.

Finally, teachers informed by CST may engage students in conversations to make explicit how students and teachers position each other in classroom interactions. For example, a teacher might tell one of her 5th-graders during a comprehension focus group, "Now you're the teacher. Come sit here and lead the others through this discussion. As the teacher, how will you invite your students to participate?" In doing so, she makes explicit different social positions, or identities, and prompts her students to think about how their discourse (both their actions and their language) might reflect those positions.

> *CST is brought to life in two vignettes: "Put It on the Train!" (p. 104) and "It's Not a Appropriate Word" (p. 129).*

These examples make clear the influence of critical social science and poststructuralism on CST. This, combined with the attention to power relations, identity, and agency, sets CST apart from other theories in this chapter and in Chapter 4. The next theory I present focuses more specifically on particular vectors of difference and how these influence literacy teaching and learning.

CRITICAL RACE THEORY

As noted previously, criticisms have been aimed at critical literacy theory, particularly its minimal attention to race, gender, sexual identity, and other historically grounded points of difference. Critical race theory (CRT) is grounded largely on a questioning of White, male, and heteronormative ways of knowing. Furthermore, combinations of experiences will come together to inform how different people may construct different understandings or "truths" regarding the world around them. CRT, including more specific standpoints or theories, such as Latino critical theory, queer theory, and some forms of feminist theory, maintains that worldviews are shaped by specific histories of inequity, and it foregrounds race in praxis. This translates into the reimagination of specific labels to emphasize the role of race in social and educational processes—for example, Urrieta's (2010) renaming of "mainstream" as "whitestream."

Critical race theorists view meritocracy, a foundational ideology in the United States, as a myth (Delgado & Stefanic, 2000; Zamudio, Russell, Rios, & Bridgeman, 2011). An example of a meritocratic discourse that has gained purchase within the popular imagination and social media is the notion of "grit" (perseverance and resiliency) as a central contributing factor to students' educational success (Tough, 2012). Critics of the "grit narrative" (Gow, 2014) argue that it overlooks very real racial, social, and economic inequities. Similarly, critical race theorists argue that a meritocratic focus on individual effort (e.g., the idea that such efforts will lead to just rewards) cloaks overt, tacit, and institutionalized racism that impedes success for many, despite individual efforts. Within schooling, where meritocracy underlies institutional and classroom policies and practices, students of color are often pushed toward the bottom rungs of achievement and,

BEYOND CRITICAL LITERACY: READING THE WORLD THROUGH A RACED AND GENDERED LENS

MARCELLE M. HADDIX, SYRACUSE UNIVERSITY

A traditional critical literacy framework moves beyond reading and comprehending texts to exploring broader, complicated themes within the larger world. Underlying a critical literacy framework is Freire's (1970) notion that literacy is about "reading the world" and seeing the world from particular frames. A critical literacy framework underscores the assumption that reading and writing are about power and that critical literacy goes beyond the individual toward an analysis and reconstruction of social identities. Moving from theory to practice, however, many versions of critical literacy circulate.

Freebody and Luke (1990) introduced the four resources model of reading, a four-tiered approach for critical literacy that identified necessary sets of social practices for literacy instruction—coding, text-meaning, pragmatic, and critical practices. In a critique of the appropriations (or misappropriations) of critical literacy, Luke (2000) notes that for many educators and scholars, particularly those within the North American context, critical literacy is often defined as higher-order comprehension skills, such as the development of metacognitive reading strategies, reader response orientations, and analysis of authorial intent. Luke (2000) also argues that the four resources model is not sufficient in and of itself for literate participation in a complex and dynamic social world. Understanding critical literacy in this way limits and negates an original intention of systemic analysis of relationships of social, cultural, and economic power. These concepts ground a definition of critical literacy that is about being situated within social practices in communities and in the world.

Many literacy scholars continue to challenge the promotion of critical literacy as a singular method or approach (e.g., Edelsky & Cherland, 2006; Haddix & Rojas, 2011; Vasquez, 2004) and instead promote the use of critical literacy in ways that provide young people with tools to critique and question the world around them as they make sense of texts, including those mediated by the school environment and by popular and media texts. A critical literacy framework should bring attention to what is included in and what is left out of a text, who is included and who is excluded. What must become clearer in the theoretical and practical application of a critical literacy framework is the "who" that we are referring to when we think about the use of critical literacy with today's youth. Further, it is important to explore the ways that a critical literacy framework is redefined and repositioned by the readers. For example, what does it mean when critical literacy becomes a tool for Black adolescent girls to read their selves into their encounters with popular media and texts?

How might critical literacy unpack and refocus issues of power and privilege when used as a literacy framework with mostly White, middle-class students? Morrell (2008) writes that "no population requires critical literacy more than today's urban youth" (p. 6). He points out that because of the realities that many urban youth confront on a regular basis, they will constantly have to interpret and critique media and texts that position them as "Other." A critical literacy framework, however, should demand that we ask, who are urban youth? Is urban really a code word for poor, Black youth? Who is included in the labeling of urban youth? Who is excluded? Who has the power to determine this? Given dominant stereotyping of people of color from low-income communities that persists within popular media and texts, a critical literacy framework can uniquely position readers to take a stance toward challenging and changing such representations. However, this stance is taken up differently based on readers' social locations, their positions of power, and their raced, gendered, and classed identities.

Luke's (2000) "redefinition" of critical literacy is a starting point for articulating a framework that is about "teaching and learning how texts work, understanding and re-mediating what texts attempt to do in the world and to people, and moving students toward active position-takings with texts to critique and reconstruct social fields in which they live and work" (p. 453). A critical literacy analysis for reading and literacy may begin with questions such as the following:

- Who was the text written for?
- Whose perspectives and narratives are omitted or silenced by this text?
- What are the cultural meanings and possible readings that can be constructed from this text?
- What is the text trying to do to me? Or, how is the text positioning me as the reader? (Luke, 2000)

However, it cannot stop there. If critical literacy is to help readers not only make sense of media and texts but also make sense of themselves and their worlds, such an analysis has to explicitly call out the role of social locations and identities. This begins by naming race, gender, class, and other identity markers when considering how readers connect with and engage with texts.

I read the word and the world as a Black woman with a working-class history, and I cannot divorce myself from my complex identities as I work to make sense of texts. The same is true for all readers—how one responds to the questions above is deeply informed by one's self-identification and awareness of one's lived experiences in the world. A critical "critical literacy" framework does not take that for granted.

oftentimes, out the school door and into the street. This has become referred to as the "school to prison pipeline" (Heitzeg, 2009; NAACP, 2005).

CRT also challenges assumptions of objectivity and neutrality in education (Ladson-Billings & Tate, 1995; Zamudio et al., 2011). As Ladson-Billings and Tate (1995) explain, "For the critical race theorist, social reality is constructed by the formulation and the exchange of stories about individual situations. These stories serve as interpretive structures by which we impose order on experience, and it on us" (p. 57). Critical race theorists question how and why some stories, or ideologies, become dominant and assumed to be coherent. In addition, this prompts those informed by CRT to place a high value on stories, in particular those told by people who have been marginalized.

From a Latino critical theory or "Lat-crit" perspective, such stories are referred to as *testimonios* (Zamudio et al., 2011) and include a process of naming one's own reality. As Beverley (2000) explains, the term *testimonio* can be related in Spanish to "the act of testifying or bearing witness in a legal or religious sense. Conversely, the situation of the reader of testimonio is akin to that of a jury member in a courtroom. Something is asked of us by testimonio" (p. 558). Building on these legal understandings, *testimonios* are akin to *evidence*, which cannot in good conscience be ignored. Beverley continues, "we are under an obligation to respond in some way or other; we can act or not on that obligation, but we cannot ignore it" (p. 558). *Testimonios* can also be thought of as counternarratives—stories that push back against dominant narratives about people of color and other subjugated groups as inferior or solely responsible for their own socioeconomic positions. Counternarratives will also embrace emotion and the role of emotion in storytelling.

The value placed on the voices and realities of those who have been marginalized also relates to CRT's critique of color blindness, which erases the voices of people of color under a false pretense of assumed sameness. Phrases like "I don't see color," or "Everyone is the same" hide the fact that White (and male, and heterosexual) ways of viewing the world are dominant and considered more coherent than others. If we are blind to race, then dominant narratives continue to assume an unquestioned superiority and benefit those in power—White people. Counternarratives work to lift false veils of color-blindness that are recruited by those in power to maintain their social and economic privilege.

Another core tenet of CRT is interest convergence. According to legal scholar Derrick Bell (1980), in his analysis of the U.S. Supreme Court's *Brown v. Board of Education* (1954) decision, interest convergence is the idea that the interests of African Americans will be achieved only when a particular action also benefits Whites—when their interests *converge*. In *Brown v. Board of Education*, desegregation occurred because it also served the United States' national interests with respect to its image of democracy abroad (Bell, 1980). The tenets of CRT are meant to help uncover White privilege, as well as male privilege and heteronormativity—the assumption that heterosexual relationships are the unspoken norm—and how privilege is reproduced and potentially challenged in the classroom.

Connecting Critical Race Theory to Curricular Models and Instructional Strategies

There are no actual curricula that are considered to be CRT instructional programs. Rather, there are key facets of instruction that are informed by CRT. Perhaps the most salient of these is taking action to improve education for students of color (Edwards & Schmidt, 2006), which is evident in Y-PAR. In addition to taking action, Zamudio et al. (2011) identify five elements of pedagogy informed by CRT:

1. acknowledge the central and intersecting roles of racism, sexism, classism, and other forms of subordination in maintaining inequality in curricular structures, processes, and discourses;
2. challenge dominant social and cultural assumptions regarding culture and intelligence, language and capability, objectivity and meritocracy;
3. utilize interdisciplinary methods of historical and contemporary analysis to articulate the linkages between educational and societal inequality;
4. develop counter discourses through storytelling, narratives, chronicles, family histories, scenarios, biographies, and parables that draw on the lived experiences students of color bring to the classroom; and
5. direct the formal curriculum toward goals of social justice and the hidden curriculum toward Freirean (Freire, 1973) education goals of critical consciousness. (pp. 91–92)

One way to take such action in literacy instruction is through conversations around texts and literary interpretation. Students and teachers may critique whiteness as a dominant frame for plot structures, character traits, and so forth. Similarly, students and teachers may critique curricular programs, canons, and the kinds of texts and topics valued in schools. This issue received national attention in the United States when the state of Arizona outlawed ethnic studies programs in 2011. In the Tucson Unified School District, which eliminated its Mexican American Studies (MAS) program in public schools, students organized and staged protests and created an organization called UNIDOS (United Non-Discriminatory Individuals in Demanding Our Studies) and the School of Ethnic Studies. Activists worked to produce significant counternarratives to resist the termination of the MAS program and the ideologies that undergird it (Cabrera, Meza, Romero, & Rodríguez, 2013).

Teachers and students can also examine and critique the relative paucity and lack of availability of children's literature that positively portrays protagonists of color or those from other under-represented or marginalized backgrounds (Bishop, 1997), such as the LGBTQ community or people with disabilities. Moreover, teachers can engage students in conversations regarding children's literature and other texts that offer counternarratives to dominant story lines. For example, in *The Paper Bag Princess* (1980), Robert Munsch ruptures dominant understandings of women's and men's intellectual and social roles. Classroom discussions and

> *Critical race theory is brought to life in three vignettes: "We're Not Going to Talk About That Stuff Right Now": (Re)presenting Racial Injustice During Reader Response (p. 141), "There Won't Be No Cure Till White Folk Start Dyin'" (p. 146), and Momentos de Cambio (Moments of Change; p. 167).*

activities could critique textbook portrayals of slavery that minimize the violence and inhuman treatment perpetrated by White people in power, including slave owners, government officials, and law enforcement during the Civil Rights Movement.

Teachers and students may also generate *testimonios* in the classroom through writing or spoken voice. Through such *testimonios* they may be encouraged to tell their own stories of injustice or other experiences that may break with dominant story lines regarding what their homes, communities, and schools are like. In classrooms, teachers and students might listen to *testimonios* in online spaces and social media, study the elements of *testimonio* as a genre, and produce and publically perform their own *testimonios*. Engagements like these reflect social constructionist theories because they question why and how some narratives regarding the world are deemed more coherent or sensible than others, while simultaneously pushing back against those story lines.

CONCLUDING THOUGHTS

Social constructionist theories are informed by critical social science and poststructuralism. They emphasize not only how knowledge is produced but also how some sets of knowledge, ways of viewing the world, and interpretations become dominant, or deemed more coherent than others. In this sense, these theories emphasize not only meaning construction but also deconstruction. This involves foregrounding counternarratives and attempting to make dominant interpretations of the world appear to be less coherent or, at a minimum, to raise questions about their assumed superiority.

A criticism of social constructionist theories is that they are often communicated through obtuse language, which turns off many teachers and researchers. And educators who align themselves with correspondence and cognitive constructivist coherence theories might argue that social constructionist theories may not support student work that is quantifiably measurable with respect to achievement outcomes. Furthermore, some educators argue that social constructionist theories do not sufficiently emphasize skills instruction. These criticisms are countered, however, with reminders that instruction aligned with these theories does not ignore skills but rather embeds them in experiences geared toward action for social justice. In addition, these theories do not preclude research that measures data in quantitative ways. However, they do argue for the emotional and social justice value of critical and deconstructionist teaching to prepare students to take up agentic roles within a democratic society.

QUESTIONS FOR PRAXIS

1. Think of a literature discussion in your classroom in which you were either participating, mediating, or observing and stepping in only when necessary. In what ways might you reimagine the conversation and your role in the discussion so that it takes a critical turn?
2. Think about the different digital tools available in your classroom and school. How might you weave these tools into your instruction in innovative ways to position students as critical consumers and text producers (i.e., in ways that do not constitute "old wine in new bottles")? What challenges exist within your instructional setting that make such uses difficult, and how might you mediate them?

RESOURCES AND ADDITIONAL READINGS

Blackburn, M. V. (2011). *Interrupting hate: Homophobia in schools and what literacy can do about it*. New York, NY: Teachers College Press.

Brooks, W. (2009). An author as a counter-storyteller: Applying critical race theory to a Coretta Scott King award book. *Children's Literature in Education: An International Quarterly, 40*(1), 33–43.

Critical Race Studies in Education Association's website: www.crseassoc.org/. This organization consists of scholar-activists who work to promote racial justice in schools.

Labbo, L. D., & Place, K. (2010). Fresh perspectives on new literacies and technology integration. *Voices from the Middle, 17*(3), 9–18.

Miller, s. j. (2008). "Speaking" the walk: "Speaking" the talk: Embodying critical pedagogy to teach young adult literature. *English Education, 40*(2), 145–154.

Razfar, A. & Yang, E. (2010). Digital, hybrid, and multilingual literacies in early childhood. *Language Arts, 88*(2), 114–124.

PART II

EXPLORING PRAXIS AND BRINGING THEORIES TO LIFE

While Part I was organized according to different families of theories, Part II is organized according to key elements of literacy instruction in K–12 classrooms. In each chapter, I present detailed vignettes of instruction and literacy practices and then connect, analyze, or critique them from multiple theoretical angles. These theorizations are not meant to be exhaustive. Rather, they are intended to highlight the different ways these practices might be understood from different theoretical frames. I discuss and at times critique each vignette with respect to two to four theories or families of theories; however, others might view them differently, drawing on other theories to make sense of the practices presented. My intention is not to provide definitive or exhaustive theorizations but rather to illustrate how practice and theory interanimate one another, or make each other come alive.

Unlike in Part I, where distinctions between instructional strategies, curricular models, theories, and epistemologies are fairly delineated, in Part II these boundaries become blurred. This is because as theories and curricular models are recruited and implemented in daily practice, they become open to revision. Furthermore, many instructional practices will animate more than one theory. These blurred lines should be understood as a natural result of the complexities of classroom life, which, as any teacher will surely attest, is often messy and unpredictable. I hope that Part I will become a resource for readers as they read the vignettes in Part II. As mentioned in Chapter 1, by viewing the vignettes through various theoretical lenses, teachers may gain alternative perspectives and a critical eye toward their own instructional practices.

CHAPTER 6

Cracking the Code

Skills Instruction and Developing
Concepts of Literacy

The emphasis on explicit code instruction (e.g., phonemic awareness, phonics, the alphabetic principle, punctuation, spelling, and grammar) in K–12 classrooms has varied over the years with the "reading wars" and the push toward "balanced" literacy (Spiegel, 1998). However, in the current political climate, with increased emphasis on standardized testing prompted by No Child Left Behind (2001) and continued with initiatives such as Race to the Top, and similar legislation and initiatives in other countries, skills instruction has gained increasing emphasis. There is broad consensus that skills such as phonics, grammar, and spelling need to be taught. There is not wide agreement, however, on *how* such skills should be taught and assessed. Indeed, how code instruction is approached and understood by teachers and researchers is tied to how we theorize literacy (Stahl et al., 1998). This chapter focuses on instruction in phonological, graphic, morphological, lexical, and syntactic aspects of language in oral and print form. In addition to explicit skills instruction, I also discuss young children's developing concepts about how print (paper and digital) and other kinds of texts function.

SKILLS INSTRUCTION ACROSS THE K–12 GRADE SPAN

In homes and communities, as well as pre-K and kindergarten settings, concepts of print and of literacy more broadly are often taught implicitly, through teacher modeling and participatory engagements in literate activities (e.g., writers' workshop, shared reading). Classroom instruction in phonics, phonemic awareness, spelling, morphology, and grammar is often explicit and taught in fairly self-contained, decontextualized, and undifferentiated ways—that is, in whole-class instructional events, with a predetermined scope and sequence, and without consideration of different students' points of development, interests, goals, or prior knowledge. Nevertheless, classroom code instruction may be contextualized through the use of children's literature or other meaningful texts. Approaches with more robust contextualization and differentiation may begin with a teacher selecting and reading aloud a text with particularly interesting features of language, like alliteration or rhyming patterns, and then focusing students' attention on those patterns, grounding explicit instruction in the text. Some teachers will also contextualize and differentiate code instruction via minilessons and writing conferences during writers' workshop using students' own writing to anchor their lessons.

Unlike teaching letter–sound relationships and spelling patterns, grammar may be taught throughout the K–12 grade span and has received renewed interest in the last decade (Andrews et al., 2004). Reasons for this resurgence include the emphasis placed on grammar in standardized tests, the CCSS and its emphasis on academic language and text complexity, and the increasing array of textual practices people engage in during their day-to-day lives (e.g., email, texting, instant messaging, podcasting, etc.), which call for monitoring different syntactic norms. While syntactic forms deemed nonstandard are frequently discouraged or even denounced in schools, increasingly teachers are expecting students to write within different registers (see Chapter 4) that are appropriate for different communication modes, contexts, and audiences (Lee, 2007; Martínez et al., 2008).

Despite evidence that isolated grammar instruction is not effective (Weaver, 1996), decontextualized practices persist, including strategies such as sentence diagramming and Daily Oral Language (DOL; Godley, Carpenter, & Werner, 2007). Other practices include sentence manipulation and combining to enhance sophistication and meaning construction in students' writing, and understanding nominalizations and other features of academic language unique to specific disciplines (Moje, 2008). One approach to grammar instruction that has gained some purchase in communities where students speak multiple varieties of English is "codeswitching," characterized by minilessons in the grammatical aspects of Standard English as contrasted with less formal varieties (Wheeler & Swords, 2004). This contrasts with more recent developments in grammar instruction that are grounded not in language *separation* (and switching between languages) but in how language forms and speakers' linguistic repertoires may be *mixed* in creative and intentional ways. This practice, termed *codemixing, codemeshing* or *translanguaging*, is not yet common in most K–12 classrooms but has been foregrounded in recent scholarship (e.g., García, Flores, & Woodley, 2012; Guerra, 2012; Martínez, 2013) and shows promise for promoting students' critical language awareness.

Grammar instruction, however, need not be limited to linguistic grammars. Recognition of multiple semiotic systems has changed understandings of what counts as "text" and prompted consideration of how different sign systems, not just language, function. Grammars of visual design (Kress & van Leeuwen, 1996) may also be addressed in classrooms, particularly given the increased prevalence of multimodal texts such as websites, social networking (e.g., Instagram, Tumblr, and Facebook), YouTube and other video sharing services, and cellphone technologies in both classrooms and the lives of youth (Lankshear & Knobel, 2003; Merchant, 2007).

The three vignettes presented in the remainder of this chapter include several elements of skills instruction, including spelling, fluency, and grammar. These vignettes span a wide age range, from early childhood to high school.

WORD SORTING IN A 3RD-GRADE MULTILINGUAL CLASSROOM

Joyce was a 3rd-year teacher and taught in a culturally and linguistically diverse city in the U.S. Midwest. Of her 19 3rd-graders, 12 were African American, most of whom spoke AAVE. Five students were of Mexican origin, spoke Spanish as their first language, and were in the process of learning English. One student came with her family from the Democratic Republic of the Congo the previous year and spoke French as her first language. One of Joyce's students was a White monolingual speaker of Standard English. (I have also presented and analyzed literacy instructional events from Joyce's classroom elsewhere; Handsfield, 2007; Handsfield & Jiménez, 2008, 2009.)

Although Joyce taught in an "all English" classroom, the descriptor "all English" is misleading. Joyce was bilingual, speaking Spanish fluently as her second language, and she often used Spanish with her Spanish-speaking students and parents. Joyce's parents immigrated from the Philippines to the United States before Joyce was born, and based on her own family history, she had a general understanding of her students' and their families' experiences learning English as an additional language. She also had an interest in her African American students' uses of multiple varieties of English. She visited the church attended by many of her African American students on at least one occasion to get a sense of the language practices they participated in there, and she conducted home visits to familiarize herself with students' families and communities. One of the students whose homes she visited was Danny (featured in the vignette), whom she took a particular interest in because of his label as a "behavior problem" and "struggling reader."

Joyce engaged in some isolated skills instruction, which was part of her district's balanced literacy approach. In addition to whole-class lessons on phonics and word study, she conducted read-alouds of culturally relevant children's literature, modeling comprehension strategies, and reinforcing those strategies during guided reading. Her students also engaged in self-selected independent reading several times a week and literature circles (Daniels, 1994). Her phonics and word study instruction were largely separate from these other activities and not grounded in authentic children's literature. Joyce characterized the lesson spotlighted in the vignette as the first in a series of phonics lessons from her district's curriculum guide. Her purpose was to support students in becoming more independent spellers when writing.

"Put It on the Train!"

As her 3rd-graders are getting situated upon returning from lunch and recess, Joyce instructs them to "take one piece of paper and fold it like a hot dog." She demonstrates as she continues her explanation: "Okay, now fold it like a hot dog again. You should have four columns." She unfolds the paper and points to the columns, counting off each one: "one, two, three, four." She slowly moves around the room spot-checking students' folding.

Moving back to the front of the room, Joyce announces, "Okay, everyone. We're going to practice spelling words. And the way we're going to do it is by thinking about words that rhyme." She asks her students to write "car." As they do this, she holds up a 3 × 5 card with the word written on it and places it at the top of one column on a pocket chart hanging from the dry erase board. She tells her students to "underline the letters *a* and *r*." She continues, "The next word I want you to think about is 'van,'" showing the word on another 3 × 5 card. A student asks, "in the second column?" Joyce says, "In the second column. Underline *a* and *n*."

Danny is tapping a ruler on his desk. Joyce takes it away and says firmly, "Get busy." She turns back to the class as a whole and says, "Next word, 'bike.' Write 'bike' in the third column." She then tells the whole class to "underline the letters *i-k-e*." She repeats the process with the word "train," so that each column has a word at the top with a different rime: *car, van, bike,* and *train.* Danny has continued playing with pencils and other items in his desk and trying to engage the boy next to him in conversation. Joyce threatens to send Danny to the office, and he begrudgingly puts his things away.

With the structure for the activity in place, Joyce introduces the focus of the lesson: "Alright. I want you to think about when words rhyme with each other; they're oftentimes spelled the same. Not always, but a lot of times." She shows them a new word card ("pain") and asks the students which of the columns it belongs in based on what it rhymes with. She asks them what the word is, and students begin raising their hands. Marie, whose first language is French, volunteers, "pen." Joyce hesitates, and Marie self-corrects to "pain." Joyce gives her the card and tells her to move to the front of the room to place it in the chart. Marie places it under "train," and the other students write it in the same column on their own papers. Joyce states loudly, "Everyone say 'pain,'" and the students chorally respond, "Pain!" Joyce then repeats, "Train, pain," indicating with a sweep of her arm for her students to repeat: "Train, pain!" Joyce repeats the process with "hike" and "Spain." Danny perks up and participates in the choral repetition. Joyce tells students to underline the parts of the words that rhyme. As she does so, she smiles at Danny.

Joyce introduces the name "Fran." Sandra raises her hand, and Joyce calls on her: "Sandra, what is this word?" Sandra does not respond. Joyce switches to Spanish: "*Mira. Escucha la palabra. Van.* [Look. Listen to this word. Van.]," indicating the anchor word at the top of the second column. Sandra still does not respond, apparently stuck on the consonant blend fr-. Joyce calls on Mariana, sitting next to Sandra: *"Mariana, ¿qué es la palabra?* [Mariana, what is the word?]" Mariana correctly reads Fran, and Joyce repeats it to confirm her response and to address the rest of the class: "Fran. Alright, Mariana said 'Fran.' This is the name of a girl or a woman. Where does it go?" Joyce gives the card to Mariana, who moves to the chart and puts it under "van." Joyce responds, *"Muy bien* [Very good]."

The next word is "star," and the process of calling on a student, reading the word, and repeating it is continued. Sandra volunteers again to read the next word, "pan," and pronounces it using Spanish phonology (the word "pan" in Spanish means "bread"). Joyce responds, "Okay, *es diferente en español. ¿Qué es en inglés?* [Okay, it's different in Spanish. What is it in English?]" Sandra hesitates, and Joyce turns to the class. They say "pan" using English phonology, and a student is given the card to place on the chart. Meanwhile, Sandra and Mariana hold a brief side conversation in Spanish about the words "pan" in English and in Spanish. Joyce notices and smiles at them.

Joyce and her students move through the words "spike" and "jar." With "jar," Joyce calls on Garibaldi, who responds and places the card on the pocket chart under "car" and "star." As he does so, Joyce tells him, "You are a star!" Joyce then says to the class, "I think this is too easy for you guys! I'm going to have to make it harder next time!" Moving on, and placing extra emphasis on the underlined words, Joyce says loudly, *"Sprain.* Look at the *letters* in it. What does it *look* like? Where are you going to *put* it?" Building on the rhythm of Joyce's prompts, Danny responds out loud and in time, "Put it on the *train!*" Joyce smiles and repeats, "On the *train!*" and gives the card to Danny, who moves to the front of the room and places it on the pocket chart.

Joyce shifts gears and asks her students if they notice the patterns on the chart. She has them read the list of words in each column chorally as she points at the words with a yard stick. Joyce then tells her students that rather than holding up a word, she will say a word out loud and they will try to spell it before placing it on the chart. The first word is "strike," and Joyce tells the students to guess where it goes and how it's spelled: "Who can tell me?" Mariana says *"s-t-r-i"* in Spanish (the letter *-i* in Spanish is pronounced like the English letter *-e*). Joyce hesitates and asks another student, who spells it conventionally with English phonology. Joyce writes it on a card and puts it on the chart. As students write the word, she stops by Mariana's desk and tells her that she noticed she was spelling it by saying the letters in Spanish but that she wanted to make sure the other students knew it was an *i* and not an *e*.

Moving on with the lesson, Joyce has the students spell "brain," "plan," and "like." Joyce says, "Boys and girls, look how well you're spelling! In closing the lesson, Joyce tells them, "Not all words that sound alike are spelled the same, but if you're writing and you don't know how to spell a word, you could think of a word you do know, and see if using the same ending works." She has her students repeat all of the words again chorally and then instructs them to put their papers away and get ready for music.

Readers will notice several features of this vignette that are worthy of discussion, from the content focus, to its interactional patterns, to Joyce's attempts to engage and respond to different students. I address each of these three areas below, focusing significant attention on the discursive patterns and expectations in the event.

Correspondence Theories

A key feature of Joyce's lesson is the controlled learning environment, content, and sequence of instruction, which animates correspondence theories, introduced in Chapter 2. This involves input that is preselected by the teacher or predetermined in the curriculum guide. The lesson also includes teacher-dominated discourse, including a quick pace and clear directives to students with repetition and immediate feedback. These features are central attributes of behaviorism.

We also see Joyce teaching component skills to target specific elements of text processing, invoking information-processing theories, which distinguish between linguistic processors, mechanisms for processing different aspects of language such as orthography, lexicon, and so forth. Specifically, her lesson connects to understandings of orthographic and phonological processing within the interactive model and distributed models of text processing. For example, the PDP model (Rumelhart & McClelland, 1986) suggests that the phonological processor works in conjunction with the orthographic processor to support word reading based on connections between sounds of words and spelling patterns. By explicitly drawing students' attention to these relationships, Joyce supports students' abilities to process words that may be familiar orally but not yet encountered in print.

> See p. 15 for a description of correspondence theories.

Her focus on word families would also be supported by stage theories of word reading and spelling (Ehri & McCormick, 2013; Gentry, 2000), which suggest that children move through different stages of alphabetic knowledge. In 3rd grade, Joyce's students would likely be in the full alphabetic phase or consolidated alphabetic phase. At this stage, students may benefit from analogy-based spelling instruction in which they are taught recurring patterns that they may use to build word families and to facilitate the consolidation of different letter sequences. The assumption is that explicit instruction can facilitate the development of readers' working memory to boost automaticity. The focus on word families in this case would also be supported by grain size theory. Joyce's focus is not on letter–sound correspondence, but rather on a larger grain size, which may be particularly helpful for her native Spanish-speaking students.

Educators who align themselves with coherence theories (Chapters 3 and 4) or social constructionist theories (Chapter 5) may be concerned about certain aspects of the vignette. There is an assumed universalism in the lesson—an expectation that all learners will benefit from the same instruction at similar points in time along a developmental continuum. What's more, the lesson is not connected to meaningful experiences with children's literature or students' writing. However, looking beyond the overall design and content of the lesson to examine Joyce's interactions with her students, there is evidence that she is attuned to the social and linguistic practices in students' homes and communities. This brings us to sociolinguistic theory.

Sociolinguistic Theory

Two aspects of Joyce's lesson reflect characteristics of sociolinguistic theory as described in Chapter 4. First, there are particular norms of interaction that characterize Joyce's classroom space, such as the traditional IRE pattern (Cazden, 2001). We see this throughout the event; for example, Joyce initiated an interaction by asking Mariana, "*¿qué es la palabra?* [what is this word?]," while holding up the word "Fran." Mariana responded by correctly reading the word, and Joyce repeated it, thereby evaluating her response. The IRE pattern, however, is not always carried out orally.

> See p. 66 for a description of sociolinguistic theory.

In response to Joyce's question, "Where does it go?" Mariana responded by walking up to the chart and placing the word Fran in the correct column, and Joyce evaluated Mariana's response with "*Muy bien.*" This common participation structure functions to maintain authority structures and aligns with transmission-oriented approaches to teaching and with correspondence theories, which operate under the assumed separation of knower and known.

However, IRE is not the only participation structure in the vignette. We also see call and response in the relatively quick-paced prompts for participation by Joyce. These "calls" have a cadence that elicits audience response in tempo. This occurs when Joyce holds up the word "pain" and calls rhythmically, "Look at the *letters* in it. What does it *look* like? Where are you going to *put* it?" Danny maintains this cadence in his response, "Put it on the *train!*" As in some African American sermons, the call and the response work together to coconstruct the text (in this case, the lesson; Foster, 1989). What's more, the call *earns* the response such that the authority of the preacher–teacher is constructed, rather than assumed. In the vignette, we see a rapport that may be attributed in part to Joyce's recognition of some of her students' (including Danny's) familiarity with participation structures such as call and response and her willingness to recruit this structure in the classroom.

Joyce's understanding of students' linguistic repertoires is also evident when Sandra reads the word "pan" using Spanish phonology. In her response, Joyce recognizes that Sandra is applying Spanish phonology not simply because she may not know the English pronunciation, but because the word also has meaning in Spanish (it is a false cognate: a word that is spelled the same or similarly in both languages, but does not share the same meaning). Joyce allows Sandra and Mariana to discuss this in a side conversation, a discursive practice not typically permitted during teacher-directed whole-class instruction. What is central from a sociolinguistic view is the importance of culturally grounded ways of using language. While the lesson is restrictive with respect to content, Joyce is adept at recognizing and using language in ways that are responsive to students from a variety of linguistic and cultural backgrounds.

Critical Sociocultural Theory

Critical sociocultural theory can help us examine how teacher and student identities and ideologies of literacy, teaching, and learning are discursively produced in the vignette. Bakhtin's (1984) ideas about language as described in Chapter 5 are helpful here. Bakhtin argued that people's language is never separated from social and historical contexts of use,

See p. 89 for a description of critical sociocultural theory.

and this is evident in Joyce and her students' interactions. While sociolinguistic theory helps us understand the social and cultural grounding of language use, from a CST vantage point, these participation structures, and the specific utterances in the vignette, do not exist in a neutral cultural or social world. Rather, they include the appropriation of words and ways of speaking that are historically grounded and infused with relations of power. For instance, when Joyce uses the phrase, "Boys and girls" to address her students, she is not simply recognizing and assuming their genders; she is using a phrase commonly associated with a traditional teacher identity. In doing so, she simultaneously positions herself as a traditional teacher and calls students into traditional gendered identities (to the potential exclusion of LGBTQ youth).

CST also helps explain student repositioning in the vignette. Danny, who has been positioned as unruly (and often takes up such an identity), shifts positions from uncompliant and nonparticipatory to compliant and participatory. Importantly, this shift is mutually constructed by Danny and Joyce in their creative use of language. The discourse in the event potentially transforms not only who Danny can be in the classroom but also the kinds of interactional norms sanctioned in the classroom (see also Handsfield, 2007).

However, it is not only Joyce and her students' utterances that invoke power relationships and identities. How they gesture and move through the classroom also contribute to these positionings (Handsfield & Crumpler,

2013). Consider Joyce's elicitation of her students' choral response with an authoritative sweep of the arm, as well as her movement among students' desks as she circulates around the room to monitor their work. These movements speak to an authoritative teacher who is the arbiter of knowledge and behavioral norms. These movements are recognized as belonging to specific teacher identities, evoking ideologies of teaching and learning—assumptions about who is in charge and how learning happens. The discourse, both speech and body movements, is constrained by expectations regarding who students and teachers are supposed to be, but also potentially shifts possibilities for teacher and student identities.

Some teachers might critique the lack of content differentiation for students in Joyce's lesson, as several students likely do not need explicit instruction on these word families. Other teachers may view Joyce's teaching style and discourse as overly monological, with few opportunities for student talk. However, there are pieces of Joyce's interactions that reveal her sophisticated knowledge of students' linguistic strengths and needs. And while her lesson is not differentiated in terms of content, she differentiates in subtle ways in terms of expectations for participation in the event. A similar complexity is evident in the next vignette, in which my young son and I tackle the task of making valentines.

MAKING VALENTINES AT HOME FROM PRE-K TO 1ST GRADE

When Nate was 5 years old and in preschool, he was asked to engage in a literacy practice that will be familiar to many readers: making valentines for his peers for Valentine's Day. His teacher's expectation was that each child, with a parent's or caregiver's help, would write each classmate's name on a valentine, which would then be distributed along with a treat (e.g., a small piece of candy or a sticker) at their class Valentine's Day party. Nate's teacher sent home a list of his classmates' and teachers' names to facilitate this process.

Nate's multi-age (ages 3–6) classroom included a reading area with pillows and chairs, lots of environmental print, a snack table, a drama/dress-up center, and shelves of activities, games, blocks, and puzzles. Nate's teacher engaged children in frequent read-alouds and shared reading, during which the children were invited to participate. Nate's teacher also emphasized students' names as a springboard into print literacy learning. The valentine-making activity fit well into this broader approach to nurturing children's development of alphabetic literacy. The vignette begins with how this task was approached in his preschool year and then extends a year back in time and then 3 years later into his 1st-grade classroom, where he was asked to engage in a similar valentine-making activity.

Dragging Valentines to the Trash

At home in the early evening, Nate and I began tackling the valentine-making project. A stack of store-bought valentines, with different cartoon characters and spaces to write the recipients' and givers' names, sat on the table. Nate took one from the top of the pile and began writing a classmate's name, copying from the list his teacher had provided. After completing a few, I suggested that he develop a system to keep track of whose valentines he had already completed so he didn't forget someone or make two valentines for one person. Nate's system is shown in Figure 6.1. You will note some interesting features of his system: He drew lines from children's names down to the bottom of the page, where he had used his pencil to darken a particular area. He also circled Molly's name and scratched out the names of others, which also had lines drawn to the bottom of the page. As I watched him complete the valentines, his process of drawing lines through students' names made sense to me—it seemed like a practical system and one that he had probably seen others use before. But I was confused by the lines drawn to the bottom-center of the page, so I asked him what they were for. He looked up at me as if I were beyond dense and replied, "I'm dragging them to the trash."

Figure 6.1. Nate's Names List for Valentine's Day

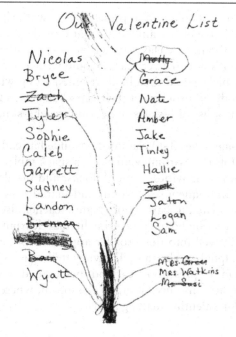

It is worth noting that Nate's classroom did not have a computer (which may explain why his teacher handwrote and photocopied the list of names). However, Nate had frequent exposure to computers both outside the classroom (at the preschool office, at the store, and at the local library) and at home and at friends' houses, where he played computer games, occasionally wrote in a word processing program, played Webkinz online, and watched and engaged peripherally while family members used the computer. This exposure carried over to his pretend play. For example, one afternoon, almost a year prior to the valentine-making event, I was writing on my laptop while sitting on the sofa. Nate (age 4) came in the room, sat down in a different chair, unfolded a piece of cardboard on which he had drawn a keyboard, and began typing, making clicking and beeping sounds as he typed. I looked up, and asked him what he was working on. "Just a second," he replied. A moment later he made some accentuated beeping sounds followed by a swoosh sound. He then closed his cardboard laptop, walked over to me and announced, "Here. I downloaded you some juice."

Now fast-forward 3 years past preschool and kindergarten to February of Nate's 1st-grade year. Nate (now 7 years old) found himself once again charged with the task of creating valentines for each of the students in his class. This time, Nate wanted to find valentines online and print them out rather than buying them at the store. After searching together, we found some that Nate liked that were both free and printable.

To facilitate students' valentine making, his 1st-grade teacher posted a list of students' names on her class website. With my laptop on the kitchen table and his valentines spread out in front of us, Nate and I navigated to the website, where we found the list of names. Using the mouse, Nate scrolled up and down through the list, and then picked up a pen and a valentine to begin writing. After finishing the first one, he took the mouse, found the name of his friend whose valentine he just finished, and highlighted it. He then hit "delete" on the keyboard. Nothing happened. He tried again, but still, nothing happened. Confused, he asked me why he couldn't delete the student's name. I explained that although his teacher had put his classmates' names online, he couldn't delete them or mark them as done on the website. He would need to figure out a different system. Because Nate liked the idea of using the computer, I copied the names from the website and pasted them into a Word file. I then encouraged him to scratch out the names (instead of deleting them) by highlighting the name and selecting strikethrough (e.g., ~~Jack~~) from the Word menu to create a record of valentines he'd already completed.

How might we understand Nate's literate activities in this narrative? There are multiple answers to this question, which depend on what we consider to be the phenomenon of interest in the vignette. Is it Nate's drawing of the lines? His manipulation of the mouse and scrolling to view names on his teacher's website? Is it his developing understanding of what the use of digital tools might accomplish? Emergent literacy theory and multiliteracies/ new literacies theory offer distinct ways of interpreting these phenomena.

Emergent Literacy

Emergent literacy theory, described in Chapter 4, explains how young children develop behaviors and understandings that approximate conventional reading and writing, and provides a conceptual system for understanding Nate's uses (real and imagined) of digital tools. As Razfar and Gutiérrez (2003) point out, emergent literacy theory

See p. 70 for a description of emergent literacy theory.

assumes that children's literacy development stems from their participation in adult-directed literacy activities and events. This includes sitting alongside a parent, sibling, or caregiver while they search for information online or download a document, which is not unlike a shared book experience (Holdaway, 1979).

Nate's play activity in which he tapped on his cardboard keyboard, and his understanding that objects such as juice can be downloaded, represent *approximations* of conventional literacy practices and emergent understandings of literacy tools and texts. He displays similar emergent understandings regarding the use and manipulation of screen-based print—specifically, the kinds of web-based interfaces that can be manipulated (Web 2.0) or not (Web 1.0). Indeed, the literacy practices and tools that young children engage with in their daily lives have changed and proliferated since Marie Clay and others (e.g., Teale & Sulzby, 1986) published their seminal works outlining emergent literacy behaviors and CAP (Merchant, 2007).

Turbill's (2001) expansion of the construct of CAP to include concepts of screen is helpful here. This includes clicking and double-clicking, scrolling, locating programs on a computer's desktop, and opening and closing programs. As evidenced in the vignette, children develop understandings of how hypertext and downloading function as they engage with digital literacies in their everyday worlds. This does not nullify concepts like directionality, concept of a word, and so on. As Merchant (2007) argues, digital spaces, such as YouTube, social networking sites, and typical webpages, require the navigation and manipulation of traditional print concepts, visual images, and concepts of screen and digital text manipulation. Indeed, in the vignette, Nate moves seamlessly from scrolling on the screen to writing with pen and paper.

In short, from an emergent literacy theory perspective, Nate's unconventional understanding that a cup of juice can be downloaded and materially produced is an approximation of the activity of downloading a document and then printing out a hard copy. Such approximations are indications of what he knows and is learning about his literate world. And notably, in the 7 years that have passed between that event and the writing of this book, Nate has seen the development of 3-D printing.

Multiliteracies/New Literacies

As the above discussion implies, we might do well to merge our understandings of emergent literacy with a multiliteracies/new literacies framework, described in Chapter 5, to explain Nate's developing behaviors and understandings. The emphasis in multiliteracies/new literacies theory on rapidly changing

See p. 86 for a description of multiliteracies/new literacies theory.

and proliferating literacy practices and tools (Lankshear & Knobel, 2003; Leu et al., 2013; New London Group, 1996) is clear in the vignette. Such changes afford new ways of *being* literate and call for radically rethinking literacy instruction.

For Nate, print has never been tied to the page. In reconceptualizing the "page" on the screen, Labbo (1996) describes "screenland" as a space of invention. Nate's experiences with digital literacies, however, are not limited to offline word processing programs. Indeed, the screen in online and interactive spaces may function in various ways, with different conventions and expectations regarding text manipulation, including hyperlinks and differences between reception-based (Web 1.0) and production-based (Web 2.0) technologies. In the vignette, we see Nate's expectations for use in relation to these concepts.

The notion of deixis with respect to literacy technologies—the fact that literacy tools are changing at an increasingly rapid pace—means that it is virtually impossible for teachers and researchers to keep up with the change, particularly in traditional teacher- and text-driven models of curriculum (Lankshear & Knobel, 2003; Leu et al., 2013). This provides another way of understanding Nate's attempts to delete students' names on his teacher's website that extends beyond emergent literacy. It could be that Nate's vision for how he might manipulate his peers' names to manage his valentine production reflects an expectation of text manipulation characteristic of Web 2.0 applications, an expectation that may surpass his teachers' professional expectations and/or the school system's framework for literacy instruction. The proliferation of digital tools and the potential of collaborative online spaces push educators to rethink transmission-oriented approaches to literacy instruction so that students are positioned as critical producers and consumers of text (Handsfield et al., 2009; Lankshear & Knobel, 2003).

The vignette also animates different components of the New London Group's (1996) pedagogy of multiliteracies. Making valentines is an example of *situated practice* as it is contextualized within authentic meaningful activity. It is also a culturally situated activity in the sense that making valentines for classmates is ubiquitous in U.S. schools, but may not be in many other contexts. In addition, I engaged in *overt instruction* with Nate while helping him figure out how to strike through text within a Word file to scratch out names. However, we do not engage in either *critical framing* or *transformed practice* because there is no explicit critique in Nate's and my interactions, nor do we attempt to carry our interactions or activity into the realm of social transformation. That said, there is a clear expansion of Nate's understandings regarding how texts might be designed and his own agency in this regard over the course of the vignette.

MANIPULATING SENTENCES IN A 9TH-GRADE ENGLISH CLASS

In the final vignette, we peer into a literature-based grammar lesson in a 9th-grade English class. Mr. Kimmel, a 4th-year teacher, has planned a discussion of Harper Lee's *To Kill a Mockingbird*, followed by a minilesson on sentence combining. Mr. Kimmel's students are largely White and Latino and represent an array of socioeconomic backgrounds. With his state's adoption of the CCSS, Race to the Top initiatives (tied to students' standardized tests scores), and political movements that seek to reduce teacher pay, benefits, and job security, Mr. Kimmel feels pressure to engage in explicit grammar instruction to boost his students' test performance. He is concerned about how their test scores will reflect on him as a teacher even though he knows teaching and learning are more complex than the stories told by test scores. His goal in the lesson is to help his students use more sophisticated language in their writing, but he also wants to give them time to respond to and talk about the powerful events unfolding in the novel. He believes that at 14 and 15 years old his students are itching for opportunities to connect what they read to the world around them.

"Dude, I Don't Know": Combining Sentences with *To Kill a Mockingbird*

It is 9:05 on a Monday morning, and as the bell rings, Mr. Kimmel's students file into the classroom. Two sentences from Chapter 17 of *To Kill a Mockingbird* are written on the whiteboard:

> The cabin's plain walls were supplemented with sheets of corrugated iron, its roof shingled with tin cans hammered flat, so only its general shape suggested its original design: square, with four tiny rooms opening onto a shotgun hall, the cabin rested uneasily upon four irregular lumps of limestone. (p. 187)

> Enclosed by this barricade was a dirty yard containing the remains of a Model-T Ford (on blocks), a discarded dentist's chair, an ancient icebox, plus lesser items: old shoes, worn-out table radios, picture frames, and fruit jars, under which scrawny orange chickens pecked hopefully. (p. 188)

As students get situated, Mr. Kimmel draws their attention to the sentences, reading them aloud. He asks if they recognize where the sentences were taken from, and students begin flipping through their books. For homework, students read Chapters 15 through 17, which include the trial of Tom Robinson, who was wrongfully accused by Bob Ewell of raping Ewell's daughter. In Chapter 17, right before Ewell takes the stand, the narrator, Scout, describes Ewell's home: a small cabin behind the town's garbage dump. Jasmine raises her hand and says, "It's where it says where he lives." "Where who lives?" asks Mr. Kimmel. Sam, his index finger comically pointing in the air, loudly asserts, "Bob Ewell!" Mr. Kimmel directs them to pp. 187–188 to reread the paragraphs including the two sentences.

Once finished, he asks them to paraphrase the description of Ewell's cabin. Several students chime in: "run down," "dirty," "in a bad neighborhood," "They're pretty poor," "They don't got no fancy things, just a messed up old car," "It's a dump!" "Junk lying all around," "They live in a dump near the dump." Mr. Kimmel affirms their observations and asks them to think about why the author has taken the time and space in this chapter to describe Ewell's cabin in such detail. A discussion follows regarding the social and economic inequalities in the southeastern United States at that time. Mr. Kimmel then underlines the words "uneasily" in the first sentence and "hopefully" in the second sentence: "Why do you think the author chose those two adverbs? What is she trying to tell us?" He prompts them to discuss this in small groups.

When the class reconvenes a few minutes later, several students argue that Lee is trying to be descriptive or to give details about how "bad" Ewell's home is. Mr. Kimmel pushes them further: "Okay, yes, but why is Lee taking all this time to describe his home in the middle of a chapter about the trial? Go back to those two words. What do they convey about his home?" Rogelio responds, "It's like uneasy, like it's not too good—like it could fall apart or you're scared it'll fall down." Building on Rogelio's comment, Sandra adds, "'Cause it's just on blocks. It's not like, solid." Mr. Kimmel responds, "OK—good. It's not solid or stable; you don't know whether it will hold, so you feel uneasy. And what about the scrawny orange chickens that pecked hopefully?" Sarah, who has been quiet until now, says, "They're hungry. When you're hungry you're hoping for food." Jasmine then says, "It's like a metaphor—I think it's like his house is like the trial, or maybe how Tom Robinson feels when he's on trial. He's worried, but he's also like, hopeful that maybe the jury will do the right thing." Mr. Kimmel responds, "Yeah, Harper Lee doesn't have to describe Ewell's cabin here, does she? I like your thinking. So maybe she's using his cabin as a metaphor. It could be how Robinson is feeling as Ewell takes the stand. That's definitely a possibility. Other ideas?" Kendra responds, "I think it's how Bob Ewell feels. It's his cabin and he's the one taking the stand." Jasmine counters, "But the author's not gonna tell us how Ewell feels bad. Tom Robinson is the one on trial and maybe didn't even do it. And Ewell's a bad guy." Sam jumps in, "Yeah but taking the stand could still be scary." Looking down at his desk, Marcus says quietly, "Ewell's a racist." Turning to Marcus, Sam responds, "Yeah, I know, he's a total loser and a racist, but I'm just sayin' he can still be scared." Marcus responds skeptically, "Dude, I don't know."

Mr. Kimmel glances at the clock and then summarizes the two points of view: "OK, so we're thinking those same two words could describe either how Tom Robinson or Bob Ewell is feeling." But Rogelio cuts him off: "But wait, it's not just about how they're feeling. It's like Ewell's house might fall down—like his story might not hold 'cause he's left-handed. It's on page 196. And he probably hit his own daughter. So it's more like his story can't hold up. It's describing Bob Ewell's story." Mr. Kimmel says, "That's a pretty convincing argument. What do you guys think?" One student says she thinks it could be both. Another short conversation ensues about the word "hopefully," but with less than 30 minutes left in the period, Mr. Kimmel shifts the focus of the lesson.

"Okay, I want to shift gears now. We've talked about why Harper Lee includes this description of Ewell's cabin, and we've focused in on two words she used to give us a picture not just of his home but also of the trial. We're going to focus now on how she writes these sentences; how she structured them. What's one of the first things you notice about these sentences?" After several seconds of silence, a student responds, "They're descriptive?" "Yes, they are," replies Mr. Kimmel. "We've established that, and that's a good start. But what else? Are these choppy, short sentences?" Several students respond, "Nooo!" Another shouts, "They're long!" Mr. Kimmel, says, "Yeah, but not too long. They're not really run-on sentences, but they are complex sentences."

Mr. Kimmel continues, "I'm noticing that many of you in your own writing are keeping your sentences really simple, even choppy. So we're going to do an activity where you break these two sentences apart into simpler chunks, or kernel sentences. Then we'll recombine them. Does anyone know what I'm talking about when I say 'kernel sentences'?" Sam replies, "No, sir! Colonel sir!" A few students chuckle, and David gives Sam a high five. Mr. Kimmel has difficulty suppressing his laughter and says, "No, not that kind of kernel. I'm talking about all the information conveyed in each sentence, but broken into short, simple sentences. We'll do the first sentence together."

Mr. Kimmel starts breaking down the first sentence, thinking aloud, asking students for input, and writing the kernel sentences on the whiteboard as he goes:

> The cabin's walls were plain.
> They were supplemented with sheets of corrugated iron.
> The cabin's roof was shingled.
> The shingles were tin cans.

The tin cans were hammered flat.
Only its general shape suggested its original design.
Its original design was square.
It had four tiny rooms.
The rooms opened onto a shotgun hall.
The cabin rested on four irregular lumps of limestone.
The cabin rested uneasily.

He asks if there's more, and Sandra says "the second to the last one, 'the cabin rested on four irregular lumps of limestone,' could be two different ones: 'The cabin rested on four irregular lumps,' and um, 'The lumps were limestone.'" Mr. Kimmel begins separating them out, when Sam says, "Wait, no, three! 'Cause you could say that 'the lumps were irregular' as another one." As Mr. Kimmel adds a third kernel sentence, a buzz of student talk ensues. Mr. Kimmel says, "I'm guessing you've found more. Talk with a partner and see if you can find even more kernel sentences."

Once they have all of the kernel sentences they can find, Mr. Kimmel asks them to look back at the original sentence and figure out what words were included in it that either changed or were not included (e.g., "so," "with"). He explains that while the kernel sentences are all "full sentences," they're not very interesting: "What would Harper Lee's writing be like if she wrote in simple sentences like these?" A few students say, "boring" and "choppy." Mr. Kimmel notices that Sarah and another student are passing notes, whispering back and forth, and asks, "What do you think, Sarah? Would you want to read *To Kill A Mockingbird* if it was written in short, choppy sentences?" Startled, Sarah says, "No" quietly, and her friend turns toward the front. Mr. Kimmel continues, still looking at Sarah and her friend, "And I don't want to read your writing when it's written in oversimplified and choppy language, either."

Turning back to the class, he continues, "So let's take a look at how Lee constructed the first sentence so that it's more interesting and complex." They identify the use of commas for sequencing and to set apart subordinate clauses, the use of prepositional phrases ("with . . ."), and the use of colons. "Alright, now we're going to play with these sentences." Mr. Kimmel erases the first sentence, leaving the kernel sentences. He tells students to put their novels away and work in groups to recombine them into one or two complex sentences. He adds, "Don't just re-create what Harper Lee wrote."

After students complete their task, each group shares their recombined sentences, and Mr. Kimmel leads them in a discussion about the similarities and differences between them and what sentence combining strategies each group used. Two of the groups come up with sentences that are very close to what Harper Lee wrote, and Mr. Kimmel makes a mental note that he might have needed to do this lesson differently in the future to avoid this, perhaps starting with the sentence kernels without contextualizing them to the novel. With 12 minutes remaining in the 55-minute period, he tells each group to go through the same process with the second sentence, identifying kernel sentences and recombining them into one or two complex sentences.

As class comes to a close, Mr. Kimmel tells them they'll share their sentence kernels and finish recombining their sentences tomorrow, and he tells them to read the next two chapters of the novel. The bell ringing, he adds that they'll also be doing sentence combining later in the week as a DOL activity.

Several features of the lesson may draw readers' attention. These include dialogic aspects of discourse in the vignette, how Mr. Kimmel facilitates student talk, and the tensions he faces between opportunities for responding to the text and teaching discrete skills. I address these and other aspects of Mr. Kimmel's instruction using sociocultural-historical theory and transactional/reader response theory.

Sociocultural-Historical Theory

In this lesson we see Mr. Kimmel's careful use of language as a mediational tool, reflecting Vygotsky's emphasis on semiotic mediation, or the idea that developmental processes are mediated by signs and tools in social contexts

See p. 62 for a description of sociocultural-historical theory.

(see Chapter 4). Mr. Kimmel offers frequent opportunities for student–student interaction (e.g., asking students to turn to a partner to discuss a point or to work in their groups to accomplish a task). However, we also see language as mediation in his scaffolding of students' interpretations. Consider his response to Rogelio's and Sandra's comments regarding Bob Ewell's cabin:

> *Rogelio:* It's like uneasy, like it's not too good—like it could fall apart or you're scared it'll fall down.
> *Sandra:* 'Cause it's just on blocks. It's not like, solid.
> *Mr. Kimmel:* OK—good. It's not solid or stable; you don't know whether it will hold, so you feel uneasy.

Mr. Kimmel synthesizes their ideas, recasting them in conventional grammar, reiterating the word "uneasy." He provides similar linguistic supports by repeating new vocabulary, such as "kernel sentences," and thinking aloud as he breaks down the first sentence. These examples point toward language use as a support for mental processes and individual development.

The book itself also becomes a mediational tool for scaffolding students into the world of reading in this high school classroom, as evident in the close references to the text. Mr. Kimmel begins by directing students to particular sentences and pages in the text, requiring them to locate specific passages. As the discussion unfolds, he refers students back to "those two words," and later we see Rogelio referencing specific page numbers on his own to support his interpretations. In this context, literary interpretation is not something one engages in without the book in hand. This expectation extends beyond the walls of Mr. Kimmel's classroom to historically and culturally grounded norms regarding reading and writing in secondary schools. In short, Mr. Kimmel uses language and other mediational tools to apprentice his students into a community of learners with specific expectations regarding what it means to read, interpret texts, and learn about language (Rogoff, 1995; Wertsch, 1991).

Transactional/Reader Response Theory

From a transactional/reader response perspective, we might view the vignette as an example of tensions between formalist or new critical approaches and transactional readings of texts (Fish, 1980). As explained in Chapter 3, transactional/ reader response theories center on the active role of the reader in constructing meaning as

See p. 50 for a description of transactional/reader response theory.

she or he transacts with the text, and they are critical of approaches that center on a search for "true" author intention (Rosenblatt, 2004). Yet we see traces of these approaches in the two portions of the lesson.

As Mr. Kimmel and his students focus on the description of Bob Ewell's cabin, Mr. Kimmel appears to steer students gently toward a desired interpretation—ultimately, the one provided by Rogelio. This is all done with an emphasis on close reading, a hallmark of new criticism and emphasized in the CCSS. It seems that in the end, interpretive authority rests with a few. Would Mr. Kimmel have kept the conversation going, rather than transitioning into the next activity, if his students had "landed" on Jasmine's interpretation?

At the same time, reader response theorists might also recognize aspects of the discussion focusing on author intent, bringing to the fore the notion that the text (and textual meaning) does not exist as an object in itself, and that specific decisions are made by authors and readers during interpretation. Mr. Kimmel also enables opportunities for alternative interpretations. From a transactional/reader response perspective, we might encourage him to ask students to connect their interpretations to their own personal experiences, and to further articulate aesthetic responses to the text. A lost opportunity in this regard was Jasmine, Marcus, and Sam's discussion of the plausibility of Harper Lee conveying to the reader Bob Ewell's feelings as he takes the stand. Marcus's response moves into aesthetic and emotional territory, yet Mr. Kimmel does not take up this conversation, instead summarizing key points so he can get the grammar portion of the lesson under way before the period ends.

In the portion of the vignette focused on sentence combining, we see traces of a formalist approach, in which the literary work is examined in a decontextualized way, disengaging the communication between the author and the reader (Rosenblatt, 2004) that transpired toward the end of the discussion. Clearly, Mr. Kimmel has made an effort to embed his grammar instruction in a meaningful text and interpretive context. At the same time, the social and historical context of the novel slips away after the transition into the sentence manipulation activity.

QUESTIONS FOR PRAXIS

1. Revisit one of the vignettes and analyze it from a theoretical frame not discussed in this chapter. What do you notice that may not have been highlighted already? What key questions arise?
2. Reimagine one of the instructional engagements or literacy practices in the above vignettes, resituating it in your own school or classroom context. How might you orchestrate it differently, and why? How would such a revision be connected to additional theories presented in Part I?
3. What connections can you draw between the third vignette, with its partial focus on complex sentences, and the construction–integration model, discussed in Chapter 3?

RESOURCES AND ADDITIONAL READINGS

Benjamin, A., & Oliva, T. (2007). *Engaging grammar: Practical advice for real classrooms*. Urbana, IL: NCTE.

Burke, A., & Hammett, R. F. (2009). *Assessing new literacies: Perspectives from the classroom*. New York, NY: Peter Lang.

Ganske, K., & Jocius, R. (2013). Small-group word study: Instructional conversations or mini-interrogations? *Language Arts, 91*(1).

National Council of Teachers of English. *Guidelines for teaching grammar*. Retrieved from www.ncte.org/positions/statements/qandaaboutgrammar

Rosen, M. (2013). *Getting the* ig *in pig: Helping children discover onset and rime*. ReadWriteThink.org. Instructional plan retrieved from www.readwritethink .org/classroom-resources/lesson-plans/getting-helping-children-discover-103 .html

Wohlwend, K. (2013). *Literacy playshop: New literacies, popular media, and play in the early childhood classroom*. New York, NY: Teachers College Press.

CHAPTER 7

Constructing Meaning with Texts

If, as many would argue, literacy is at its core a meaning-making process, how do we determine what instructional components of literacy fit within a chapter on constructing meaning with texts? Comprehension is quite complex and is considered to be an unconstrained skill. Unlike decoding and grammar, it is not mastered within a brief period of development but rather is developed in variable ways across longer spans of time (Paris, 2005). That said, when someone speaks in a syntax that is considered appropriate for a given context, or that is recognizable in a particular language, it is more likely to be meaningful to others within that context or language community. Similarly, if you are not able to connect a symbol system with the ideas it is meant to represent, you will be unlikely to make meaning with it. What is more, I have yet to meet a teacher who would claim that literature discussions, persuasive writing, and other literacy engagements do not involve constructing or conveying meaning. Accordingly, we could argue that any aspect of literacy and literacy instruction contributes to meaning-making. Nevertheless, in school literacy programs, meaning-making tends to be construed more narrowly, limited to comprehension and vocabulary instruction. In addition, because fluency is also closely associated with students' comprehension of text (Rasinski, 2010), it may be included under the umbrella of meaning-making along with vocabulary and comprehension.

FLUENCY, VOCABULARY, AND COMPREHENSION INSTRUCTION

Throughout the elementary grades, teachers support students' fluency development in a variety of ways. One of the most widely used approaches is readers' theater, which involves students reading from a book with a significant amount of dialogue while using minimal (if any) props. However, some teachers will have students create a script from a book or use commercially produced scripts (Rasinski, 2010). Another approach to fluency instruction is fluency-oriented reading instruction, which includes structured repeated reading (Stahl & Heubach, 2005), which can improve not only reading rate but also word recognition and expression. Some teachers will have students self-monitor their repeated readings using a voice recorder. Additional approaches include engaging students in shared reading experiences or at reading stations, where students can follow along as they listen to a text on an MP4 player or computer.

Unfortunately, reading rate, and to a lesser extent accuracy, are often emphasized over other elements of fluency (pacing, expression, and phrasing). This is evident in one-minute reading assessments within programs such as Diagnostic Indicators of Basic Early Literacy Skills (DIBELS). A principal concern with one-minute assessments is that they do not allow readers sufficient time to recognize text features or to build an understanding of the text, and they prompt students to read as quickly as possible without attending to meaning. Teachers may mediate these limitations by using authentic literature and allowing students time to read the first page or two prior to timing. One-minute reading rate assessments may also be supplemented with more holistic assessments, such as the Multidimensional Fluency Scale (Rasinski, 2010).

Vocabulary knowledge has long been known to predict academic achievement (Stahl & Fairbanks, 1986) and, more specifically, reading comprehension (Beck, McKeown, & Kucan, 2013). Furthermore, word knowledge has been shown to be a central area of difficulty for students reading in English as an additional language (Genesee, Lindholm-Leary, Saunders, & Christian, 2006). With the wide-scale adoption of the CCSS, increasing emphasis is being placed on academic language—discourses and registers of different academic fields, marked by different syntaxes and text structures, as well as vocabulary, and educators are under increasing pressure to teach academic vocabulary (Flynt & Brozo, 2008). Unfortunately, the practice of having students look up words in the dictionary and write definitions still exists in many classrooms despite the fact that it is insufficient for learning the complexities of words and word meanings (Fisher & Frey, 2014). Research on vocabulary instruction supports different instructional approaches, including explicit instruction in word meanings, teaching strategies for learning new words in context, and analyzing morphology (teaching affixes and word roots) (Adams, 2013).

Oftentimes teachers wonder which words to explicitly teach. Beck et al. (2013) differentiate between Tier 1, Tier 2, and Tier 3 words. Tier 1 words are high-frequency words that permeate everyday language use (e.g., "lunch," "uncle," "store," "small"). Tier 2 words do not permeate everyday use but are common enough that they may be used within a variety of contexts (e.g., "explosion," "injuries," "justice," "mountainous"). Tier 3 words are less common and more specific to particular contexts or content areas (e.g., "igneous," "immunotherapy," "hypotenuse," "Hellenistic"). It is recommended that teachers devote more energy to teaching Tier 2 words because their use spans a variety of contexts and content areas. Tier 3 words would be taught as needed within content area instruction. However, students learning English as an additional language may require instruction in Tier 1 words as well, particularly those with irregular spelling patterns. In addition, teachers may not need to teach words that English learners may be able to identify using cognate strategy or morphological analysis.

The RAND Reading Study Group's (2002) definition of comprehension as a "process of simultaneously extracting and constructing meaning through interaction and involvement with written language" (p. 11) is widely accepted among educators. While decoding and literal understandings may be necessary for comprehension, they are not sufficient in themselves. Moreover, others have argued that comprehension goes beyond integrating textual meaning with prior knowledge to include critical analysis of texts (McLaughlin & DeVoogd, 2004). This includes not only constructing meaning but also deconstructing dominant understandings (analyzing whose voices are privileged and excluded within texts and literature discussions) and then reconstructing alternative meanings.

Strategy instruction has gained wide appeal and is now regularly practiced in classrooms throughout the primary, intermediate, and middle grades. Specific strategies include predicting, making connections, questioning the author, visualizing, paraphrasing and translating, summarizing, clarifying meaning, scanning texts, identifying important text features, and so forth. While considerable evidence links approaches like TSI to higher achievement on curriculum-based and standardized measures of comprehension (Pressley, 2000; Reutzel, Smith, & Fawson, 2005), it has also been the subject of criticism (McKeown, Beck, & Blake, 2009; Palincsar, 2007; Palincsar & Schutz, 2011), particularly in linguistically and culturally diverse classrooms. For example, Handsfield and Jiménez (2009) argue that in linear and inflexible approaches, in which strategies are taught in undifferentiated ways, strategy display becomes more important than strategic reading. These limitations may disadvantage culturally and linguistically diverse students, whose "ways with words" (Heath, 1983) may not involve or privilege procedural display.

Students may also articulate strategies simply to please the teacher or because they believe it will help them understand the text; however, they are not always clear about how or if strategies like making connections support understanding (Harvey & Goudvis, 2000). Teachers may also overemphasize strategies like making connections (e.g., text-to-text, text-to-world, text-to-self) and not invite students' *dis*connections—different kinds of experiences or perspectives from those in the text or the world around them (Jones et al., 2010). Finally, strategies may not always be an accurate indicator of comprehension. As Serafini (2011) argues, "Being able to predict what happens next in a story may, in fact, reveal the shortcomings of the plot of a particular story, not necessarily the comprehension skills of the reader" (p. 239).

Below I share two vignettes to illustrate meaning-making instruction and practices. The first describes a series of one-on-one tutoring sessions with a 3rd-grader, and the second depicts strategic reading in a literature discussion group in a 4th-grade bilingual classroom.

FLUENCY INSTRUCTION WITH A 3RD-GRADE READER IN A ONE-ON-ONE TUTORING CONTEXT

Lydia was an undergraduate teacher candidate in an elementary education program. Part of her pre–student teaching coursework included an 11-week one-on-one literacy tutoring experience in which teacher candidates worked with elementary students two times a week for approximately 30 minutes. After getting to know their students and conducting a range of assessments, tutors articulated specific instructional goals and designed and carried out lessons intended to support their students in those areas. Lydia's student, Diana, grew up speaking both English and Spanish and was enrolled in a monolingual English 3rd-grade class. While Lydia did not know Spanish, she learned about strategies for teaching bilingual students in her coursework.

Using VoiceThread and Inquiry to Boost Vocabulary and Fluency

Based on her initial assessments, Lydia noted that Diana was interested in the natural world. While Diana enjoyed reading for school, she read slightly below grade level, and her reading was not very fluent, either in rate or expression. She read in stops and starts, frequently stumbling over two- and three-syllable words. Lydia was concerned that Diana's issues with fluency might inhibit her comprehension, and so she decided to focus her instruction on fluency and vocabulary development.

During their fourth meeting, however, Lydia's plans were temporarily set aside. Diana told Lydia that she and her family would be leaving at the end of the week to visit her father in Guatemala for 2 weeks. After briefly conferring with Diana's teacher, Lydia learned that Diana's father had been deported 4 months previously. At their next meeting, Lydia gave Diana a disposable camera and a journal and asked her to document her trip in photos and writing. Lydia hoped this experience would be generative of experientially based writing and reading activities within which she could embed some fluency and vocabulary instruction once Diana returned.

Upon Diana's return, she excitedly shared her journal with Lydia and gave her the camera to get the photos developed. Diana talked a mile a minute, describing the most exciting part of her trip (other than seeing her father): a family excursion to a town situated next to a majestic volcano. Their entire tutoring session was filled with Diana telling Lydia all about the volcano and showing her a book she checked out from the school library about volcanoes.

Not surprisingly, Lydia decided to build fluency and writing activities around Diana's newfound interest. To do this, she turned to VoiceThread, an online multimedia tool in which users upload photos and video and narrate them in writing and/or audio (voicethread.com). Lydia proposed the idea of a project in which Diana would create a radio broadcast about volcanoes. Diana liked the idea and wanted to make it about an eruption.

Over two sessions, Lydia taught Diana about the features of radio broadcasts (especially what they sound like), connecting those to features of fluent reading. She had Diana listen to a radio broadcast about the 2010 magnitude 8.8 earthquake in Chile on Lydia's laptop. As they listened, Lydia occasionally paused to point out key moments, such as how the announcer began the broadcast, what sorts of details were included, when the announcer's voice indicated excitement, or when the announcer interviewed someone affected by the quake. Lydia also used the broadcast to introduce elements of fluency, such as pacing, juncture between sentences and clauses, and expression.

During the next several sessions, Lydia and Diana went to the school's media center to look for books about volcanoes and do a web search, seeking information about different types of volcanoes, why they erupt, and effects on local communities. As they engaged with texts, Lydia modeled fluent reading, occasionally asking Diana to note her rate, expression, juncture, and so forth. Lydia integrated word work to support Diana's fluency and comprehension of these texts, many of which were challenging for Diana. As they read books and browsed websites, identifying and documenting key information about volcanic eruptions, Lydia identified words she considered important for understanding the texts and taught Diana several strategies for identifying unknown words. Focusing on Tier 2 words (e.g., "converging," "injuries," "mountainous") and Tier 3 words (e.g., "seismometer," "sulfuric acid," "subduction," "tectonics"; Beck et al., 2013), they created a glossary in Diana's notebook and word cards with a concept map on one side and a photo illustrating the word on the other. Using these words, Lydia taught Diana specific affixes and their meanings (e.g., con-, -ous, sub-). Finally, she taught Diana how to recognize Spanish–English cognates, and together they identified cognates in the texts (e.g., "thermal-*termal*," "magma-*magma*," "minerals-*minerales*," "eruption-*erupción*").

After reviewing some of the new vocabulary, Lydia used these texts to model how to segment sentences into meaningful phrases. She then asked Diana to reread portions of the texts, sometimes two or three times. Her hope was that the focused vocabulary instruction, fluency strategies, and repeated readings would enhance Diana's automaticity with multisyllabic words, as well as her phrasing. Lydia made sure to point out moments when Diana's reading reflected key elements of fluency that they discussed. After these sessions, Lydia helped Diana think about how to plan and begin writing the broadcast, and the process of composing began.

Fast-forward five more tutoring sessions. Diana had composed, revised, and edited her radio broadcast and was excited about recording the radio show on VoiceThread. However, Lydia reminded her that she needed to practice reading it several times before producing a final broadcast. Using an iPad Mini, Diana recorded herself reading her broadcast. But after playing it back, she was dissatisfied, saying that she sounded "boring." Lydia noted that Diana's first reading lacked expression and that she stumbled on some of the new words they had studied previously. Lydia said she needed to run down to the office for a few minutes and told Diana to practice a few more times while she was gone. When Lydia returned several minutes later, Diana had already recorded herself two additional times, and she replayed the latest recording for Lydia. The difference from the first recording was stark: Lydia read with virtually no stumbles or repetitions and read with appropriate expression and juncture. She was ready to do the broadcast on VoiceThread.

After a couple of takes, they got a recording that Diana was pleased with. Their last task was to select accompanying photos to upload into VoiceThread. They revisited Diana's photos of her trip to Guatemala. Once they selected a few photos, Lydia showed Diana how to use an app on her smartphone to scan and edit the photos. After sending them to her laptop, Lydia showed Diana how to upload them to VoiceThread to complete the project. After conferring with Diana's teacher, Lydia played the radio broadcast for Diana's class and passed the link on to some of the other teachers, who then played it for their own students.

In the ensuing discussion, I focus on how Lydia's skills instruction, although embedded within meaningful experiences, animates key elements of information-processing and stage theories, and also connects to sociocultural-historical theory.

Information-Processing and Stage Theories

To be clear, teachers operating from the perspective of information-processing theories may be less likely to contextualize instruction according to students' interests and cultural experiences like Lydia did.

See p. 21 for a description of information-processing theories.

That said, when we look closely at Lydia's skills instruction, we see the influence of the information-processing theories described in Chapter 2. In keeping with the PDP model, which identifies four processors—orthographic, phonological, meaning, and context—that work interactively during reading (Adams, 2013), Lydia did three things to support the activation of connections between these processors. First, she read aloud the texts that she would later expect Diana to read on her own, providing a model to facilitate Diana's phonological processing while supporting conceptual understanding. Second, Lydia explicitly taught Diana to recognize specific morphemes—affixes and their meanings. In doing so, she facilitated connections between orthographic and meaning processors. Third, Lydia engaged Diana in repeated readings of words and texts, which, according to the PDP model, activates connections across processors to promote automaticity, or fluent reading.

Repeated reading is also consistent with the automatic information processing model. A key element of this model is attention. LaBerge and Samuels (1974) argued that if too much attention is being devoted to decoding, then comprehension will suffer. By systematically engaging in morphemic analysis, cognate strategy, and fluency work and by engaging Diana in repeated readings, Lydia reduced the attention Diana needed to devote to decoding, thus supporting comprehension. Recall that automatic information processing was revised to include a top-down component, in which readers may recognize specific words, which are then sent directly to semantic memory (Samuels, 1994). Lydia's decision to read the texts aloud that Diana would later read on her own, and then explicitly teach specific words that might prove challenging for Diana, is supported by the revised version of the model.

From the perspective of stage theories, we can surmise that Diana is in the consolidated-alphabetic stage of word knowledge development (Ehri & McCormick, 2013). In this stage, readers can consolidate larger units of letter–sound correspondences by recognizing spelling See p. 33 for a description of stage theories. patterns. This recognition is supported by Lydia's attention to specific affixes of focal words. Stage theories would also provide support for Lydia and Diana's repeated reading practices to build automaticity, as well as the writing component of the project.

While correspondence theories do not emphasize meaningful contextualization of instruction or the role of teacher–student interactions, these were key elements of Lydia's instruction. These elements also animate sociocultural-historical theory.

Sociocultural-Historical Theory

Lydia's instruction exemplifies how educators may use Vygotsky's concept of ZPD, as described in Chapter 4, to push students to accomplish tasks they cannot complete on See p. 62 for a description of sociocultural-historical theory. their own. While Vygotsky (1978) developed the idea of ZPD as a concept for advancing children's problem solving (rather than simply measuring what they know; Vygotsky, 1978), use of the concept has expanded to other domains, such as teaching and learning specific skills. By engaging in word work and repeated readings, Lydia scaffolds Diana's ability to read texts she would likely struggle with in the absence of support.

By engaging alongside Diana and collaborating on the project, Lydia also apprentices Diana into a community of readers and writers (Rogoff, 1995). Of course, in the vignette, Lydia and Diana are the only two people present. However, the community that Diana is entering extends beyond the immediate context of the tutoring. Rather, it is a broader literacy community in which people read for meaning, research concepts online and in books, synthesize information, and compose texts for authentic audiences. In this sense, the vignette exemplifies sociocultural-historical theory's view of learning as a historical and social process in which new concepts are internalized through cultural practices (Smagorinsky, 2009).

Lydia also taps into Diana's cultural and linguistic funds of knowledge (González et al., 2005) to support her language and literacy development, a practice that is consistent with sociocultural-historical theory's emphasis on learning as socially and historically grounded (Smagorinsky, 2009). For example, Lydia teaches Diana how to use her knowledge of Spanish to identify unknown vocabulary (cognate strategy). Although it is not foregrounded in the vignette, her family experiences of immigration and her father's deportation also mediate how she understands the world. By viewing Diana's bilingualism, her father's deportation, and her trip to Guatemala not as deficits (framed according to terms such as *Limited English Proficient, illegal,* and *truancy*) but instead as funds of knowledge—culturally grounded experiences and ways of viewing the world (González et al., 2005)—Lydia is able to recruit Diana's experiences to support her emotional and academic development. Providing Diana with a camera and a journal also helped frame Diana's trip as not only significant for her and her family but also potentially generative of learning. Lydia did not assume that Diana should or would write about immigration, deportation, and living without her father or about "my trip to Guatemala." While Diana could have chosen those topics to write about, consistent with sociocultural-historical theory, Lydia took her cues from Diana when designing instruction. All too often in schools, students from marginalized backgrounds become defined solely according to their differences from the mainstream (Spanish-speaking, immigrant family; Gutiérrez & Orellana, 2006). Lydia's approach helped avoid such essentializing practices.

Language is not the only mediational means by which people become participants in cultural worlds. Learning is also mediated by tools, such as pencils, books, cameras, computers, and websites. Notably, the use of digital tools supported Diana's engagement and literacy development while also mediating her identity as digitally literate. The complexities of semiotic mediation are also evident in the next vignette.

STRATEGIC READING AND WORD IDENTIFICATION
IN A LITERATURE DISCUSSION GROUP

Isabel, a White, middle-class woman in her early 30s, was a 3rd-year teacher when this event was documented. Fluent in English and Spanish, she taught a bilingual 4th-grade class at Southend Elementary School in the U.S. Midwest. Isabel's teaching situation was unique in that her class consisted entirely of eight boys, all of whom spoke Spanish as their first language. Her students' families came from various countries of origin, including Mexico, El Salvador, Guatemala, and the United States, and represented different degrees of English proficiency. Isabel used English most of the time, particularly during whole-group instruction. However, her students frequently used Spanish with each other. Teachers in Isabel's district used a reading series with a strict scope and sequence, but Isabel supplemented the series with literature discussion groups and a commercial curriculum designed to teach comprehension strategies.

In the vignette described below (also discussed in Handsfield & Crumpler, 2013), a literature discussion group consisting of six of Isabel's students (Alejandro, Avery, Jesús, Esteban, José, and David) devote approximately 10 minutes to identifying an unknown word ("booger") in their novel, *Get Ready for Gabí: A Crazy Mixed-Up Spanglish Day* (Montes, 2003). Isabel assigned Alejandro and Avery the roles of co–discussion directors. Alejandro was considered to be a leader socially within the group, and of Isabel's students he was also the most fluent in English. Avery did not have the same social status, and teachers characterized him as having limited oral language skills in both English and Spanish. However, the interactions in the vignette paint a more complex picture of his linguistic and literate repertoire.

"It's Not a Appropriate Word"

It is mid-April, and the literature discussion group has assembled in a corner of the classroom, seated at a sofa and on chairs around a coffee table. Isabel is also there, seated on a chair next to the sofa. They are each holding their own copy of the novel. *Get Ready for Gabí* is the story of a spirited elementary-aged girl and her relationship with her classmate Johnny (her "worst enemy"). Gabí is bilingual, and as she interacts with Johnny, who is monolingual, her emotions get the best of her, and she begins mixing Spanish and English. The group chose the book from among four short novels that Isabel selected from her supplemental curriculum.

As they get started, some of the boys occasionally refer to small white slips of paper they took from an accordion folder sitting on the coffee table. Each paper has a discussion prompt (e.g., ask a question, make a prediction, etc.) designed to help them manage their discussion and to use comprehension strategies. Isabel had previously assigned Avery and Alejandro the role of discussion directors, and as the others in the group get ready to share their responses to the prompts, they each vie for the floor by both trying to call on the others. Isabel intercedes by asking them to clarify where they are in the book (she was absent and had a substitute the day before). They say they are reading and discussing Chapter 8, titled "My Secret Identity." This chapter begins with a conversation between Gabí and her father about what she can do to control her temper with Johnny:

> "But, Papi," I said, "Johnny makes me see red." "I thought you liked red." "I like red, not *Johnny*!" I said his name with my upper lip curled up—the way I say *booger*. (Montes, 2003, p. 51)

Isabel asks Alejandro and Avery if their group members understand the book so far, and they nod yes. She then prompts them to take over, stating, "Well, get started."

Avery points to José, whose hand is up, and José says, "Uh, I don't get this word, this *b-o-o-g-e-r*. What does that mean? Bogar? Boooger?" He looks to Isabel for assistance. The use of the word "booger," from the excerpt above, is metaphorical, a metaphor for how Gabí feels about Johnny. To pick up on the metaphorical meaning, however, the reader must attend to the use of italics for both the word "booger" and the name "Johnny," as well as the context of the story. The formation of the mouth in English when articulating the -er ending of the word (curling up the upper lip) also offers contextualization (a facial expression of disgust) for the word's meaning.

Isabel gestures the word's meaning to José, bringing her finger to her nose, but the other boys don't notice. José throws his head back, and with a smile on his face says, "Aagh, ugh!" in feigned disgust. Isabel then initiates a discussion regarding the word:

> *Isabel:* Wait what—what's this talk about a booger? You're talking about a *booger*? Where is a booger at?
>
> *José:* There. It says right there in the book. It says right there in the book.
>
> *Avery:* Look. Put it—right there.
>
> *Isabel:* No, but I mean in the book were there boogers? Was somebody flinging boogers? Or putting them under their desk or something?

Isabel's intention is to prompt them to consider whether there are actually boogers in the text, or whether the word is being used metaphorically. However, they do not respond, and so she asks José to reread that portion of the text. After his rereading, Isabel initiates a discussion of the meaning of the phrase "seeing red":

Isabel: Okay, so first of all, what does—she says, "Johnny is making me see red."

Jesús: She doesn't like Johnny.

Isabel: Is she like painting something red? [Motioning with hands as if painting something]

Students: No!

Isabel: No. What does that mean?

Jesús: She makes him mad.

Alejandro: Making her mad.

Isabel (to Alejandro): Why do you think that?

Jesús: Because he does bad stuff to her?

Alejandro: Because your face turns red when you're angry?

José: She—she—she doesn't like Johnny.

Avery: I thought—I thought—I think—I thought red, like you see in the dark.

Isabel: Like you see in the dark.

Alejandro (to Avery): Huh?

Isabel: Well, generally when you say "That makes me see red—" And red is? What do we think about red?

Alejandro: Fire.

Isabel: Fire? Or what emotion would you think red?

Avery: I was—

Alejandro: Angry.

Isabel: Angry. It makes me see red.

Avery: I—

Isabel: Her dad's like, "You like red."

Avery: I was thinking—I, uh, I thought that it was—like he—she had eye vision.

José: Or maybe Johnny was wearing red!

Isabel (to Avery): You thought she had eye vision? [Spoken skeptically]

Despite Isabel's discursive scaffolding, they do not arrive at either the word's literal or figurative meaning.

Isabel tells them to continue on their own, and she steps away to confer with an aide, who was working with David. But instead of continuing on, the boys return to the word. With an air of confidence, Alejandro offers a potential definition: "It's a booger that you pick your nose with." But not everyone is convinced:

Jesús: Maybe—maybe a hambooger.

Avery: No, like booger. Like booger. Like booger.

Unknown: [Unintelligible] hamboooger.

Alejandro: Dude, hamburger is spelled *h-a-m-b-u-r-g-e-r*. The booger that he's talking about is spelled *b-o-o-g-e-r*.

Avery: The booger that you're talking about must be like someone is a booger.

Jesús: Uh, I don't know [spoken quickly and skeptically].

Avery: Like, like booger means to a person, which—that means it's a yuh [referring to the word's -er ending].

Alejandro: I know what we could check!

Alejandro, José, Jesús: The dictionary!

Avery: The dictionary doesn't have booger.

Alejandro: It has words! Why do you think they call it a dictionary?!

Avery later argues to Alejandro, "Dude, it's not a—uh, a appropriate word." But despite Avery's assertion that it won't be in the dictionary, Alejandro and José jump up and make their way across the classroom to find the dictionaries. Jesús follows, and Esteban and Avery bring up the rear.

David now joins the group, and the others fill him in on what they are doing. They spend the next 5 minutes looking for the word in a variety of dictionaries, dispersing around the classroom, speaking in both Spanish and English. Ultimately, Isabel intervenes, calling Alejandro over to her. Avery follows, and José and Esteban are also nearby. Directing her words to Alejandro, Isabel prompts them to recall different strategies they can use to figure out an unknown word:

Isabel: What can you do if you can't find it in the dictionary or you don't know what it is? What did we talk about?

Esteban (to José): No sé en español [I don't know in Spanish].

José: Computer!

Isabel: Nooo . . .

Avery: Reference [pronounced *reeference*]—

Alejandro: Context clues?

Isabel: [Quietly] You can infer.

Avery: We can't infer.

Alejandro: We don't know the words.

Avery: We don't have the picture. We don't have the words. We don't have the clues.

As they are talking, Avery appears to stumble and almost knocks Alejandro over. Isabel gently takes him by the shoulders, says "Watch what you're doing, Avery," and moves him off to the side. Directing her words to Alejandro, she then says, "Right now you are taking a lot of time to find just one word. So what can you do to bring your group back together at some point?" Avery, listening in, yells to the group, "Keep going," while beckoning with his arm to return to the sofa. Isabel, missing his gesture and thinking he's telling them to continue searching the dictionaries, says, "Keep going?!" Meanwhile, Alejandro shouts, "Let's wrap it up!" and the other group members follow in a line behind Alejandro back to the sofa. Isabel says to Alejandro, "Way to go, Director!"

Back at the sofa, Alejandro is frustrated that they couldn't find the word and no longer attempts to lead the group. Avery says to José, who first asked about the word, "Too bad, so sad. You cannot find the answer." With confidence, he commands the others to "*¡Cállate!* [Shut up!]" and "*¡Da me eso!* [Give me that!]" as he refocuses and redirects the conversation. They ultimately abandon their attempt to identify the word.

Unlike earlier vignettes, I explore this event from three different cognitive constructivist perspectives: schema theory, psycholinguistic theory, and the construction–integration model. I then explain the identity work in the vignette using CST.

Schema Theory

The boys' comprehension of the text illustrates key aspects of schema theory (Chapter 3), which explains comprehension as the activation of readers' schemata to form hypotheses about textual meaning (Anderson & Pearson, 1984).

Importantly, the boys do not lack schemata regarding the meaning of the *concept* of booger. This is made clear by José's disgusted response to Isabel's gesture and Avery's assertion that it won't be in the dictionary because "it's not a appropriate word." However, they do not have a clear understanding of the *English word* for the concept or of its metaphorical use. They analyze the word's structure, revealing their prior understandings of affixes, as when

See p. 42 for a description of schema theory.

Avery suggests that a booger is a person who does something, emphasizing the -er ending. And Alejandro corrects another student's suggestion that it's like a hamburger based on phonetic similarities. Finally, they recruit their prior knowledge and understandings of different comprehension strategies, as well as dictionary use, to ascertain the word's meaning. In other words, they try to use their schemata regarding language and context to identify the word. However, these do not prove useful given the metaphorical use of "booger" in the text. Thus, despite the time and effort spent to identify the word, in the end, they never arrive at its meaning as used in the text.

Connecting the event to Anderson's (2013) six functions of schemata, we can see that they were attempting to assimilate new information from the text (the word "booger" and its morphology) into mental "slots" to make sense of the word. However, the schemata they activated did not enable them to go beyond the literal, perhaps because their schemata for figurative language were not considered or sufficiently recruited when deciding what information from the text was most important. Isabel attempts to scaffold the students' understanding of figurative language by focusing their attention on the phrase "Johnny makes me see red," perhaps trying to build or activate prior knowledge regarding figurative language. However, while the students arrive at a basic understanding of "seeing red," they do not transfer their understandings regarding figurative language to the word "booger," likely because Isabel did not return to that word within the discussion. Isabel might have pursued further schema building and activation attempts related to figurative and metaphorical language by asking them to talk about such uses of language in Spanish and then transferring that knowledge into an explicit conversation about the use of the word "booger" in their novel.

Psycholinguistic Theory

The boys' use of different cueing systems (graphophonic, syntactic, semantic, and pragmatic) to generate hypotheses about the word reflects the core elements of psycholinguistic theory, as explained in Chapter 3. The vignette does not offer a window into one child's reading and problem solving, so we do not have a pattern of miscues to analyze. Nevertheless, the boys offer different hypotheses regarding the meaning of the word "booger," and we can see how they draw on different cueing systems as a group to try to make meaning.

Recall that K. S. Goodman and Burke's (1973) research showed that less proficient readers over-rely on the graphophonic cueing system and less on the semantic cueing system. Complicating the situation in this vignette is the fact that the boys are reading in their second language. Thus, the word "booger," which is a commonly known word to native English speakers in the United States, was unknown to them. Also, given

See p. 45 for a description of psycholinguistic theory.

the word's metaphorical use in the text, they were unable to use context clues to figure out its meaning. Thus, they could not rely on the semantic cueing system. Jesús recruits his knowledge of English graphophonics, suggesting that the word might be related to "hamburger" given its partial phonemic and graphic similarities. Avery, on the other hand, draws on both morphosyntactic and pragmatic knowledge. Specifically, he suggests that the word might refer to a person, emphasizing the word's -er ending, and suggests that they won't find the word in the dictionary because "it's not a appropriate word." His use of the pragmatic cueing system could have been supported by Isabel's earlier gesture to José.

The vignette highlights some of the difficulties that emergent bilingual readers may face when attempting to draw on different cueing systems when reading in a language in which they are not yet fluent. In this case, the word is not a cognate and its use in the text was figurative. This minimized their ability to draw on their knowledge of Spanish. So what might have been the most useful course of instruction? Provide the word to the students so that they could continue reading the text? Teach a minilesson on figurative language and then return to the text later or the next day? Or, as Isabel did, prompt students to exhaust their resources and move on if the word is left unknown? Of course, hindsight is 20/20. Perhaps Isabel could have pretaught specific vocabulary, moved their discussion of figurative language into the part of the text that used the word in question, or just ensured that when she indicated the word's meaning with her gesture, all of the students were paying attention. However, this is not a simple instructional problem, in part because of the complexity of the text.

The Construction-Integration Model

The metaphorical use of the word "booger" in the text is arguably the primary complicating factor impeding the students' ability to understand the word. The construction–integration model can help us understand processes of meaning construction with complex texts. This model suggests that comprehension involves the

See p. 48 for a description of the construction-integration model.

construction of both a textbase and a situation model. The *textbase* refers to the words on the page whereas the *situation model* refers to the meaning ascribed to the text in the reading process (Kintsch, 2013). When normal reading breaks down, readers will turn to different strategies, devoting extra effort to render the text meaningful (Kintsch, 2013). Isabel's students do just that in their attempts to construct a textbase. They make their questions about the text explicit, analyze the word's phonology and morphology, and apply strategies such as inferring based on other information in the text. However, the microstructure of the text (the network of propositions) is fairly complex with its use of figurative language and metaphor, and these strategies are not enough.

Again, the portion of the text under consideration reads as follows:

> "I like red, not *Johnny*!" I said his name with my upper lip curled up—the way I say *booger*. (Montes, 2003, p. 51)

The ideas, or propositions, in this excerpt are many: I like red. I don't like Johnny. I said his name. My upper lip curled up when I said his name. I curl up my upper lip up when I say booger. However, the meaning goes beyond these ideas to include the idea that *Johnny* is a *booger*. This complexity places the textbase beyond their reach, at least without further scaffolding by Isabel. To construct a situation model, readers will recruit their prior knowledge about boogers (e.g., they are disgusting and unpleasant), about the articulation of the upper lip in English when uttering the -er suffix (which partially resembles a look of disgust), and about managing peer relationships and language politics in classrooms. It is clear from the vignette that the students needed further support to construct both the textbase and a situation model.

Isabel could have provided further linguistic scaffolding to activate and build students' prior knowledge, in both Spanish and English, regarding the word "booger" and the use of metaphor and figurative language. However, there are indications that meaning construction may not have been Isabel's and the students' only objective in the event. Indeed, we can also examine the event to understand not only how meaning is constructed (or not), but how, in the process of meaning-making efforts, student identities are constructed. This brings us to CST.

Critical Sociocultural Theory

While some may critique Isabel's decision to allow the students a full 10 minutes to try to identify one word, she felt that was time well spent because of the opportunities it provided for social interaction and for collaborative attempts at strategy use. As Vygotsky (1978) noted, such student–student interaction can mediate students' problem solving (such as textual interpretation or word identification), particularly problems they may not be able to solve on their own. However, unlike Vygotsky and later sociocultural theorists (e.g., Rogoff), CST also focuses attention on power relationships and social identities.

What is particularly interesting from this theoretical angle is Alejandro's and Avery's discourse—both their language and their body movements—as they jockey for leadership positions within the group. At first, this comes more easily to Alejandro, whose facility with oral English surpasses Avery's. For example, he quickly rattles off answers to Isabel's questioning, spells the words "hamburger" and "booger" with ease and speed, and uses colloquial terms such as "dude," a staple of U.S. boys' peer interac-

See p. 89 for a description of critical sociocultural theory.

tions (Kiesling, 2004). Avery also uses the term "dude," but most of his attempts to use colloquialisms or to respond to Isabel's questioning are marked by stops and starts, indicating a difficulty smoothly articulating his thoughts in English.

Until the end of the event, the boys respond to Alejandro's suggestion to look in the dictionary (even given Avery's argument that booger won't be found there) over Avery's suggestion to analyze the word's morphology. Avery's knowledge of strategy use (the idea that they can't infer not only because they don't "have the words" but also because they don't have the clues or pictures) appears stronger than Alejandro's. However, Alejandro's status as a peer leader and his facility with English seem to buy him recognition for his academic arguments despite the fact that Avery's academic arguments are more sophisticated. Alejandro also gets more uptake from Isabel, both in their initial conversation about "seeing red" and toward the end as she responds to their separate attempts to reconvene the group. Things only seem to change at the end when Alejandro's strategy clearly fails. At this point, Avery is finally able to recruit his stronger academic position to achieve a more robust peer-group position.

Critical sociocultural theory brings to the fore how discourse and power operate in the event, and it illustrates how constructing meaning is tied up with constructing social and academic identities. It is unlikely that Isabel was consciously privileging Alejandro's attempts at leadership over Avery's simply because of Alejandro's communicative repertoire in English. That said, the event does show how powerful Discourses (Gee, 1996; such as the privileging of English communicative competence) may be reproduced in the classroom.

QUESTIONS FOR PRAXIS

1. Considering the first vignette, think of a student you have worked with who might have faced similar challenges in literacy as Diana. How might you learn about and recruit that student's experiences and cultural and linguistic funds of knowledge to support his or her literacy development in a one-on-one intervention context?

2. Put yourself in Isabel's shoes. How might you reimagine the event, and how might such a revision animate one or more of the theories discussed in Part I?

RESOURCES AND ADDITIONAL READINGS

Aukerman, M. (2008). In praise of wiggle room: Locating comprehension in unlikely places. *Language Arts, 86*(1), 52–60.

Database of Spanish–English cognates from the 146 International Reading Association's Teachers' Choice books for the years 1998–2012: www.angelfire.com/ill/monte/teacherschoices.html

A 5th-grade teacher models how he's present in the moment of reading a story and develops theories about the characters: www.teachingchannel.org/videos/theories-of-character.

Flynt, E. S., & Brozo, W. G. (2008). Developing academic language. *Got words? The Reading Teacher, 61*(6), pp. 500–502.

CHAPTER 8

Literature Discussion, Response, and Critique

The use of high-quality literature is a hallmark of literacy instruction; even most basal reading series will include children's literature. And teachers using more scripted skills-based curricula may supplement such programs with read-alouds, literature discussion groups, and self-selected reading. Some readers may question how (or even *if*) the instructional practices highlighted in this chapter should be distinguished from those in Chapter 7 on meaning-making. Indeed, I know few teachers who would argue for teaching comprehension without also prompting discussion and response, and teachers engaging students in literary response and critique surely recognize the importance of comprehension within those engagements. And yet, these are often considered separate curricular areas and are treated as distinct in literacy research. By separating these practices into two chapters, I admittedly maintain a false separation between the meaning-making practices highlighted in Chapter 7 and literature response, discussion, and critique in this chapter. However, this distinction may be helpful as readers attempt to connect these practices to their own instruction and district curricula. I invite readers to notice significant overlaps between the instruction described in Chapter 7 and the vignettes that follow.

LITERATURE DISCUSSION, RESPONSE, AND CRITIQUE IN K–12 CLASSROOMS

Literature discussion, response, and critique span the K–12 spectrum and occur in different sorts of classroom configurations. These range from whole-group read-alouds and conversations to individual or partner self-selected reading, reading conferences, small-group reading such as literature circles, guided reading, and comprehension focus groups. In literature group discussions, students may relate their own experiences to those of characters within a novel. For example, a student who has a sister with Asperger's syndrome may describe her own family experiences and relationships in the context of reading *Mockingbird,* by Katherine Erskine (2010), a story told from the perspective of Caitlin, an 11-year-old girl with autism whose older brother is killed in a school shooting. Such discussions may prompt further inquiry, with students learning more about topics such as gun violence or specific conditions such as autism and theories about its causes. In yet another classroom, a teacher and students might question representations of different cultural or socioeconomic groups in popular films and books, such as *The Lion King* or *The Hunger Games* trilogy by Suzanne Collins.

In middle school and high school classrooms, students will be expected to engage in more sophisticated literary analysis and critique. Traditionally, this has been focused on helping students closely attend to texts, including literary elements and plot structures, and to decipher authors' intended meanings, an approach known as new criticism (Appleman, 2009). And in other schools and classrooms, middle and secondary students may read short stories from an anthology textbook while selecting novels or other literature, sometimes from an approved district list, to read independently and report on.

The kinds of instructional engagements spotlighted in this chapter may also be distinguished in part by their discourse conventions, or participation structures, as they typically include significant opportunities for student–student interaction. Unlike the IRE structure, which situates the teacher as the primary arbiter of knowledge and authority, literature discussion, response, and critique are often characterized by responsive-collaborative participation structures (Gutiérrez, Rymes, & Larson, 1995), in which students and teachers respond to and build on one another's ideas as interpretations are mutually constructed.

Within a variety of curricular approaches to literature discussion, activities often include written products ranging from traditional book reports; to completing response sheets with specified questions regarding characters, plot, intertextual connections, and essays; to letter writing and poetry. Teachers may also have students respond to literature or other texts using multiple semiotic modes through art projects (e.g., dioramas, mobiles), music (e.g., composing a rap), or drama (e.g., skits or plays). Process drama, for example, borrows elements of theater to support students' learning, interpretations of texts, or understandings of power relationships (O'Neill, 1995) and to imagine new social possibilities (Edmiston, 2007). (See inset discussion on p. 54.) Some scholars have been critical, however, of response activities that are removed from real-life or authentic reading engagements. Serafini (2011) writes,

> We do not know anyone who has finished a great book and gone looking through their garage for a cardboard box to make a diorama, or cut up magazines to make a mobile of one of their favorite characters. Unfortunately, these things happen all too often in classrooms under the guise of developing lifelong readers. (p. 238)

The three vignettes presented below illustrate a range of literature discussion and response practices and span a wide range of grade levels, from 1st through 12th grade.

RESPONDING TO LITERATURE ABOUT
CIVIL RIGHTS IN A 1ST-GRADE CLASSROOM

Mrs. Green teaches 1st grade at Ridgeway Elementary School, located in an urban area of a large metropolitan city in the U.S. Ridgeway's student population is mostly low-income and predominantly African American, and Mrs. Green's class reflects these demographics: She has 24 students, 21 of whom are African American, two of whom are White, and one of whom is biracial. Mrs. Green is a middle-class White woman in her early 30s with 9 years of teaching experience, 7 of which have been at Ridgeway.

This vignette occurred in February, and like many schools in the U.S., Ridgeway had been celebrating Black History Month. Mrs. Green felt it was important for her students to explore civil rights during that month, and she believed that children's literature offered a way into exploring historical events and figures, including the struggle for civil rights in the 1960s. Mrs. Green had asked students in a literature response group to bring one object, activity, or document to share that represented what they thought to be an important part of the text they were reading, *Happy Birthday, Martin Luther King* by Jean Marzollo and J. Brian Pinkney (1993). During this portion of the event, Jamal attempts to talk about present-day racial injustice. Mrs. Green, however, is not prepared for what she considers to be a sensitive topic and resists the discussion.

"We're Not Going to Talk About That Stuff Right Now": (Re)presenting Racial Injustice During Reader Response

---

This vignette is provided by Terry Husband, Illinois State University, a researcher in early childhood education and former 1st-grade teacher.

Mrs. Green makes her way to the kidney table where six 1st-graders are waiting for her anxiously, books in hand. Mrs. Green had prompted the students to select a book from the classroom library related to the theme of Black history and civil rights and to be prepared to discuss the book during literature circle time. The group decided on the book *Happy Birthday, Martin Luther King*.

"Is everybody ready? Okay Jamal, would you mind giving us a brief summary of the book please?" said Mrs. Green. Jamal nodded and began talking about the major events in Dr. Martin Luther King's childhood and young adult life as documented in the text: "Martin Luther King Jr. was born in Atlanta . . ." When Jamal finished, Mrs. Green responded, "Thank you very much! Does anyone have anything to add to Jamal's summary?" Several students contributed additional facts about the life of Dr. Martin Luther King that were not explicitly stated in the text.

Mrs. Green continued, "Thank you! Now, I would like us to talk about what you thought the most interesting part of the book was and to share the artifact, document, or activity you brought to represent this part of the book." Thomas, a White student, began discussing the famous "bus boycott" involving Rosa Parks. He displayed colorful photographs of this event that he found on the Internet and had printed out at home. Mrs. Green assisted the students in discussing this event in greater depth. "Thank you very much, Thomas! Okay, Jessica, please share with us an interesting part of the book." Jessica began discussing the portion of the text that documented Dr. King's life as a Baptist preacher, and she brought in images of Ebenezer Baptist Church from her trip to Atlanta, Georgia, the previous summer. "Thank you very much for sharing, Jessica! How about you, Jamal?"

Jamal began discussing the part of the book that documented when Dr. King was arrested and thrown into the Birmingham jail, and he displayed a copy of the letter Dr. King wrote from jail. Mrs. Green looks at the document in surprise. She had not expected such a young student to produce such a powerful document as a response to the book. Unsure as to what exactly to say about the letter, Mrs. Green moved on to the next part of the discussion.

"Okay, now we're going to talk about connections. We'll start with text to world, and then move to text to text and text to self. Let's start with you, Jamal. What text to world connections did you make while reading the book?" Jamal carefully removes a large image from an 8 1/2 by 11 inch manila envelope. He turns the photo over so that everyone in the group can see. Almost simultaneously, Mrs. Green and other students gasp. The photograph contains an image of several protesters holding a sign that says, "Please Don't Shoot." Jamal decided to display a picture from the infamous protests in Ferguson, Missouri, from summer 2014. Mrs. Green asked him to explain his photograph and the connection to the text at hand. Jamal began discussing how the racism that Dr. King experienced in the book continues to happen today. Although he did not use this terminology, he passionately explained how racial profiling and police brutality is a reality for many African American males (e.g., "People get pulled over 'cause they're Black, not because they did anything wrong").

An awkward silence ensued for several seconds after Jamal finished talking. Mrs. Green was caught off guard by the connection he had made. She did not know if she should continue probing deeper regarding the topic or if she should retreat from this politically and ideologically charged discussion. On the one hand, she saw the topic as a powerful teaching opportunity to engage her students in dialogue related to issues of social justice in general and racial justice in particular. On the other hand, she was mortified by the threat that this dialogue could pose, worrying that it could possibly offend a student or a parent and potentially threaten her job. Rather than assume this risk, Mrs. Green decided to take the politically safe option and avoid the discussion in its entirety. "Okay, that's nice, Jamal! We're not going to talk about that stuff right now. Who else has a text to world connection to make?"

With Mrs. Green's abrupt transition to give a different student the floor, this vignette illustrates the tensions that may emerge when discussing topics of racial disparities and violence in primary classrooms. Rather than beginning with Mrs. Green's negation of Jamal's connection, I start by connecting the event to schema theory and sociocultural-historical theory. I then move into a discussion of the vignette from the perspective of CRT.

Schema Theory

Making connections to texts is a hallmark of CSI and an entryway into literature discussion that is grounded largely on schema theory, outlined in Chapter 3. Activating schemata, as Mrs. Green prompts her students to do, supports the process of ideational scaffolding, or opening up "slots" for assimilating information from the text. According to Anderson (2013), schemata also help readers edit out extraneous details and

See p. 42 for a description of schema theory.

summarize important information in a text, which we see play out as Jamal provides a brief summary of the book *Happy Birthday, Martin Luther King*. Specifically, he identifies the main points in the text while filtering out unnecessary information or minor details.

Schema theory can also help explain how Jamal connected the text to the demonstrations in Ferguson, Missouri, after the fatal shooting of Michael Brown, an unarmed teen, in 2014. As Anderson (2013) explains, schemata enable inferential elaboration. That is, they provide a base upon which readers can make inferences to go beyond literal meanings. Jamal's connection to Ferguson requires inferential elaboration beyond the context of the 1960s Civil Rights Movement to consider current issues of racial inequity. In fact, the book is written in the past tense and does not explicitly address current issues of racial injustice except to argue for the power of Dr. King's ongoing legacy as celebrated annually on his birthday. While other students' connections remained contextualized to the historical time period of Martin Luther King Jr.'s life, and referenced subjects included in the text (e.g., Ebenezer Baptist Church, the Montgomery bus boycott), Jamal's text-to-world connection required inferential elaboration beyond the text and time period. As a member of the African American community, Jamal may have had a heightened awareness and sophisticated schemata regarding racial justice and violence.

Sociocultural-Historical Theory

While schema theory might explain the internal cognitive processing of textual information to support meaning-making, sociocultural-historical theory draws our attention to how understandings are semiotically mediated. This is evident in the vignette in how Mrs. Green creates opportunities for interaction around the text and the artifacts that students bring into class. Sociocultural-historical theory also understands literacy development as mediated by culturally and historically situated practices and experiences. Jamal's cultural funds of knowledge, including his family's and community's frame of reference regarding events in Ferguson, likely mediated his understandings of the text as connected to current issues of police brutality and racial justice. Jamal's ability to tap into his funds of knowledge was partially facilitated by Mrs. Green's selection of culturally relevant children's literature.

See p. 62 for a description of sociocultural-historical theory.

The discussions and artifacts do not just mediate students' learning; they also mediate students' apprenticeship into the classroom community. Rogoff (1995) argued that apprenticeship involves active participation with others in culturally grounded activities. Through guided participation, more expert members of the community guide novices' participation. As novices change their participation to more closely fit the norms and expectations of the community, a process referred to as participatory appropriation, they develop into community members who can successfully participate without guidance. In the vignette, Mrs. Green is the expert member who directs the guided participation of her more novice students. As Jamal takes the conversation to an area that is deemed to be outside the bounds of participation within the literature discussion activity, Mrs. Green becomes flustered and guides him and the other students not so subtly back into sanctioned community discourse.

As noted in Chapter 4, guided participation is not a process of acquisition but rather one of becoming. This raises important questions regarding students' academic and cultural identities. What happens when the norms of the classroom community do not value or sanction debate about current racial injustice? What does this mean for Jamal's identity as a learner and as a Black male within a classroom traditionally dominated by White middle-class expectations regarding what topics of discussion are valued or taboo? Sociocultural-historical theory does not say much about these issues of power and identity, nor does it foreground issues of racial inequity. For this, we turn to CRT.

Critical Race Theory

Why does Mrs. Green decline to entertain discussions regarding current-day racism in the discussion? Some might argue that such topics are not appropriate in early childhood classrooms. However, Terry Husband's (2010) research and the work of other literacy scholars (e.g., Rogers & Mosley, 2006; Vasquez, 2004) have debunked that claim. So, what does this vignette look like from the vantage point of CRT?

When discussing the vignette from the perspective of schema theory, I pointed out that Jamal's contribution to the discussion with his photo of the demonstrations in Ferguson, Missouri, is the only one that extends beyond the historical time period of the text, *Happy Birthday, Martin Luther King*, into the present day. Some teachers may assume that Jamal's parents provided him with the photo to bring to school. However, people of color, including young children, often develop a "double consciousness" (Du Bois, 1903), or a critical consciousness regarding race and racism that is experienced on a day-to-day basis, leading to fairly sophisticated understandings regarding racial and social injustice (T. Husband, personal communication, April 6, 2015). From a CRT perspective, Jamal's connection constitutes more than just an inferential or intertextual link across time and context; it forefronts racism by inserting a counter-story to the dominant narrative of the 21st century as postracial. The effect is to make racism real and current, challenging the myth of meritocracy. When Mrs. Green tells Jamal, "We're not going to talk about that stuff right now," she essentially declares that his connection to current-day issues of racism is not welcome in the classroom, or at least that it makes her uncomfortable, keeping the topic of race and racial injustice at a safe historical distance. The discomfort Mrs. Green feels when Jamal connects the book about Martin Luther King Jr. to the shooting of Michael Brown supersedes the discomfort and pain that so many people of color experience with continued systemic racial injustice. In this sense, Mrs. Green asserts White privilege, constructing racism as something that should not be dealt with or talked about at school.

See p. 92 for a description of critical race theory.

The next vignette also illustrates how a teacher responds to students' racially charged literary interpretations. In this case, however, we jump to the other end of the K–12 spectrum.

LITERATURE DISCUSSION IN AN 11TH-/12TH-GRADE MODERN WORLD LITERATURE CLASS

Mrs. Cardona's Modern World Literature class is discussing Albert Camus's (1947) novel, *The Plague*, which details a bubonic plague outbreak in the Algerian city of Oran. The narrator, Dr. Rieux, describes the city's initial denial and gradual recognition and response to the epidemic. Mrs. Cardona's students take up a central theme of the novel—that disease and death affect everyone equally, regardless of wealth and stature or innocence and guilt.

They also connect the novel to the 2014 Ebola outbreak in West Africa and its feared spread to the United States.

Mrs. Cardona is an experienced Latina teacher in a racially and economically diverse district in the Pacific Northwest. The class featured in the vignette consisted of 16 students: six African Americans, one second-generation Korean American, one student of Chinese descent, three fourth-generation Japanese Americans, one Latino originally from El Salvador, one student originally from Ghana, and three White European Americans.

Mrs. Cardona's students brought up Ebola early into the novel, and in response, she introduced extension activities, including analyzing media reports about the outbreak. Now they are three-quarters of the way into the novel, when the plague epidemic is at full throttle. In preparation for discussion, students were to have read the beginning of Part IV (pp. 169–197), in which Camus details the tortured death of a child and a subsequent conversation between Dr. Rieux and Father Paneloux regarding faith, innocence, and the brutality of the disease. They were to prepare three in-depth questions for discussion. Mrs. Cardona's goals were threefold: (1) to consider contextual similarities and differences in Camus's fictive plague outbreak and the 2014 Ebola outbreak, (2) to explore how these differences impact how stories of these outbreaks are told in the novel and in the media, and (3) to have students engage in close reading and to support their claims with reference to the text. She organized the discussion as a fishbowl: Half the class was in an inner circle that was expected to engage in a conversation about the novel. The students in the outer circle did not participate orally but were to actively listen and participate via a digital back channel. They could pose questions, relevant links, and commentary via cellphones or iPads. The comment feed was projected on the wall, but without students' names, so their contributions were anonymous, although as we see in the vignette, this anonymity was only partial.

"There Won't Be No Cure Till White Folk Start Dyin'"

Mrs. Cardona initiates the discussion by asking Miranda to start the conversation. Miranda reads one of her questions: "On p. 195, after M. Othon's son dies, Tarou asks Castel, 'Will you have to start it all over again?' It being the serum to cure the plague. Castel nods 'with a twisted smile.' Why do you think Castel smiles? Support your answers with the text." Darrius says that maybe his smile is "sarcastic because it's 'twisted,' and also because Castel has spent so much time trying to find a cure." Omar responds, "I think it's twisted in a creepy way. All he cares about is his work, not really about the people. 'Cause he says on p. 196 that 'after all he put up a surprisingly long resistance.' So even though Othon's son dies, it shows the serum might help.

But it means he also might suffer more; Paneloux said that like a page earlier. So it's more about making a serum and like, his reputation."

As the conversation unfolds, comments and questions appear on the back channel. Mrs. Cardona notes that James participated in this way; shortly after she saw him tapping on his phone, the following comment appeared: "It don't matter that an innocent child was killed. There won't be no cure till white folk start dyin.'" Mrs. Cardona noticed over the past week that James had not been keeping up with his reading, and she suspected that he had not actually read the portion of the novel under discussion. But James's comment catches Mikaela's attention in the inner circle, and she responds, "Well I don't know if that comment is about Ebola or the plague. I don't know. I think the point is that innocent people are dying. You can't get more innocent than a little kid." Another student, Bokeo, responds, "Yeah but with Ebola kids are dying all the time and mostly Africans, and they're innocent too. And there's like vaccines or things they're doing, like giving people blood of people who survived it and an experimental medicine—Z-something—and only the White people have gotten it. It doesn't matter if you're innocent or not." Mikaela nods and says, "Well yeah, I think that's what the author is saying—the plague will kill anyone, even innocent people." Bokeo says, "But that's not what I mean. I don't know how to say it." Monique offers, "In the book there's no treatment yet, but there are things with Ebola that doctors can do." Bokeo adds, "Right, but the guy in Dallas didn't get Z-Mapp—that's what it's called—and he died. But the White doctors, they got it and lived." Omar now chips in and says, "Racism, people." Darryn says, "Yeah, but that's Ebola, not the plague in, what? The 1940s? The doctor—Rieux—couldn't do anything. He had to sit there and watch the child die."

The conversation continues in this vein, and comments appear with more frequency on the screen: "Racism." "Don't you think if they could cure Ebola they would??" "Why is it racist? Spanish priests got a drug." "Didn't some African doctors got experimental vaccines?" "i agree its racism." "Volunteers are risking their lives to go over to Africa to help." "dude spanish people are white." Mrs. Cardona is conflicted. While she thinks the conversation is an important one, she also wants them talking about and within the text—*The Plague*—and the conversation has drifted to solely focus on Ebola and the present day. Moreover, the conversation is becoming more heated, and the structure of the fishbowl is dissolving.

James says, "Ain't no way it's not racism. Black lives don't matter to White people." Jocelyn, in the inner circle, turns to James and says, "That's not true. White people do care. And besides, you didn't even read the book." James retorts, "Dang, I ain't got to read no book to know that!" A link to a CNN commentary appears on the screen, in which the writer argues that the Ebola crisis is leading to implicit racism and racial profiling (www.cnn

.com/2014/10/09/opinion/wright-ebola-racism/index.html?hpt=op_t1). A few other students start navigating to the commentary on their own phones, tablets, and iPods.

At this point, Mrs. Cardona interjects: "This conversation is extremely important. James, it's true, you don't have to read the book to know that, but you do have to read the book for my class. Let's talk about this some more, but in the context of the book. I hear Bokeo, James, who else? Monique, saying there are racial disparities in how the Ebola outbreak is being addressed. Others—Darryn, and some who've commented on our back channel—disagree. Then we have still others, let's see, Jocelyn and Mikaela referring us back to the text, which is in a different time and place—1940s Algeria.

"I want to talk about both—possible inequities and the context of the book. We've already talked about Algeria in the 1940s. What do we know about it? Caitlyn?" Caitlyn hesitates and then asks, "What do you mean?" Mrs. Cardona rephrases, "What do we know about Algeria at that time? Who was there? Who was in power?" Caitlyn says, "It was a colony of France." Mrs. Cardona confirms her response, and adds that there were many people of French descent there, including Dr. Rieux, and she reminds them that Camus was a Frenchman born in Algeria. "We also talked about similarities between the Ebola outbreak and bubonic plague: quarantine, the exponential rate of growth for both epidemics, the human and economic toll. Right now we're going to pause the fishbowl discussion. I want you to get with a partner, go back into the text, and see if Camus talks about any inequities in treatment of the plague in Oran."

Five minutes later, they resume the discussion, and this time, Mrs. Cardona reminds them to "stay close to the text." Jocelyn says that she and her partner didn't find anything in the text about inequities with who gets the experimental vaccine, except that Othon's son gets it, "maybe because Othon is an important person—a magistrate." After a bit of discussion, Miranda says, "I don't get why Camus doesn't really talk about it. I mean, if it was a French colony and under French rule, wouldn't there be divisions between the French and the local—you know, Arab people who were there first?" Omar responds, "Yeah, the French probably got better treatment." Mrs. Cardona interjects, "But does it say that in the text?" Omar says, "No, I—I don't think so. But it could've been that way." Bokeo adds, "Yeah, 'cause Camus was French," but Mikaela interjects, "He was born in Algeria, though." Bokeo retorts, "Well, yeah, but he's still French. He's White or European. So did he just like ignore that? I mean, no way was it equal there."

Soon the class period comes to a close. As the students gather their things and head out the door, Mrs. Cardona feels like she needs to catch her breath, and she wonders how she can help them continue the conversation the next day.

The discussion in Mrs. Cardona's class was clearly racially charged and conveys an intensity that invites discussion according to theories that acknowledge multiple kinds of responses and stances to texts, as well as issues of social justice.

Transactional/Reader Response Theory

It is not difficult to see key elements of transactional/reader response theory in the fishbowl discussion. This theory's main premise, that reading is a transaction between readers' subjective experiences and understandings and the text, suggests that students' own experiences with racism would play into their responses to both the text and to each other. This is most evident with James. Accordingly, the range of opinions expressed by Bokeo, Omar, Monique, Mikaela, and

See p. 50 for a description of transactional/reader response theory.

Darryn in response to James's back-channel comment demonstrates the transactional principle that different readers will approach texts from different stances, respond to the same texts differently, and construct different meanings. Different experiences with racial disparities may explain the students' varied responses to the text and to one another.

According to transactional/reader response theory, stance is reflective of people's purposes for reading and will therefore impact what a reader attends to while reading (Rosenblatt, 2004). Mikaela's question prompted a focus on themes of justice, innocence, and equity. This pushed students to engage both aesthetically and efferently with the novel and even to diverge from the text to discuss the Ebola outbreak and how it relates to issues of race and racism. Some students assume a stance of resistance (Sipe, 1999), questioning the text, plot, and author's language choices, particularly when they do not reflect their own social and cultural realities. James, for instance, resists many texts at once. First, he resists the separation between the novel and the Ebola outbreak as framed in the activity. Next, he resists the "text" or structure of the fishbowl discussion, which enables only certain kinds of conversations to ensue. In doing so, he also resists Mrs. Cardona's requirement of "close reading" to highlight what he views as the most important issue: current racial inequities in the world's response to the Ebola outbreak. In actuality, the text does not serve his needs because Camus does not address such inequities in any substantial way in the novel. Rather, Camus's message is that disease affects everyone equally—a message that does not reflect the reality James sees playing out in the case of Ebola.

James's decision to disengage with the text by not keeping up with his assigned readings or staying "close to the text" is questionable with respect to his ultimate success in Mrs. Cardona's class. Nevertheless, Mrs. Cardona takes up his insights to help the class address these issues in ways that *do* relate back to the text. In other words, she allows space for this stance of resistance, signaling the value of James's participation and potentially engaging him more deeply with the text. James's stance of resistance can also be understood from the perspective of CRT.

Critical Race Theory

CRT suggests that because race has been the primary dividing line framing social and cultural life in the United States (and indeed in other countries that participated in the slave trade), it should be a central feature of attempts to understand and alleviate racial inequities. James brings this topic to the fore with his back-channel comment, "It don't

See p. 92 for a description of critical race theory.

matter that an innocent child was killed. There won't be no cure till white folk start dyin.'" This is taken up by other students and Mrs. Cardona, who recognizes the relevance of the discussion and works to integrate it into the analysis and subsequent critique of the novel. A core concept within CRT is interest convergence, the idea that measures benefiting Black people will not prevail unless they also benefit White people (Bell, 1980). James and Bokeo argue this point, suggesting that no cure or vaccine will be developed for Ebola unless it will clearly benefit White people.

Camus's point in *The Plague* was an existential one—that diseases know no racial, moral, or economic boundaries. All are affected, regardless of whether one is an innocent child or a criminal. Some view his novel as an allegory for the Nazi occupation of France, with the plague representing the Nazis, and the efforts to fight the disease as the French resistance. Camus's emphasis was arguably on saving lives, regardless of religion or culture, a tacit reference to the Holocaust. However, the Holocaust was not highlighted explicitly in the novel. These are dominant readings of the novel and are certainly supportable. However, from a CRT perspective, asking *why* racial or cultural injustices were not addressed more explicitly in the novel might be a valid point of critique, and understandable given the saliency of racial tensions in the United States in 2014. And because race was not forefronted in the novel, it is a point of critique that James must step away from the novel to address. Given contextual differences between the United States in 2014 and 1940s North Africa, James could not "stay close to the text" to make his point, either with respect to Ebola or the plague in the novel.

The next vignette also illustrates how a teacher and her students manage conversations about difference. However, unlike the first two vignettes, this one centers around representations of individuals with physical disabilities and issues of bullying.

STEPPING INTO ANOTHER'S SHOES IN A
6TH-GRADE LANGUAGE ARTS CLASSROOM

Out of My Mind, by Sharon Draper (2010), is a novel told from the first-person perspective of Melody, an 11-year-old girl with severe cerebral palsy. Melody has a photographic memory, particularly for words, which we learn at the very onset of the novel. Yet, she is unable to walk, write, or speak, and has for most of her life been unable to communicate with her family, teachers, and peers beyond rudimentary ways. She finds herself relegated to tedious basic skills instruction at school, such as learning the alphabet over and over. Melody is going "out of her mind." The reader becomes privy to Melody's frustrations, as well as what unfolds when she finds a way to claim her voice. The following vignette illustrates how Ms. Jackson engages her 6th-graders in a reader response activity that prompts students to step inside Melody's mind.

Ms. Jackson has been teaching Language Arts at Eaglewood Middle School for almost 10 years. Although she is an avid user of social media herself, she wants her students to develop a critical eye toward some of the perils of social media, as well as the benefits in terms of accessing information and communicating outside of one's immediate and everyday context. Her goals in this regard stem from recent high-profile bullying incidents involving social media reported in the national news, as well as incidents of bullying at Eaglewood over the past year. The bullying, and Ms. Jackson's desire to support her students in thinking more carefully about difference, has prompted her to begin the school year with *Out of My Mind*. She believes the novel will be a fairly easy read, which may be appropriate for the beginning of 6th grade. This will allow her to devote less class time to working on difficult vocabulary and spend more time thinking about broader themes such as friendship, belonging, and understanding difference.

When Ms. Jackson introduced the response activity in the vignette, students had read 11 of 33 chapters and had an understanding of who Melody was, her developing friendship with Rose, and her experiences in school. Ms. Jackson wanted her students to think about how others see Melody and to compare that to how she understands herself. To this end, she had her students design a mock Facebook page for Melody based on what they learned about her in the text.

Being Melody: Stepping into Role Through Social Media

It is a warm morning in late September, and Ms. Jackson's 6th-graders begin filing into her first-period Language Arts class. To her students' surprise, they see a Facebook page projected onto the screen. As students sit down in their desks, they start pointing to the Facebook page and chatting with one another. Noah asks, "Whose page is that?" And Maggie asks, "You do Facebook before school, Ms. Jackson?"

As students get settled, Ms. Jackson says, "I'm sure some of you are wondering what a Facebook page is doing up here. This is actually my sister's page, and she let me show it to you today. How many of you have Facebook pages, or Instagram or Tumblr?" Twenty-two of her 24 students' hands go up. The two who did not raise their hands have family or close friends who use those sites. Ms. Jackson asks them what you can learn about a person from their Facebook page, and students' hands shoot up. Samira says "the different things they like," and Ms. Jackson asks how. Samira points to the left of the screen, and explains, "if you scroll down you can see what other pages they like." Isaac adds, "and the books and movies and music they like, too, right above that; it's just not called 'likes.'" Ms. Jackson responds, "Okay, so I can learn about someone's interests. What else?" Omeed responds, "You can see what they're thinking about. Like in their posts, you can see if they share something that just happened or ideas they have, or if they just did something fun." Lizzie clarifies, "It's in their status update, so you can see what they post on their timeline." Ms. Jackson says, "So I can learn about what sorts of things might be going on in their lives, and maybe how they feel about it? Okay. Anything else?" Ryan explains that people can have a profile photo and share other photos as well as videos. Max then states, "You can also follow other people and like their posts. So like, if your sister follows something, I don't know, like—" Ms. Jackson says, "Like the middle school band?" Max says, "Yeah, okay. So if the band posts something, your sister will see that and she can like it." The conversation continues, with students offering information about other features of Facebook, such as lists of friends, mutual friends, and the like.

At this point, Noah asks, "Why are we doing Facebook?!" Ms. Jackson acknowledges his question and introduces their response activity: "Well, as I was thinking about Melody in *Out of My Mind*, I began to wonder what her Facebook page might include. If she could create a Facebook profile, what might she include in it? What would her likes be? What might she say in some of her posts? Turn to a partner and talk about what Melody's page might include and why." As students are doing this, Ms. Jackson navigates away from her sister's profile page and brings up what looks like a Facebook page but is actually a mock page, created using the web tool Fakebook. The page she brings up is made for Rosa Parks (www.classtools.net/FB/1248-H3y2Ri), whom they had studied at the end of 5th grade.

"Okay, what have you all come up with?" Students offer various ideas. Omeed says she'd probably post about being frustrated, and Julia adds that she'd post about words she likes. Sarah responds that her profile picture would be her in her wheelchair, but another student counters that she could make an avatar that "shows what she would look like if she wasn't in a wheelchair, or even an object or something. My mom's profile picture is a pink ribbon for cancer awareness." Ms. Jackson then responds, "Okay, so it doesn't have to be a photo of yourself; it could be a thing, or even a photo of someone else, like a family member.

"Over the next few days, you are going to be working in partners to design Melody's profile page, not on Facebook, but on Fakebook. When you do this, I want you to really think about what Melody would convey about herself to others, as well as what others might post on her page." Max blurts out, "Can we pick our own partners?!" Ignoring this, Ms. Jackson tells them they'll need to attend to the different conventions of social networking sites. Using the Rosa Parks Fakebook page as an example, she explains that "typically, posts on social networking sites are not lengthy, and if they are, they may appear out of place." Marisa points out the advertisements on the Fakebook page, and Ms. Jackson says that she's unsure whether or not you can control those advertisements, but she says, "That's kind of how it is on Facebook, too, right?"

They examine other features of the Fakebook page, such as who Rosa Parks's friends are, and Ms. Jackson tells them they'll need to think about who they'll include for Melody's friends. "You could consider having Melody be friends with characters from other books you've read or historical figures." As she does this, she shows them how they can add friends within the tool and select photos or images to go along with them. Finally, she reminds them that their choices must be supported by the text: "If you want to make Melody be friends with the character August Pullman from *Wonder*, you can. That would make sense, wouldn't it? But would it make sense for her to be friends with SpongeBob?" Laughing, a few students shout, "Nooo!" and Ms. Jackson says, "Yeah, probably not."

Wrapping up the class period, Ms. Jackson assigns the students to partners and provides them further information and guidelines on the assignment, including a graphic organizer to help them think about what they'll include, and information about accessing Fakebook. As the week progresses, Ms. Jackson has students share their pages under construction, such as Omeed's and Julia's (see Figure 8.1). As they discuss students' pages, they address the use of conventions, such as multiple exclamation points and hashtags, and how these are realistic given who they think Melody is based on the book.

As they continue reading the novel, they discuss how Melody is treated by some of her peers and how that treatment surfaces in students' Fakebook pages. She uses these discussions as a platform to engage students in critical conversations about bullying at Eaglewood and beyond through cyberbullying. Ms. Jackson invites two 8th-graders who participate in a program called Eagle Friends to talk with her students. Eagle Friends is a program in which able-bodied students and students without identified learning disabilities are paired with and spend their study hall period engaging socially with special needs students. This conversation has a significant impact on some of Ms. Jackson's students, who themselves go on to become Eagle Friends as 7th- and 8th-graders.

Figure 8.1. Omeed and Julia's Fakebook Page for Melody in *Out of My Mind*

Ms. Jackson's instruction raises questions regarding the use of social media and how it may be used to support both students' interpretations of texts and critical awareness of social issues, such as bullying.

Transactional/Reader Response Theory

The Fakebook activity that Ms. Jackson facilitates is a fairly classic example of a reading response activity. It serves as a venue for students to articulate both expressed responses (reflecting on the

See p. 50 for a description of transactional/reader response theory.

meaning of a text) and expressed interpretations (continued efforts to clarify meanings after reading; Fecho & Meacham, 2007), key aspects of meaning construction within a transactional/reader response framework. By speaking from Melody's perspective and making decisions regarding what sorts of information to include in her Fakebook page, students must go beyond the literal and make inferences regarding the kinds of things Melody might post, who her friends would be, what kinds of books and movies she would like, and so on. In the process, and as they continue reading the novel, they come to new understandings regarding Melody as a character.

Furthermore, from this theoretical vantage point, the students construct understandings as transactions occur between students' schemata regarding disabilities such as cerebral palsy, their understandings of uses of social media, their prior knowledge and experiences with respect to social interactions and bullying, and the events in the text. This results in the students' constructing understandings of the text that may differ substantially from one another.

Importantly, transactions between text and reader are not linear, nor do they occur unidirectionally. That is, just as readers' schemata will impact constructed meanings of the text, those constructed meanings can alter readers' understandings about the world. This occurs as students recalibrate their ways of thinking about people with disabilities, and, potentially, their interactions with their peers at school. As students engage in conversations around Melody's feelings of exclusion, and equitable treatment of those with ability differences, they take up multiple stances toward the text.

Multiliteracies/New Literacies Theory

A central characteristic of multiliteracies/new literacies theory is the emphasis on broadened conceptualizations of literacy, including multimodality and rapidly changing literacy technologies. The response activity clearly recruits new digital technologies as tools to support students in stepping into Melody's shoes. However, we

See p. 86 for a description of multiliteracies/new literacies theory.

may question why Ms. Jackson had them use Fakebook rather than real social networking pages in which they could have taken on multiple character identities and used online tools to communicate with one another in role.

We may also consider the vignette using the New London Group's (1996) four elements of a pedagogy of multiliteracies (overt instruction, situated practice, critical framing, and transformed practice). Ms. Jackson engages in overt instruction through the explicit discussion and explanation of conventions of social media sites. She also models specific tasks within the Fakebook tool, such as adding friends and photos. There is an element of situated practice because she grounds her instruction in a meaningful social practice (social networking) that her students are familiar with. In doing so, she taps into their popular culture knowledge, as well as previous academic instruction (using a sample Fakebook page portraying Rosa Parks). While there appears to be space within Ms. Jackson's lesson for critical media literacy, particularly with respect to the presence of advertisements within social networking tools and mock sites such as Fakebook, Ms. Jackson does not push her students to consider the issue. However, consistent with some of her initial pedagogical goals, Ms. Jackson does use the novel and the response activity to critically frame issues of difference and bullying and to prompt students, even if somewhat indirectly, to take social action (transformed practice) through the Eagle Friends program.

Finally, the vignette can be framed within the concept of designing (New London Group, 1996), which includes three features: *available designs* (resources for making and representing meaning), *designing* (the process of working with and changing available designs), and *the redesigned* (new meanings or representations produced through designing). Both the novel and Facebook (or Fakebook) could be considered available designs. Students' construction of Melody's profile page is a process of designing (including conversations and decision-making processes about what to include and how), and their end products would constitute the redesigned. (One limitation of Fakebook, however, is that students cannot edit their pages once they have been saved. That is, they cannot save their work in progress and then return to the tool at a later date to continue their process of design.) Also, if we consider bullying and existing interactional norms around issues of disability as texts to be "worked on," or altered, we can think of students' transformed practice through Eagle Friends as a process of designing and redesigning texts.

QUESTIONS FOR PRAXIS

1. Another way to engage students in conversations about texts is through blogging. How might blogging fit in or alongside the instructional engagements in the three vignettes? How might students' caregivers become involved in these conversations?

2. In the three vignettes, the teachers engaged their students in conversations about difference, including race and racism, inequities in the Ebola outbreak, the holocaust of slavery, and rethinking ability differences. In what ways have you engaged your students in conversations about difference through literature? Thinking about your practices in this regard, what theoretical connections can you make?

RESOURCES AND ADDITIONAL READINGS

Clarke, L. & Holwadel, J. (2014). "Help! What is wrong with these literature circles and how can we fix them?" *The Reading Teacher, 61*(1), 20–29.

Davis, S. (2014). View from the chalkboard: Rethinking reading logs. *The Reading Teacher, 68*(1), 45.

Hunter, J. D., & Caraway, H. J. (2014). Urban youth use Twitter to transform learning and engagement. *English Journal, 103*(4), 76–82.

Question–answer relationships: Question–answer relationships (QAR) is a strategy for framing the kinds of questions students may ask and respond to in literature conversations: Right there questions (the answer is stated explicitly in the text), think and search questions (answers come from different parts of the text and must be integrated to respond to the question), author and you (students must blend information from the text with their prior knowledge), and on my own (students may answer based solely on their own understandings or experiences. www.readingrockets.org/strategies/question_answer_relationship

Thein, A. H., Guise, M., & Sloan, D. L. (2011). Problematizing literature circles as forums for discussion of multicultural and political texts. *Journal of Adolescent & Adult Literacy, 55*(1), 15–24. doi:10.1598/JAAL.55.1.2

CHAPTER 9

Writing and Writing Development
Authoring Texts, Authoring Lives

Educators generally use the word "writing" to mean the production of print text. However, what happens when we get more specific? Does writing refer to composing the content of messages or of putting those ideas down in print? Should writing instruction be limited to print texts? Which conventions and mechanics matter, and to what extent, given the multimodal nature of communication in the 21st century?

In times and places where most people were not proficient in print literacies, people would hire a scribe to create records of economic transactions or other official business (Kalman, 1999; Samuels, 2007). The word "scribe," which is derived from the Latin word *scriber*, makes appearances in all sorts of related terms, including "describe," "proscribe," "subscribe," the Spanish word *escribir*, and even the word "scribble." Scribes were trained in the mechanics of linguistic representation to inscribe, or write, what they wanted to say; thus, the term is often meant as someone who creates *copies* of texts rather than *composing* original texts. Indeed, the word "compose" is etymologically unrelated to "scribe" and its derivatives. Rather, it comes from the Old French word *composer*, which means to put together or arrange to convey meaning—hence its use in music and its connotations with more original or agentic processes than copying. In short, when we talk about writing, we are not always talking about the same thing.

WRITING INSTRUCTION IN K-12 CLASSROOMS

At times, teachers may engage students in activities more akin to the work of scribes, such as taking dictation (this is an activity included in Marie Clay's [1993a] *An Observation Survey of Early Literacy Achievement*) or copying sentences or words from a book or a classroom whiteboard. Teachers of young children often emphasize mechanics, such as letter formation, and 3rd- and 4th-grade teachers may still instruct students in cursive, stressing form over function. Teachers frequently accentuate development in particular writing skills, such as grammar and spelling. On the worksheet shown in

scribe (copy) vs. composition (create)

Figure 9.1, for example, the phrase "good sentences" is understood to mean complete sentences rather than sentence fragments.

At other times, however, teachers emphasize composition, teaching students how to arrange and design texts to meet particular genre or pragmatic conventions. Part of this process involves considering audience and voice, and teachers may emphasize function over form, stressing the importance of communication rather than conventionality. The conversation regarding how much instructional attention should be devoted to mechanics or composition has a corollary in the tension regarding the relative importance of product versus process in writing (Calkins, 1994; Graves, 1983). With the development of workshop approaches came increased emphasis on process and teaching students what writers *do* as they move from conceptualizing a piece of writing to its completion, different genres and purposes for writing, and writers' tricks of the trade, or craft (Ray, 1999).

Reading and writing often occupy distinct curricular identities in K–12 classrooms, particularly at the elementary level. Reading and writing instruction are typically slotted into different times of day, with reading workshop occurring over a 90- to 120-minute block, and writing workshop over 60 to 90 minutes. Even in some secondary classrooms, students may have both a literature class and a composition or writing class, which includes grammar instruction.

However, these distinctions, and assumed oppositions, between reading and writing, product and process, and between skills and composition are false ones, much like the artificial separation between theory and practice. Our sentence structure, punctuation, and spelling matter because our

Figure 9.1. A Worksheet and Teacher Feedback Emphasizing Writing Skills and Conventions

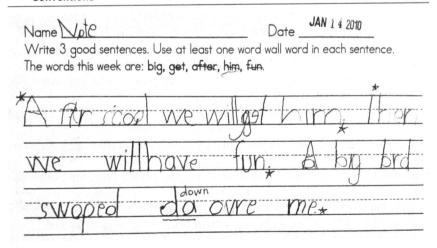

choices about these elements carry different weight as we write for different purposes and audiences. What is more, we recruit different forms of language and other semiotic systems not just to conform to or challenge conventions but to construct meaning.

These processes are about more than authoring texts; they are also about authoring lives. Maxine Greene (1995) wrote that "writing has to do with that recognition of an 'I'" (p. 106). She continues, "It is by writing that I often manage to name alternatives and to open myself to possibilities" (p. 107). In the same vein, Katie Wood Ray (1999) explains that she and her students use writing to say, "This is who I am, this is what I wish for, and this is what I care about" (p. 7). From this angle, writing is not simply a process of producing texts but also of imagining, producing, and reshaping identities. The two vignettes in this chapter highlight relationships between form and function, process and product, as well as the interconnectedness of authoring texts and authoring lives. The first illustrates small moments writing in a 1st-grade English monolingual classroom, while the second describes autobiographical writing in a 4th-grade bilingual classroom.

SMALL MOMENTS WRITING IN A
1ST-GRADE MONOLINGUAL CLASSROOM

Kay Coulson is a Reading Specialist at Sangamon Elementary School in Mahomet, Illinois, a bedroom community of Champaign-Urbana, where the University of Illinois is located. Students in Mahomet come from predominantly White monolingual homes, and there is a substantial degree of socioeconomic diversity in the district. Kay has over 20 years of teaching experience at the primary level, and prior to moving into her current position as a Reading Specialist, she spent 16 years teaching 1st grade.

As a 1st-grade teacher, Kay implemented a unit from Calkins's *Units of Study for Primary Writing* (K–2) called Small Moments: Personal Narrative Writing (Calkins & Oxenhorn, 2003). The purpose of this unit is to support students in writing with detail by elaborating on different events within their narratives. Teachers begin by asking students to focus on one small everyday moment or event, such as falling off a bicycle, scoring a goal in soccer, or eating a favorite dessert. In subsequent parts of the unit, the focus shifts to specific skills, such as word writing and planning for writing, and then moves on to revision strategies, editing, and publishing lengthier stories that include detailed accounts of several small moments. Rather than illustrating a specific moment of Kay's teaching and her students' small moments writing, this vignette details her general approach to the unit, including her adaptations to the published curriculum.

Small Moments Writing: Adaptation and Experimentation

As recommended by Calkins and Oxenhorn (2003), Kay's implementation of small moments writing began with an introductory minilesson including a read-aloud of a text with significant detail about specific moments or events. For the first session, Kay typically used one of the texts suggested in the unit, such as Keats's *The Snowy Day* (1976), or another text that highlighted specific moments with substantial detail. Using *A Chair for My Mother* (Williams, 1982) in big book form, for example, Kay talked with her students about how the author offers very specific details about the moment when the characters discover that their home and belongings have been destroyed by a fire. She framed this as a small moment within the longer narrative.

Mentor text

Over the course of a few sessions, Kay engaged her students in composing detailed narratives of one particular moment in time. For each small story, she required students to include dialogue, sound effects, and words describing their feelings. For example, one student wrote about spilling her water bottle on her desk. She included dialogue and exclamations, such as "Oh no! Everything is all wet!," a sound effect ("Whoosh") to represent the water rushing over her desk, and adjectives, such as "soggy." Students composed their small stories on white lined paper with spaces above them for illustrations. (See Figure 9.2.)

Kay encouraged students to use different resources to support their spelling. For high-frequency words, she expected them to use the classroom word wall, and for more difficult words she encouraged invented spelling. To support them in their invented spelling, she conducted minilessons in which she showed students how to stretch out the sounds in words and to try to represent all of the sounds they hear in a word. She also taught them to consider common spelling patterns they already knew by using high-frequency word wall words (an analogy approach). For example, she taught her students that by listening for words that rhyme, they could use word wall words ("game," "name") to spell words they did not already know ("blame," "tame," "shame," "fame").

As students wrote independently, they often conferred with one another informally, showing each other what they were writing, or chatting about their small moments. Kay also conferenced with writers one-on-one during this time, reading over students' writing or asking students to read their writing aloud for her. She would ask clarifying questions about event sequences, details, and the elements of small moments writing that students were integrating into their stories (e.g., sound effects, dialogue, etc.). Kay also used these writing conferences to reinforce strategies taught during minilessons. For example, when a student struggled with how to write "bottle," Kay prompted her to say the word slowly, stretch out each of the sounds, and then

Figure 9.2. A Student's Small Moments Story Draft

write down the letters she heard. Slowly, with additional prompts from Kay (e.g., "And what sound do you hear next?"), the student wrote, "Botol." The same student spelled several word wall words conventionally (e.g., "come," "on," "going," and "mom"), and less frequent words and phrases by matching sounds and letters (e.g., "gys" for "guys," "dulivry" for "delivery," and "les clen up" for "let's clean up"). Other students used the analogy approach—for example, using the word "down" to spell "clown" and the word "people" to write "steople" (for "steeple").

In their unit guide, Calkins and Oxenhorn recommend that teachers make small books, stapling papers together with a construction paper cover, for students to use when composing. While the curriculum guide does not emphasize revising, editing, and publishing this particular episode of writing, Kay took her students through these steps with these small moments stories prior to continuing on with the unit. Kay would help her students revise and edit their writing during conferences, as described above, but would then transcribe their writing herself onto the computer. As she did this, she would make their spelling and punctuation conventional. She included a series of lines at the end of each book for people her young authors shared their books with to sign their names. Once printed out, she stapled the pages together, including a title page and a construction paper cover with spaces for the students to include their illustrations. (See Figure 9.3.)

Part of Kay's reasoning for typing students' stories for them was so that they later had access to reading their own writing in conventional form, with the expectation that reading their own stories repeatedly with others would support their word recognition and fluency. Kay used the students' handwritten drafts for assessment purposes, but the computer-produced ones served as the published narratives.

However, a few years ago, Kay began taking classes to attain her reading specialist certificate. As part of her coursework, she read the work of Katie Wood Ray and Matt Glover (Glover, 2009; Ray & Glover, 2008), whose ideas also informed writing instruction for the kindergarten teachers in her

Figure 9.3. A Student's Published Small Moment Story

district. These authors emphasize the importance of young writers taking on authorial stances, and they suggest that children have the opportunity to edit and publish books themselves. Although Kay's inclinations as a self-described perfectionist were to "tidy up" her students' writing, she wondered how her students would write and publish their own books having just moved from kindergarten into 1st grade. She also wondered whether they might take more ownership of their writing if this process were completed on their own. With the encouragement of one of her professors, Kay shifted away from transcribing and correcting students' small moments stories and began having her students revise, edit, and publish their handwritten small stories.

Because Kay's school had discontinued their computer lab because of funding issues and reallocation of limited school space, and because she had only two computers in her classroom, she felt it was not feasible for her students to publish their stories digitally. Thus, she shifted how she approached the publishing process, moving away from the computer and back toward student produced books, made by hand. These took the same basic form as the books published on the computer but included lines for students to write on. Her desire to provide lines to guide students' handwriting was to prompt her students to attend to conventional forms of writing with respect to page orientation and letter formation. In short, she felt that the lined paper would help her students transition into "1st-grade writing" with respect to state standards.

Once Kay grew accustomed to the handwritten final products, despite their imperfections, she began using these alongside their earlier drafts to assess her students' writing development. This offered Kay a richer set of texts to use when understanding her students' spelling. In the process, she also noted that the extra time they took to produce "clean" copies of their writing by hand prompted edits to their spelling and conventions that built on her additional minilessons. Kay placed each student's writing across the school year into three ring binders, which became portfolios for writing assessment and for showcasing students' writing development for parents.

Kay's implementation of, and adaptations to, the small moments writing unit invites rich discussions of how to support young students' understandings of narrative composition, the writing process, their development of voice, and their spelling development. In what follows, I analyze Kay's teaching using stage theories of spelling development and emergent literacy theory.

Stage Theories

Kay used her knowledge of the array of developmental stages of word knowledge and spelling (described in Chapter 2) of her 1st-graders (mostly semiphonetic to transitional) by teaching specific spelling strategies, such as stretching out the sounds in a word, listening for rhyming patterns, and using the word wall. In doing so, she offered her students strategies that are considered developmentally appropriate given their respective stages and that also push their development into subsequent stages and ultimately to conventional forms.

Kay's initial use of computer-generated final products within the small moments writing unit were produced in part to provide her students with opportunities for repeated reading of conventional texts, as they reread their own writing. Repeated reading has been documented as a useful strategy for fluency development and word recognition (Stahl & Heubach, 2005) and is consistent with stage theories of word knowledge. Furthermore, developing readers' word recognition and spelling are both connected to phonological awareness and occur concurrently (Stahl & McKenna, 2000). This connection is brought to life in the vignette as Kay prompts her students to stretch out and listen for each sound in a word they are trying to spell.

See p. 33 for a description of stage theories.

As noted in Chapter 2, stage theories such as Gentry's (2000) focus on fairly linear sequences of development and finer components of language learning (spelling, phonics, phonemic awareness). However, Kay brings stage theories to life within the context of meaningful writing rather than in decontextualized skills instruction. This reflects the idea that, in practice, stage theories are not necessarily inconsistent with constructivist theories of reading and writing development. Gentry (2000) views children's invented spelling, such as Kay's student's rendering of "bottle" as "Botol," as a way of understanding children's thinking about how print works. When explicit instruction in word recognition and spelling is embedded within authentic and meaningful literacy pursuits, such as the personal narratives and small moments writing described above, students are given tools to construct new understandings about language and communicating meaning in print.

Emergent Literacy Theory

A common practice in early childhood classrooms, and one that we see in Kay's implementation of small moments writing, is the use of explicit modeling and mentor texts, which students will then attempt to approximate as they engage in their own small moments writing. Specifically, Kay used *The Snowy Day* (Keats, 1976) and *A Chair for My Mother* (Williams, 1982) in big book format to ground her introduction of detailed description. This use of authentic high-quality children's literature is consistent with social constructivist coherence theories like emergent literacy, which emphasize developing writers' approximations of conventional forms and practices as they become apprenticed into literate communities.

See p. 70 for a description of emergent literacy theory.

Kay's instruction also relied heavily on social interaction, which is a key element of emergent literacy theory. This was evident in several portions of the unit. First, her students were allowed, even encouraged, to confer with one another as they wrote. Second, she engaged in detailed conferences with students about their writing. In doing so, she focused not only on finer skills such as spelling but also on the content of their narratives and their attention to detail in constructing their small moments. Such conversations allow both speakers and listeners (students and teachers) to draw on their previous understandings, language, and cultural knowledge as they construct meaning with texts. They also allow Kay to understand more than just her students' writing skills, as she learns about them as writers and individuals in their classroom community.

Kay's shift away from transcribing her students' writing onto the computer in conventional form is consistent with emergent literacy's focus on student-produced texts and valuing students' invented spelling and other aspects of their writing as approximations of conventional forms (Holdaway, 1979). Her emphasis moved from one in which conventional forms serve as the primary measure of student success (a practice that is more reflective of correspondence theories) to one in which students' invented spelling offers windows into each individual's understandings about how print works (consistent with coherence theories). This shift offered a richer sampling of students' writing that Kay could use for "roaming around the known" (Clay, 1993a, p. 12) regarding children's developing understandings of spelling and composition. The next vignette similarly highlights a teacher's in-depth knowledge of her students and the contextualization of classroom writing practices.

AUTOBIOGRAPHICAL WRITING IN A 4TH-GRADE BILINGUAL CLASSROOM

Patricia Valente teaches bilingual 4th grade at Cedar Ridge Elementary School in Bloomington, Illinois. The district's transitional bilingual program (officially meant to transfer students into all-English classes) serves a Spanish-speaking Latino community and includes one to two bilingual classrooms across the K–5 grade span. A few years previously, the district moved from a skills-based reading series to a reading and writing workshop model coupled with designated writing units at each grade level. For 4th grade, this included narrative, memoir, and expository essays, among other genres. The district also aligned its literacy instruction with the CCSS. Patricia valued the CCSS's emphasis on critically analyzing texts, close reading, and pushing her students to read complex texts.

The following vignette features a memoir unit in Patricia's classroom focused on "*momentos de cambio* [moments of change]," which filtered into comprehension instruction and additional writing engagements. The unit prompted public speaking events involving her students, and ultimately *"momentos de cambio"* became a theme that framed students' learning and self-assessment across the school year. I documented these events during a participatory action research project on reading comprehension and identity that Patricia and I conducted in her classroom.

Patricia approached her instruction with social justice in mind. While she grew up in a White middle-class community, her husband immigrated to Illinois from Mexico, and they speak both Spanish and English at home with their two daughters. Patricia has witnessed many of the injustices her husband has endured based on his language and his skin color, which has motivated her to support her students in achieving academically to dispel the deficit thinking that swirls around them. She has mentioned to both her students and their parents on more than one occasion that there are people, even teachers, "who think we can't do it *porque somos hispanos* [because we are Hispanic]. They won't ask you to do as much because they assume you can't. So you have to work that much harder to prove to them that you can."

Patricia's class included 13 students, all of whom were bilingual in Spanish and English. While most of her students were born in either the United States or Mexico, a few families came to the United States from Guatemala. Approximately half of her students were with her for 3rd grade, and already knowing many of the school's Latino families, Patricia was quick to get to know her students' strengths and needs.

Momentos de Cambio (Moments of Change)

In the memoir unit, Patricia wanted her students to connect deeply with themselves and their life experiences. Reflecting on her own experiences, she focused her students' attention on moments of change—key events that changed their day-to-day lives and how they viewed the world. She knew that many of her students had experienced significant life events, both positive and negative, ranging from the birth of a sibling to a parent being incarcerated, and she understood these events as generative of learning. While most teachers consider topics such as incarceration, drug use, and crime to be taboo, and best left at the schoolhouse door, Patricia wanted to create a space where students could tell these stories.

Patricia began by reading examples of memoir to her students and examining features of the genre. They then brainstormed moments of change in their own lives, identifying specific details of those events. Patricia wanted her students to move beyond "beginning, middle, and end" to explore different forms of writing within the genre. These objectives influenced the structure she asked her students to employ when composing their memoirs, which included five different chapters.

The first chapter consisted of a conversation between themselves and another person involved in the moment of change, as well as a brief description of the event. She pushed her students to consider how a conversation can help readers understand the relationships involved in the narrative and invite readers into a story. In the second chapter, students described what life was like before the moment of change, while the third chapter was devoted to describing the event in detail. Within this chapter, Patricia emphasized to her students the importance of "exploding" particular events with detail, much like small moments writing. The fourth chapter included a description of life after the moment of change, and in the fifth chapter, students composed a letter to someone involved in their moment of change (possibly the person in the conversation in the first chapter). Patricia required her students to write their memoirs in Spanish to further develop and maintain their native language skills.

During minilessons, Patricia modeled how they might go about composing each chapter, using sentence frames (e.g., *"Antes del momento de cambio, me sentí. . . . Por ejemplo, . . .* [Before the moment of change, I felt. . . . For example, . . .]"). Students composed, revised, edited, and published their stories over the course of 6½ weeks. During this time, Patricia used examples of students' writing to conduct additional minilessons on revising and editing.

What Patricia did not anticipate was how the unit would take on a life of its own and seep into other areas of her instruction. A few weeks after the unit, for example, Patricia was working with a comprehension focus group on making inferences using Aesop's fable *Ponle el Cascabel al Gato* [Belling the Cat] (Paxton, 1990), in which a group of mice devise a plan to address the addition of a cat in the house where they live. During the discussion, Danny's face lit up as he said, "The mice had a moment of change!" Patricia built on his connection, using the idea of a moment of change, including what life was like before and after the event, to further their conversations regarding the fable. Similarly, when analyzing a clip from the movie *Finding Nemo* to discuss character development, students immediately asserted that Marlin, Nemo's father, had experienced a moment of change when his wife and all of their eggs but Nemo's were killed. Patricia followed students' lead by asking them to articulate how Marlin changed as a result of that event. The phrase *"momentos de cambio"* was also used during classroom conversations regarding students' personal and family experiences throughout the year.

During late fall Patricia attended a conference on bilingual education and learned about Latino critical (LatCrit) theory, including the concept of *testimonio* (see p. 95, Chapter 5). As a Christian, Patricia felt that *testimonio* bore a resemblance to the kinds of testimonies given in church or other religious spaces, and she wondered if it might have a place in her classroom with respect to her students' life experiences. She began connecting *testimonio* to students' memoirs. In conversations with students, she referred back to their moments of change, telling them that they had important and unique understandings and experiences to share with the world. And in a side conversation during a literature discussion group, when she stopped to remind her students to attend to each others' ideas, she said "You sometimes just wait to see what I say, but you are the experts. You have ideas and experiences that others haven't had. You each have something to teach the world. You need to use your voice and give your own *testimonios*."

In January she initiated a new project aligned with her district's writing curriculum, which included persuasive writing. She wanted to make this project meaningful not only to students' own lives but also to their local school context. Thinking about her students' bilingualism and their minority status within the school, she asked her students to take a stand on bilingualism—is it a benefit or a detriment in their lives? Although she invited them to take either stance, all of her students decided to argue for bilingualism as a benefit. Their unanimity in stance may have been related to Patricia's ongoing advocacy for their bilingualism across the school year.

In preparation for writing, they read articles on the Internet about being bilingual, and they engaged in whole-group discussions regarding their own language experiences translating for family members or being able to read books and other texts, such as signs in restaurants and stores, in two languages. As she did in her unit on memoir, Patricia supported their writing through minilessons, in which she modeled how to conduct an interview, strategies for composing main idea sentences, addition of supporting details, and construction of coherent paragraphs. However, Patricia kept returning to the idea of her students sharing their writing with a wider audience. She wanted to give her students voice and create an opportunity for them to "give testimony" to others regarding their lives.

In late February, I invited Patricia to talk with a group of practicing teachers enrolled in my graduate class on social and cultural contexts of reading and literacy. Patricia suggested that she bring along a couple of her students. She felt that this might be a good opportunity for some of them to articulate their own linguistic and cultural experiences to teachers who may otherwise misunderstand Latino and immigrant students or view them from deficit perspectives. Patricia selected three students, but word quickly spread, and they all implored Patricia to participate. After checking with me, she invited all 13. She also invited preservice teachers who were working with some of her students, as well as her students' families, and I invited some university faculty. Within 2 weeks, the event had blossomed into an evening potluck scheduled in April at Illinois State University, with an expected attendance of 70 people.

Because many of the attendees did not speak or read Spanish, Patricia had her students revisit their memoirs and generate one-page summaries in English. She also gave her students the responsibility of planning the event. They created invitations in English and worked in small groups to translate them into Spanish. Patricia asked students if this should be a formal occasion, a semiformal one, or a casual one, and together they brainstormed how they would communicate expectations for attire to those who were invited. And because so many different people would be there, the students created conversation prompts and getting-to-know-you games for attendees so they could get to know one another as they ate dinner. Students decided to read their memoirs and persuasive essays aloud in groups, sort of like panels, and each group devised a set of questions to ask audience members to prompt conversation about the readings.

The event went smoothly. Proud parents took video and snapped photos as their children stood and read their memoirs and essays. After the group readings and discussion, Patricia thanked the attendees, in particular the families, for their support of their children's learning. She also reiterated her belief that their children's experiences and abilities needed to be heard. She was very animated and remarked that they had all heard her students' *testimonios* regarding their bilingualism and their moments of change, and that with continued support, their children could "change the world." This prompted a series of statements from audience members. One student's mother stood up and addressed the crowd, stating that they wanted more bilingual education throughout the K–12 system, and encouraged other parents to speak out. Others spoke about the impact on their families of hearing their own children's stories. Others simply stood up and thanked the children and Patricia. One teacher, who did not speak Spanish or have experiences working closely with Spanish-speaking students and families, stood up and told the crowd how much she had learned from the students and her conversations with family members, and explained that the event would mark a moment of change for her as a teacher.

Critical Literacy Theory

In both the memoir unit and the persuasive writing project, we see Freire's (1970) emphasis on reading the word and the world, as discussed in Chapter 5, as Patricia's students write from their own experiences. Further animating critical literacy theory, Patricia engages her students in dialogue through which they could further understand and critique their world. This embodies reading both the word and the world, as well as what

See p. 79 for a description of critical literacy theory.

Freire (1970) referred to as "*conscientização.*" Patricia's students explore their own lives and their own positions within social and institutional systems that tend to devalue bilingualism and the kinds of experiences that they and their families have had.

One of Patricia's goals was to empower her students; she sought to give them voice beyond the classroom walls. In addition to *conscientização*, she extends the two writing units beyond students' personal reflection and their written products. By engaging her students in public presentations of their writing, she moves what was at first just "schoolwork" into a realm of possibility for social and political transformation. The composition of the audience that was invited to the culminating event is important. Recall that for Freire, *conscientização* is necessary not just for the oppressed but also for the oppressors, or the dominant classes. Social transformation will occur only through dialogue between those in power and those who have been marginalized (Freire, 1970). This collective effort plays out by bringing students, families, prospective teachers, practicing teachers, and university faculty to the table during the event.

We might question, however, to what extent critical reading and writing occur in the persuasive writing unit. Patricia nudges her students toward a particular position: that being bilingual is a benefit. Critics might view this as another form of colonialism, in which a dominant power (the teacher) imposes particular ways of thinking on those in less powerful positions (her students). To be fair, dialogue framed daily interactions about texts in Patricia's classroom. She consistently invited respectful disagreement and pushed her students to state their views and support their assertions with evidence. Patricia was passionate about language, however, and seeing the impact of inequitable practices on her own family and on her students, she may have assumed that she and her students would take the same position on the issue.

Critical Race Theory

Patricia was explicitly influenced by LatCrit theory, a subcategory of CRT. In particular, she viewed her students' writing and performances as *testimonios*. Recall from Chapter 5 that CRT is a "race conscious" approach to understanding social inequalities and systems of oppression

See p. 92 for a description of critical race theory.

(Zamudio et al., 2011) that places race at the forefront of analyses regarding inequity. LatCrit more specifically is grounded in the inequities and experiences of oppression of Latinos in the United States.

LatCrit resonated with Patricia, particularly with respect to her own hybrid identity as a bilingual White woman whose husband and children are Latinos. She took a keen interest in *testimonio* work, which is consistent with CRT's valuing of alternative ways of knowing, such as story, through which dominant narratives about race and equity might be challenged and alternative voices might be heard. Memoir is a genre that requires students to go in depth and reveal elements of their own lives, even things that may have been private or not welcome in school (Jones, 2004). Patricia imported *testimonio* work in obvious and explicit ways into the memoir unit, including sharing aloud students' sometimes difficult-to-hear narratives.

At the end of the event, when Patricia addressed the audience, she made clear to those in attendance that they had just heard *testimonios*. In doing so, she positioned the audience as witnesses. She tacitly sent the message that the students' experiences, including the benefits of being bilingual, could not be ignored. Citing Levinas (1994), Alarcón, Cruz, Jackson, Prieto, & Rodriguez-Arroyo (2011) describe *testimonios* as requiring

> a deep learning, necessitating an openness to give oneself to the other. It requires what Emmanuel Levinas (1994) described as "receiving the lesson so deeply [that] the lesson of truth is not held in one consciousness. It explodes toward the other" (p. 80). (p. 370)

Arguably, the public statements made by audience members at the end of the event represent such "explosions toward the other," as in the teacher who pinpointed her own professional moment of change at the event.

It should be noted, however, that CRT scholars might view *testimonio* as something that cannot be assigned or mandated, that it is an oral practice, rather than a written one, that is meant to project the voice of the speaker rather than that of a mediator (e.g., a researcher or teacher; Beverley, 2000). Given that students were writing and sharing their writing at the request and invitation of their teacher, we might question whether this would truly be considered *testimonio*. Nevertheless, it is difficult to dispute the impact that LatCrit had on Patricia's practice; like other models or theories, it may be taken up in real classroom spaces in altered and sometimes unexpected ways.

New Literacy Studies

In the vignette of Patricia and her students, we see ways of writing and speaking grounded in local contexts of practice, which is a particular focal point of NLS, as described in Chapter 5. For example, students' writing about the benefits of being bilingual is anchored in part in their own personal histories and experiences of bilingualism in their own local communities. NLS also assumes that all literacy practices are socially and culturally

See p. 83 for a description of new literacy studies.

situated and ideological, a principle that is manifested in the vignette. The two writing engagements created spaces in which students' home languages and family experiences, which might not otherwise be welcomed in school, could be framed as valuable for student learning. At the same time, the students also wrote within genres that were prized in school—memoir and persuasive writing—and thus their practices reflected particular institutional, or global, ideologies regarding language and literacy. Patricia reframed these writing projects as *testimonios*, language and literacy practices that convey very different ideologies regarding expertise and evidence.

Students also had to learn elements of public speaking and organization for the event. As they acquired new (little d) discourses, and put them into practice, the students were able to position themselves and take up new (big D) Discourses, or "ways of being in the world" (Gee, 1996, p. 8) as potential community leaders.

We also see a contextualization of literacy practices in the classroom as the students prepared for the culminating event. As Patricia turned elements of the planning over to the students, they had to consider the audience and their language needs. Because the audience was diverse, with individuals from different linguistic and socioeconomic communities, they developed conversation starters and games to promote conversation during dinner. They also included information about what to wear for families, some of whom had never been to the local university, and translated writing for those who could not speak Spanish.

QUESTIONS FOR PRAXIS

1. In the first vignette, Kay engaged her students in small moments writing and shifted her instruction to allow students to create their own final products. Imagine that Kay taught in a classroom with a richer array of digital tools, such as laptops or iPads. How might such tools be utilized in the creation of small moments stories?
2. In the second vignette, Patricia frames students' writing and sharing of their memoirs and persuasive essays as *testimonios*, building on LatCrit theory. Consider how *testimonio*, or other forms of counternarratives, might be integrated with writing instruction in your own classroom.
3. In what ways might the instructional ideas you generated in questions 1 and 2 speak both to the CCSS (or other state standards) and to potential shifts in power relationships in your classroom?

RESOURCES AND ADDITIONAL READINGS

Berg, D. (2014). Unit plan: Crossing boundaries through bilingual, spoken-word poetry. International Reading Association. Retrieved from www.readwritethink.org /classroom-resources/lesson-plans/crossing-boundaries-through-bilingual-30525 .html

Gibney, T. (2012). Memoir in the elementary classroom: A genre study approach. *The Reading Teacher, 66*(3), 243–253.

Jones, S. (2004). Living poverty and literacy learning: Sanctioning topics of students' lives. *Language Arts, 81*(6), 461–469.

National Council of Teachers of English. (2014). Position statement: NCTE beliefs about students' right to write. Retrieved from www.ncte.org/positions /statements/students-right-to-write

CHAPTER 10

Disciplinary Literacies in the Content Areas

When I was a 4th-grade teacher in the 1990s, educators did not use the term *disciplinary literacies*; we talked only about "content area reading." Prior to having my students read their social studies textbook or another informational text, I would typically use a prereading strategy, such as a DR-TA, to support their understanding of a text. Although such practices may have some value for supporting students' comprehension of content area texts, they do not constitute *disciplinary literacy*. While content area literacy is focused on instructional strategies to support students in understanding texts within and across disciplines, disciplinary literacy is meant to teach students to read and write as historians, mathematicians, musicians, scientists, literary critics, and so on. As Draper and Siebert (2010) explain, to teach disciplinary literacy is to teach students "to negotiate (e.g., read, view, listen, taste, smell, critique) and create (e.g., write, produce, sing, act, speak) texts in discipline-appropriate ways or in ways that other members of a discipline (e.g., mathematicians, historians, artists) would recognize as 'correct' or 'viable'" (p. 30).

C. Shanahan and T. Shanahan (2014) argue that disciplinary literacy is essential because general reading and writing practices are not sufficient for engaging students in the specific ways of reading, writing, and indeed thinking that are unique to different content areas or academic disciplines. This stance is aligned with the CCSS, which delineates what students should know and be able to do as they prepare to enter the 21st-century workforce. The CCSS articulate disciplinary reading standards at the middle-school and secondary levels, but not for the elementary levels. Yet, discipline-specific texts still appear in the elementary grades in the form of primary source documents, maps, diagrams, data tables embedded within textbooks, nonfiction children's literature, science reports, and so forth (C. Shanahan & T. Shanahan, 2014).

TEACHING DISCIPLINARY LITERACIES

Disciplinary literacy instruction involves several elements that extend beyond general text comprehension strategies and support. An obvious element of discipline-specific knowledge is vocabulary. This is not just about teaching words unique to specific content areas but also about the *kinds* of words students will encounter in different disciplines, such as words with Greek and Latin roots in science (C. Shanahan & T. Shanahan, 2014). Disciplinary vocabulary instruction will attend not just to word meanings but also to morphology. Such understandings can be particularly supportive for emergent bilingual students who speak a language grounded in Latin (French, Spanish, Portuguese), as they will likely find a higher percentage of cognates in science texts than they might in fiction. Examples include words like *solución salina* or *condensación*, which share morphological components with their English counterparts: "saline solution" and "condensation."

In addition to vocabulary, teachers may also support students' engagement with content concepts and texts by teaching the unique syntactic features of texts and discourses within particular disciplines. This may include the use of nominalizations (e.g., crystallization, oxidation, mutation), as well as the passive voice. In the natural sciences, both passive voice and nominalizations establish a detached voice and a sense of objectivity (Gee, 1996). And within literary criticism, readers must attend to imagery, irony, and figurative language. Furthermore, in many disciplines, students must learn to deconstruct complex sentences, which can be a frustrating characteristic of some historical and legal documents.

In addition to supporting students' understanding of disciplinary vocabulary and syntax, teachers must familiarize students with genres and relevant textual elements and features characteristic of texts within a target discipline. One way that teachers do this is by examining the features of a particular text prior to having students read independently or in groups. Such previewing can be used to engage students in conversations about the purpose of those features (e.g., diagrams, maps, headings, and inset photos with captions) within texts.

During disciplinary literacy instruction, teachers will also engage students in reading multiple texts on a topic (C. Shanahan & T. Shanahan, 2014). Pennington, Obenchain, and Brock (2014), for example, describe instruction in a 5th-grade classroom to scaffold students' reading and historical understandings of Martin Luther King Jr.'s *Letter from Birmingham Jail* (1994). Students had to think about the purpose, context, and audience of the text and examine it alongside other documents. While some documents may communicate first-person accounts, such as Martin Luther King Jr.'s letters, others may include journalistic reports (e.g., a radio broadcast or newspaper article), sermons, or legal documents. Each of these contains different discourses—ways of using and structuring language. Reading multiple kinds of texts requires students to know the expectations for reasoning in different disciplines and to understand what counts as evidence within those disciplines so they can evaluate claims made in these texts. In the two vignettes that follow, we see two different teachers, at the elementary and secondary levels, supporting students' disciplinary literacy and content knowledge development.

CHARTING PLANT GROWTH IN A 4TH-GRADE BILINGUAL CLASSROOM

First, we return to Isabel's 4th-grade bilingual classroom (also highlighted in Chapter 7). In April and May, Isabel engaged her students in an extended plant life unit. Although not part of her district's 4th-grade science curriculum, Isabel's students always enjoyed the unit, which they could connect to personally, as her students' parents all had gardens at home or had worked in agriculture.

The unit began with a class fieldtrip to a local nursery, where they interacted with staff about gardening and plant life. Throughout the unit, Isabel encouraged her students to talk with family members about what they were learning, and students each planted and maintained vegetables, such as tomatoes, zucchini, and potatoes. Isabel's classroom had a door that led directly outside to a south-facing patio. The plants were kept on a movable "greenhouse," a tall multi-shelf cart with a plastic cover that could be wheeled into the classroom in inclement or unseasonably cold weather. Prior to planting, and throughout the unit, Isabel had her students research different possibilities for plant food on the Internet and experiment with them on their plants. These included soda, pet food, coffee, milk, and tea, among other everyday household substances. Each student planted and maintained two plants from the same seed packet. One received only water, and one was fed an alternative food. They wrote observations and measured and recorded their plants' growth twice a week over 2 months in their science journals.

I also discuss this unit elsewhere (Handsfield, 2012). Note that while the unit as a whole actually occurred, the minilesson, conversations, and impromptu conference between Isabel and one of her students that I include in this vignette are fictional. The vignette begins 6 weeks into the extended unit.

"My Tomatoes Don't Like Soda": Experimenting with Plant Foods

---

It is a Monday afternoon in late May, and students file into the classroom from recess. In the third week of the unit, when students' seedlings began to emerge, Isabel had them begin recording their plants' development and other observations of each plant every few days. She supported their journal writing by keeping an ongoing graffiti-style chart of vocabulary they might need to use (e.g., *hypothesis*, *precipitation*, *peat pellet*, and *condensation*). Today, she introduces ways for her students to chart their plants' growth based on the data they recorded in their observation journals.

She begins by showing them examples of different charts that record comparisons between one or more items on a growth measure. For example, she shows a plot chart from the students' math textbook that compares two boys' times in five consecutive 100-meter-dash races. She also pulls a bar chart from an article from a previous science unit showing changes in fuel emissions in U.S. and Japanese cars over the past 25 years. They examine the features of each chart, and she writes these features on the whiteboard: a key, x-axis and y-axis, a numerical scale, different colored lines and bars, and a title.

After this discussion, she asks her students why someone would want to make charts such as these. José responds, "To tell about the things." Isabel asks for clarification, "What things?" José says, "How things are, like how fast the kids run." David jumps in, "To show how two things are different or how they change!" This satisfies Isabel, and she rephrases: "Yeah, to compare two or more things over time. But why can't I just write that? Why put it into a chart?" Students mull this over, and Alejandro says, "'Cause it's easier to see it on a chart." "Okay. Other ideas?" asks Isabel. David says, "So you can see it. It stands out." Isabel agrees and also suggests that it's like a special language for scientists: "Even if a scientist was reading this in another country and didn't speak English, they could understand it."

Isabel then models for the students how they might chart their plants' growth. Using her two zucchini plants as an example, she shows them how she could create a plot chart with a red line representing her plant that she fed coffee and a green line representing the one she fed only water. She wraps up by telling them that they need to begin recording and plotting their plants' growth in their science observation journals.

The students head outside and spend the next 20 minutes checking their plants' moisture, measuring water or experimental foods (e.g., coffee, milk, dog food, soda) and feeding their plants, and closely observing their leaves and stems for signs of health or distress. As they work, Isabel's students move around about the classroom space and the outdoor patio and chat with each other and Isabel about their observations.

Over the extended 3-day weekend, one of Avery's tomato plants had begun to droop, and its leaves were beginning to yellow. Jesús, standing next to Avery, says, "Man, your plant is sick." José adds, "His plant is sagging!" He proceeds to walk in a slouched fashion, with his pants inched down, and says, *"Mira! Soy Avery's tomato plant* [Look! I'm Avery's tomato plant]!" Jesús and José giggle, and Avery smiles. Alejandro then comments with a critical tone, "You got to give it water, man!" Avery defends himself by responding, "This is my experimental plant. It's not supposed to get water. Duh." Jesús says, "Hey, that's cool, *pocho.*" (According to *Urban Dictionary*, the term *pocho* originated as a derogatory term for someone from Mexico who has lost his or her Spanish, although it is now often embraced and used amicably and sometimes with a "defeatist sense of humor"; www.urbandictionary.com/define.php?term=Pocho&utm_source=search-action.)

Avery moves his things next to Esteban and Tomás and records his findings in his journal. "What are you feeding it?" asks Tomás. As he writes, Avery says that he's giving it Coke. "I'm testing it to see if it grows with soda. I said in my *hipótesis que no creciera*. [I said in my hypothesis that it wouldn't grow.]" He then approaches Isabel with his plant to show her: "Look, Ms. Schmidt, this plant is . . . it's . . . like falling down." Isabel says, "Yeah, it's kind of drooping isn't it?" Avery responds, "Yeah, it's drooping." Isabel continues, "That's interesting. I wonder why it's drooping." Avery explains that this is the tomato plant that he was feeding soda, but Isabel presses: "Yes, but what does that mean?" Avery says, "My tomatoes don't like soda?" "But what is it about the soda that your tomatoes don't like?" asks Isabel. Avery suggests that maybe there's something in the soda that makes plants sick, and she advises him to do some research to find out. Avery goes outside to retrieve one of the soda bottles next to the mobile greenhouse and begins reading the label. However, this does not tell him what ingredients may be detrimental to plant growth. Isabel suggests that the next day he go online to find information but that for now he should begin creating a chart to show his plants' growth.

The next day, Avery goes online, Googles "giving plants soda," and starts reading an article on the Gardening Knowhow website (www .gardeningknowhow.com/garden-how-to/soil-fertilizers/using-soda-on -plants.htm). When Isabel checks on his progress, he begins reading part of it aloud to her. In the process, he stumbles on unfamiliar vocabulary. The text from the article is presented below, followed by Avery's reading, including his miscues:

Text: Therefore, pouring soda on plants, such as Classic Coca Cola, is inadvisable. Coke has a jaw dropping 3.38 grams of sugar per ounce, which would certainly kill the plant as it would certainly be unable to absorb water or nutrients. Other varieties of Coke such as Coke Zero, Coca Cola C2 and Coke Black have little to no sugar but neither do they seem to have any added benefits over tap water, and they are significantly more costly than tap water.

Avery's reading: Therefore, pouring soda on plants, such as Classic Coca Cola, is in—inad—inadvis—able. Coke has a [2-second pause] jaw dropping 3.38 grams of sugar per [pause] ouncie? [mispronunciation of "ounce"; Avery looks up at Isabel, then continues], which would certainly kill the plant as it wouldn't be able to absorb water for nu—nutrients [long pause] water or nutrients. Other varieties of Coke such as Coke Zero, Coca Cola C2 and Coke Black have little to no sugar but either do they—[pause] but neither do they seem to have any additional benefits over tap water, and they are significantly more costly than tap water.

Isabel asks him what he thinks that means, and Avery continues reading:

Text: Basically, the end conclusion is that sugary sodas do not aid in a plant's development and, in fact, can retard the absorption of nutrients and water, resulting in death.

Avery's reading: Basically, the end conclusion is that sugar sodas do not aid in a plant's development and, in fact, can [pause; Avery looks up at Isabel, then back at the text] retard? [Spoken quietly. Avery asks Isabel, "Isn't that a bad word?" Isabel says it's an inappropriate word to use when talking about people with disabilities, but here it means something different. Avery continues] retard the ab—ab—sorp—tion of nutrients and water, resulting in death.

Avery says he doesn't get the phrase, "retard the absorption," and so Isabel asks Avery to "read it again, but use a different word there that might make sense." Avery reads the paragraph silently, and then reads it again aloud. Upon rereading, Avery uses the word "stop," and then says "Oh! The soda makes it so it—so the plant can't absorb the water?" Isabel responds, "Okay, but what about the soda makes that happen?" Avery scans the article again and then almost shouts as he figures it out, "The sugar!" Isabel laughs, "Yeah, the sugar. So if the plant can't get any water, what happens?" Avery responds, "It falls over. It—" "It droops," adds Isabel. Avery: "Yeah, it droops."

Isabel continues, "So you have your plot chart, and all your observations, and now you've found this out. I want you to include this information when you write your report. But wait, let's go back to this word ("retard"). You're right, it's not a nice word to use when you're talking about someone, but scientists use that word to mean that something isn't developing—that it's growth is stunted, *un retraso de crecimiento* [like a delay in growth]." Avery asks, "So I should write that in my report?" Isabel says, "Yes, using it in your report is fine, and it actually sounds like how a scientist would say it."

Several aspects of the vignette stand out, including Isabel's minilesson on creating charts to represent the students' plants' growth over time, her impromptu vocabulary lesson in response to Avery's questions about the use of the word "retard," and the student-to-student interactions about their plants. I address these as I consider the vignette from three different theoretical angles: NLS, sociolinguistic theory, and psycholinguistic theory.

New Literacy Studies

New literacy studies' focus on context and literacy practices often manifests itself in authentic literacy engagements within classrooms, much like Isabel's plant life unit. It is significant that Isabel took her students on a fieldtrip early in the unit rather than waiting until the end. See p. 83 for a description of new literacy studies. This decision suggests that the visit to the nursery is not an add-on or simply a fun excursion to celebrate their learning or accomplishments in the unit. Rather, it was purposeful, giving students the opportunity to see what people who specialize in plant cultivation do on a daily basis, to hear them talk about their work, and to learn particular tricks of the trade. As her students spent several weeks growing their own plants and experimenting with different plant foods, Isabel asked them to talk, read, and write like scientists. This is evident in her minilesson on charting plant growth based on data noted in their journals. She explained the practical value of data charts by referring to their use as a universal language of scientists.

Isabel also engaged in impromptu instruction in discipline-specific vocabulary when she worked with Avery to help him make sense of the Internet article on the effects of soda on plant growth. Avery was particularly perplexed by the phrase "retard the absorption of nutrients." In Avery's experience the word "retard" was taboo—an epithet used to describe people identified with cognitive disabilities. However, Isabel clarified for him that scientists use it to describe a delay in development or growth, and that within science, it's not only okay to use it but using the word would make him *sound* more like a scientist. In short, we see Isabel supporting her students in doing what scientists do: engaging in authentic scientific activity, including reading and writing in ways that are specific to the discipline. Because NLS draws our attention to the discursive conventions that govern specific contexts and academic disciplines, it is a fairly easy fit with disciplinary literacy instruction. However, we can also examine the language use in the vignette from the perspective of sociolinguistic theory.

Sociolinguistic Theory

Notable characteristics of Isabel's plant life unit are its authentic and meaning-based activities and opportunities for student interaction, which reflect sociolinguistic theory's focus on language-in-use—how people use language as they interact within specific contexts or communities—and language variation (Cazden, 2001; Gumperz, 1982). We see these principles enacted as Isabel's students interact with one another as they monitor their plants, feed them, measure them, and record their observations in their journals. Three things are notable about their language use. First, they play with language, joking about Avery's plant and how it slouches, much like the stylistic slouching of some youths' pants and gait. Their interactions may appear off-task to some; however, from a sociolinguistic standpoint, they demonstrate linguistic and conceptual flexibility as they quite accurately and imaginatively describe Avery's plant.

See p. 66 for a description of sociolinguistic theory.

Second, the boys use content vocabulary in meaningful ways with one another; for example, Avery uses the term "experiment" and explains to Tomás that he's "testing [his plant] to see if it grows with soda. I said in my *hipótesis que no creciera.* [I said in my hypothesis that it wouldn't grow.]" Here Avery engages in codemeshing—the purposeful and crafty intermingling of two language forms. Interestingly, it is immediately after Jesús calls Avery a *pocho* that Avery meshes Spanish and English when addressing Tomás, perhaps as a way to re-establish his credibility as Mexican. The relationship between language and identity is an important connection from a sociolinguistic perspective because from this theoretical vantage point, language is a core aspect of who people are, signifying social and cultural belonging.

Third, in addition to language in use, sociolinguistic theory attends to linguistic scaffolding, or the mediational uses of language for student learning (Cazden, 2001), which is evident in Isabel's recasting and rephrasing of students' utterances using academic language. For example, when Avery tells her that his plant is "falling over," she rephrases his observation: "Yeah, it's kind of drooping isn't it?" Avery then takes up her language: "Yeah, it's drooping." Isabel also scaffolds language learning through repetition, adding, "I wonder why it's drooping," and uses similar scaffolding in her minilesson. For instance, when she asks her students why someone would make plot or bar charts, José says, "To tell about the things." Isabel asks him to clarify, prompting him to use more precise language. She also rephrases student contributions by stating, "Yeah, to compare two or more things over time."

While sociolinguistic theory draws our attention to social and mediational uses of language in the vignette, psycholinguistic theory focuses on how readers cognitively recruit language systems during reading and writing.

Psycholinguistic Theory

In the vignette, Isabel has the opportunity to listen to Avery read aloud from the Internet article, and he miscues on several occasions. This enables Isabel to ascertain Avery's thinking about the text, a primary focal point of psycholinguistic theory. Specifically, Isabel can garner an

See p. 45 for a description of psycholinguistic theory.

understanding of how Avery solves problems on the run (Y. M. Goodman & K. S. Goodman, 2013) by drawing on and integrating the four cueing systems (graphophonic, syntactic, semantic, and pragmatic) to make sense of the text.

In the first portion of text, Avery reads, "Coke has a [2-second pause] jaw dropping 3.38 grams of sugar per [pause] ouncie? [mispronunciation of "ounce;" Avery looks up at Isabel, then continues], which would certainly kill the plant. . . ." He reads "ounce" as "ouncie," which is a meaning-changing miscue because "ouncie" is not an actual word. While this goes uncorrected, understanding the word "ounce" is not necessarily a prerequisite for making meaning according to Avery's purpose: to understand how soda inhibits plant growth. He appeals for assistance by pausing, using a questioning tone and glancing up at Isabel, but when she does not respond, Avery continues. Her lack of response requires Avery to self-monitor—to determine for himself if it makes sense, whether that matters, and what he should do about it.

Avery miscues again at the end of the same sentence when he reads "for nu—nutrients." He pauses, then self-corrects by going back and repeating "water or nutrients." Avery may have over-relied on the syntactic cueing system when he read "for" instead of "or" and then self-corrected because "for" did not make sense. His use of the semantic cueing system to self-correct is indicated by his return to the word "water" to self-correct, rather than just back to "or." He seems to recognize that both water and nutrients need to be absorbed by plants. Of course, to gain a better understanding of Avery's psycholinguistic processing, Isabel could perform a retrospective miscue analysis (RMA) or simply ask Avery to note and then comment on his miscues and self-corrections. However, the purpose of his read-aloud was not for assessment; rather, it was to learn about how soda may have been detrimental to his tomato plant's growth.

As noted in my analysis of the vignette through the lens of NLS, Avery and Isabel's discussion of the word "retard" is significant. Avery stopped at the word both because it did not make sense to him and because he questioned its appropriateness. In short, he self-monitored his comprehension and drew on both the semantic cueing system to ask whether the word made sense, and the pragmatic cueing system to determine if the word was misplaced or offensive. The next vignette also illustrates the value of disciplinary literacy instruction as students attempt to make sense of content area texts.

RESEARCHING JAPANESE INTERNMENT IN A CULTURALLY DIVERSE 10TH-GRADE HISTORY CLASS

Thomas Aquino has been thinking about this unit for months. Over the summer he attended an educational technology conference to learn new ways in which he might use the laptops that his school's history department recently purchased for student use. While he did not have a laptop for each student, he had a cart of 12, which would allow his students to use them with partners or in small groups. At the conference, he learned about WebQuests (inquiry based engagements involving the use of online sources to explore a topic [Dodge, 1995]) and how to design them to support content learning. He felt that the unit on Japanese internment during World War II in his 10th-grade U.S. history class would provide an ideal focus around which to design a WebQuest.

Thomas teaches in a suburban high school in the Pacific Northwest, and several of his students are of Japanese American heritage. He is fairly sure that some of his students' grandparents experienced internment as children. The assignment guidelines for the WebQuest are shown in Figure 10.1. I recommend that readers look over these guidelines before reading the vignette.

The vignette joins Thomas's class on the second day of the unit, where we see a few students watching the introductory video on removal and internment, and then reading and trying to make sense of Executive Order 9066 (www.pbs.org/childofcamp/history/eo9066.html), in which President Roosevelt empowered the secretary of war to create internment camps for U.S. citizens deemed to be threats to national defense.

Figure 10.1. Japanese Internment WebQuest

You are a U.S. citizen. You were born here. You have never been outside of the United States, although you have dreams of traveling. But things are tense right now politically. People worry that the war, which has been escalating, will come to U.S. shores. Then it happens—the bombing, the fear, the discrimination. And you somehow become a "foreigner" and a prisoner in your own land.

This happened, and it happened right here in the Pacific Northwest and all over the country during World War II. In fact, it may have happened to some of your own relatives. In 1941, after the Japanese bombed Pearl Harbor, thousands of Japanese Americans were forced from their homes and imprisoned in internment camps throughout the United States.

This WebQuest will be done in small groups and will serve as an introduction to our studies of Japanese internment in the U.S. After the WebQuest, we will read *Farewell to Manzanar*, by Jeanne Houston and James D. Houston (1973), which tells Jeanne (Wakatsuki) Houston's own experience of being imprisoned at the Manzanar concentration camp in 1942, when she was 7 years old. By the end of the unit, each group will make a digital presentation (a video or a slideshow) presenting a particular aspect of Japanese internment. You could write about children's experiences in internment, the experience of evacuation and leaving one's home, life and conditions at the camps, what it was like to return, or a different topic. Your presentation must be at least 3 minutes long. You may borrow and "remix" images and texts found in your WebQuest, but you MUST cite the sources you use.

The WebQuest includes video testimonials and interviews by people who were held prisoner, the executive order that called for the internment of Japanese Americans, historical websites, newspaper articles, and letters from imprisoned high school students to their teachers. See the class website for graphic organizers and response sheets to complete as you visit the following websites. **You must complete these and turn them in at the end of the week!** You may investigate these websites in any order, but I recommend beginning the WebQuest by navigating to the first link, a YouTube video that offers an overview of removal and internment.

Removal and Internment: www.youtube.com/watch?v=MoeVaJtPz94&list=TLzym Mo1x7QGk&index=6

Historical information about Japanese Internment: www.pbs.org/childofcamp/
history/index.html. There are several links that you can explore within this
website. The following is required reading: Executive order 9066, calling for
the removal of Japanese and Japanese Americans: www.pbs.org/childofcamp/
history/eo9066.html

Interview with George Takei regarding internment in Arkansas: www.youtube.
com/watch?v=4N7oaJ9pvVs

Testimonies on the Denosho Project YouTube channel:

Rae Takekawa: www.youtube.com/watch?v=ovrDyiLdTXY&list=PL61D73465
14907B72&index=38

Norm Minetta: www.youtube.com/watch?v=FsWfYhSZ17c

Newspaper articles:

depts.washington.edu/civilr/news_colasurdo.htm

www.sfmuseum.org/hist8/sfevac.html

Letters from Seattle high school students who were imprisoned back to their
teacher: www.lib.washington.edu/exhibits/harmony/Exhibit/willis.html

---

"I Know the Words, but I Don't Get How They're Used":
Reading Historical Documents in a WebQuest

Lily and Christy sit at a table along with Dylan and Marco, each pair with a
laptop. They begin by working separately, but when Lily and Christy go back
to the first YouTube video in the WebQuest on removal and internment to
watch it for a second time, Dylan and Marco walk around the table to look
over their shoulders. At time marker 1:42, a survivor talks about her memories
of being moved to the Portland Livestock Center, where they were brought
during evacuation, and a still photo is shown of a man wearing a white tag. Lily
pauses the video and says, "Oh my God. What is that?" Christy says, "Wait,"
and goes back to time marker 1:38, which showed another photo of children
with tags. "I think they're ID tags." Marco adds, "That's so screwed up." Lily
and Christy continue watching the video while Marco and Dylan return to
their side of the table.

Back at their own laptop, Dylan goes to the next link in the WebQuest,
a website at PBS.org with historical information about internment. They
each read the website quietly, and near the end, Dylan says, "Dang, the
government didn't apologize until 1998. That's the year I was born." When
Marco finishes reading, Dylan clicks on the link to the signed apology, which
has an earlier date: 1993. He then goes back and rereads the part of the
previous website about the apology and learns that it was "reparation" that
ended in 1998. "What's reparation?" Marco replies, "I think it's where they

repay or give you compensation." They read the apology signed by President Clinton in 1993. Dylan then clicks on the link to the Civil Rights Act of 1988, but Marco stops him, navigating back to the historical overview page, and reminding Dylan that they have to answer questions about the original page and also read the executive order. Lily and Christy are answering the two questions about the historical overview, which are fairly basic questions that can be answered in the text itself. Marco and Dylan do the same.

After answering the questions, Marco navigates to Executive Order 9066, and begins reading:

> Whereas, the successful prosecution of the war requires every possible protection against espionage and against sabotage to national-defense material, national-defense premises and national defense utilities as defined in Section 4, Act of April 20, 1918, 40 Stat. 533, as amended by the Act of November 30, 1940, 54 Stat. 1220, and the Act of August 21, 1941, 55 Stat. 655 (U.S.C.01 Title 50, Sec. 104) . . .

When Dylan finishes writing their answers, Marco says, "Dude, what? I don't get this," and reads the first sentence aloud for Dylan. By the third line, his reading becomes monotone, and he trails off near the end. Marco once more begins to reread, but when he gets to the phrase "as defined in Section 4 . . ." he says, "blah de blah. It's just a list of stuff. So, 'Whereas all of that stuff . . .'" He then moves on to the next paragraph, still reading aloud:

> Now therefore, by virtue of the authority vested in me as President of the United States, and Commander in Chief of the Army and Navy, I hereby authorize and direct the Secretary of War, and the Military Commanders whom he may from time to time designate, whenever he or any designated Commander deems such action to be necessary or desirable, to prescribe military areas in such places and of such extent as he or the appropriate Military Commander may determine, from which any or all persons may be excluded, and with respect to which, the right of any persons to enter, remain in, or leave shall be subject to whatever restriction the Secretary of War or the appropriate Military Commander may impose in his discretion.

But by the time he gets to the sixth line, he is lost. "That's like the longest sentence ever." Dylan says, "Okay so the first paragraph is the 'whereas,' and this one is 'therefore.'" Marco responds, "Yeah, but . . ." Dylan continues, "So it says 'I hereby authorize and direct the Secretary of War and the Military Commanders . . .'" He then rereads at a whisper, mostly to himself. Marco interjects, "There, where it says 'the right of any persons to enter.'" Dylan keeps reading but says, "That doesn't make sense."

They refer back to a question that Mr. Aquino gave them: "What did Executive Order 9066 give the Secretary of War the power to do?" Marco notes that the executive order "doesn't say anything about Japanese

Americans, but it's supposed to be the order that says they can be put in internment camps." Dylan suggests that they just write that, but Marco protests: "But it doesn't actually say that." While Marco tries to reread the second paragraph, using the words "whereas" and "therefore" as signposts, Dylan asks Christy and Lily what they wrote for their answer.

At this point, Thomas approaches the table, and Marco says, "Mr. Aquino, we don't understand the executive order." Dylan clarifies, "Well we know that it made it so Japanese Americans would be put in the camps, but we don't see where it says that." He starts reading the executive order aloud, tracking the text as he goes. It is then that Thomas realizes that he has not fully prepared his students for the complex nature of this historical document. He then addresses the rest of his class: "How many of you have already read the Executive Order?" Out of his 23 students, Lily, Christy, Marco, Dylan, and four others raise their hands. Thomas asks, "And how many of you understood the language in the document? Be honest." Only Christy and Lily raise their hands.

Thomas transitions into an impromptu minilesson, bringing the executive order up on the computer. He asks the students to pause their work and says, "I probably should have given you some information about how to read documents like this. It's not easy reading. Let's talk about what makes it difficult to read. Who has some ideas?" A student says she doesn't understand some of the words, and Thomas asks her to be more specific. But when she points them out ("designate," "prosecution," and "national defense utilities") she hedges, and says, "Well, I know the words, but I don't get how they're used." Thomas writes, "how words are used" on the whiteboard. Marco says, "The sentences are too long and confusing," and Thomas writes "long and confusing sentences" on the board. Another student says she has trouble with "all the laws and stuff" in the document, and Thomas adds this to the list. He then asks, "What kind of a text is this?" Students offer different responses: "A document." "A government text." "An executive order." "A legal text." "A law." "A confusing text." Thomas laughs, and says that in truth, they're all correct. "But the text is written in legal language, and that's what makes it confusing, especially for those of us who haven't gone to law school. Texts like this often start with the word 'whereas.' Why?" Lily says, "Because it says why they're doing it. It says—it gives the reasons for the order." Thomas responds, "Okay, and what are those reasons?"

The minilesson continues in this fashion, with Thomas leading the students through the different parts of the text and highlighting specific features unique to this type of legal document, including specific vocabulary ("whereas," "therefore," "by virtue of," "hereby," "shall") and syntax (long, complex sentences, beginning a sentence with a conjunction, such as "whereas"). Dylan again raises his point that nowhere in the document does it say anything about Japanese Americans. Thomas responds by asking the students to think about the context and to talk about whether or not this was directed at Japanese Americans. A student says that in the letter of apology from President Clinton, he says the internment was driven by racism, so that was probably the reason. Christy says, "They couldn't say that it was only against Japanese Americans, but it really was." Thomas pushes them further: "Why? How do you know?" Christy responds, "Because it wouldn't be written if the Japanese hadn't bombed Pearl Harbor, so they didn't have to say that it was against Japanese Americans. Everybody knew it." Another student, Jessica, says, "Mr. Aquino, go to the YouTube video of—of Norm Minetta. He talks about how after September 11th people wanted to put Arab Americans in concentration camps" www.youtube.com/watch?v=FsWfYhSZ17c). Jessica and her partner, Ryan, had already watched that video. Thomas wondered whether he should move the discussion to that portion of the WebQuest. After all, he wanted them exploring these web resources on their own. But given the other students' responses to Jessica's comment (e.g., "No way." "What?!"), he decided to show it.

Most students were shocked by Minetta's testimony although not all were. Thomas then posed the following question: "Could this happen again here in the U.S.? Could specific cultural, religious, or racial groups be imprisoned like this again in the U.S.?" The students debated the question for several minutes. As class time drew to a close, Thomas told his students to keep asking critical questions about fairness and civil rights and making connections to other historical events as they continued the WebQuest.

A salient feature of this vignette is the complexity of the executive order. I address this by discussing the vignette from the perspective of the construction–integration model. I then interpret conversations regarding social justice in the vignette using critical literacy theory.

Construction-Integration Model

Thomas's impromptu minilesson, in which he walks through Roosevelt's executive order, is meant to support students' comprehension of a complex text. He provides explicit instruction about text features and facilitates a discussion to help students connect the information in the document to more recent historical and political debates (the wars in Afghanistan and Iraq and continu-

See p. 48 for a description of the construction-integration model.

ing tensions with the self-proclaimed Islamic State in Iraq and Syria). In the language of W. Kintsch's (2013) construction–integration model, these instructional conversations scaffold students' ability to construct both a textbase and a situation model of the executive order.

In Chapter 4, I introduced the construction–integration model by prompting you to consider the effort that must be invested in reading difficult texts. When readers like Thomas's students encounter such difficulties—when normal reading is impeded—they move into active problem-solving mode, devoting more energy to comprehension (W. Kintsch, 2013). Thomas's students, for example, paraphrased the text ("So, 'whereas all of that stuff'"), tried using key words such as "whereas" and "therefore" as cues, and reread portions of the text. Such problem solving is particularly important in content area classrooms, where students engage with discipline-specific texts written in registers that may be less familiar, such as the legalese in Roosevelt's executive order.

After Thomas realizes they are struggling, he provides additional instruction to support students' construction of the textbase—propositions, or idea units, that combine words into units of meaning (W. Kintsch, 2013, p. 808). This is important because one of the more difficult text features of the executive order is that each sentence contains several propositions, some of which include legal terms. In other words, it is the microstructure of the text that is so complex. Thomas also shows students how particular aspects of the text might connect to their understandings of racial politics and discrimination both at the time and currently with respect to the treatment of Arab Americans post–September 11th. By doing this, he supports his students' ability to construct a situation model, the integration of prior knowledge, experiences, and readers' goals. However, while this process of construction and integration may explain textual comprehension, it does not provide insight into how students might critique the political and social structures that enabled the internment of Japanese Americans.

Critical Literacy

The students' reactions to the injustice of the incarceration of U.S. citizens illustrates their collective critical reading of the historical events, bringing elements of critical literacy theory to life, (See Chapter 5). The fact that this occurred through dialogue is significant, as Freire (1970) argued that dialogue, in which multiple perspectives are invited and heard, See p. 79 for a description of critical literacy theory. is considered essential to critical literacy. The conversations at the end of the class period regarding the frightening potential of political and military actions such as internment occurring in the students' own lifetimes indicates the critical stance Thomas's students begin to take. Specifically, Thomas asked, "Could this happen again here in the U.S.? Could specific cultural, religious, or racial groups be imprisoned like this again in the U.S.?" prompting further dialogue among his students. This student-centered problem-posing approach, in which Thomas follows the students' lead to facilitate critical conversations, is central to critical literacy theory. Through this process, Thomas's students read both the word and the world. From this view, specific literacy skills pertaining to the discipline of history are not ignored but rather are recruited to engage with real and important issues of equity and justice.

Through dialogue regarding the experiences of everyday people, in particular those who have been marginalized, and by reading both the word and the world, students may come to *conscientização* (Freire, 1970). However, critical literacy theory also stresses transformative action, something we do not see in the vignette. Thomas and his students engage in critical dialogue regarding Japanese internment and issues of racial discrimination, and it is possible that Thomas and his students might engage in extension activities to raise awareness among their peers within their school or in their community regarding the history of Japanese internment or the present treatment of Arab Americans post 9/11. That said, neither the WebQuest nor the culminating project require or explicitly invite students to take action for social justice.

QUESTIONS FOR PRAXIS

1. In the first vignette, Isabel creates ample opportunity for student interaction for both social and academic purposes. In what ways do you enable student interaction in your classroom to support students' social and academic language development?
2. The two vignettes in this chapter illustrate disciplinary literacy instruction in social studies and science. Think about instruction in a different content area (perhaps math, art, or computer science) in your own classroom or in the classroom of a colleague in your school. What kinds of disciplinary literacy instruction might be helpful to students within that content area?

RESOURCES AND ADDITIONAL READINGS

Draper, R. J., Broomhead, P., Jensen, A. P., Nokes, J., & Siebert, D. (Eds.). (2010). *(Re)imagining literacies for content-area classrooms*. New York, NY: Teachers College Press.

Literacy expert Dr. Elfrieda Hiebert unpacks claims about text complexity with the CCSS: textproject.org/frankly-freddy/claims-about-text-complexity-within-the-ccss

Shanahan, T. (2012). Disciplinary literacy is NOT the new name for content area reading. Blog post, Shanahan on Literacy. Retrieved from www.shanahanonliteracy.com/2012/01/disciplinary-literacy-is-not-new-name.html

WebQuest.org: webquest.org/index.php

Wineburg, S., Reisman, A. & Gillis, V. (2015). Disciplinary literacy in history: A toolkit for digital citizenship. *Journal of Adolescent & Adult Literacy, 58*(8), 636–639. doi:10.1002/jaal.410

CHAPTER 11

Teacher Inquiry and Praxis

Throughout Part II, I have presented an array of vignettes that bring different theories of reading and literacy to life. And yet, these examples capture only finite moments in the pedagogical lives of teachers. With one or two exceptions, these snapshots are just that—still frames of practice that differ from one another but do not illuminate how individual teachers' pedagogies may shift over longer periods of time. To be sure, teacher development may indeed occur in micro-timescales, as specific moments or events shift our thinking about our work in powerful ways. And yet, our teaching practices and professional identities are more likely to shift over longer timescales, over the course of a summer, a school year, or several years.

In this chapter, I address teacher development over longer scales of time (Lemke, 2000), beginning with a narrative of one teacher's pedagogical and theoretical shifts over 10 years. I use this vignette to open up discussion regarding teacher inquiry and how theories of reading and literacy intersect with teacher professional development. Teacher inquiry and development can take many forms, from informal inquiry (e.g., a teacher's summer reading to explore new curricular possibilities), to study groups and district-supported learning opportunities, to graduate coursework. In this chapter, however, I focus specifically on literacy coaching and classroom-based research as pedagogically and theoretically rich contexts for inquiry that push at the boundaries of praxis—that dialogic dance between practice and theory.

ONE TEACHER'S PEDAGOGICAL AND THEORETICAL SHIFTS OVER TIME

Melinda Spears began her teaching career in the early 2000s in a suburb of Chicago when she was 23 years old. She completed her undergraduate teaching degree and took a position as a 5th-grade teacher in a district near where she grew up. Two years later, she moved to 2nd grade, and then 3 years after that to 3rd grade in a district closer to the city. After completing a master's degree in reading a year ago, she took on a position as a literacy coach. She now works with teachers to support their literacy instruction, coplanning with them and sometimes coteaching. These experiences prompted her to think about her own professional development and shifts over the course of her career.

Professional Development in Motion

When she began teaching, Melinda viewed reading as a skills-based process and felt at home in her district, which implemented a balanced literacy approach. She believed that if students had phonics and morphological knowledge, had large vocabularies, could read fluently, and could apply specified strategies to texts, their reading development would progress. She taught reading groups using leveled texts, and she determined students' reading groups according to benchmark reading level assessments involving running records, structured retelling of passages, and comprehension questions.

During reading groups, she taught various comprehension strategies, such as making connections, predicting, and making inferences. She also engaged in discussions to provide background knowledge to students about the topics of their reading. She believed this would support the development of schemata, which could in turn support comprehension. During these groups, other students completed independent seatwork consisting of test preparation packets, skills worksheets, or writing projects, such as summaries and responses to writing prompts. She administered weekly spelling tests and occasionally engaged students in readers' theater to support fluency development.

This was in the midst of pressures to make Adequate Yearly Progress, as required by No Child Left Behind (2001). While not fond of standardized tests, Melinda felt compelled to prepare her students as well as she could for state assessments, and she viewed balanced literacy as consistent with this goal. Over several years, she gained respect as a teacher who was organized and who successfully engaged in regular assessment of her students and progress monitoring. New teachers sought her out for tips on classroom management, differentiating reading instruction, and student assessment.

And then things began to change. One afternoon, during a series of indoor recesses due to a pattern of inclement winter weather, Melinda watched as her 3rd-graders played board games, completed puzzles, played with Legos, and pulled well-worn comic books and magazines out of their backpacks to share with one another. Girls huddled in pairs and groups of three, giggling and feverishly writing notes to one another. A group of boys played Monopoly. She listened to their conversations, in which they shared expertise, took up different roles, debated monetary calculations, gave directives, argued over rules while referring to a manual, and mediated each others' disagreements. Students whom she characterized as struggling readers, quick to disengage from classroom literacy activities, took up leadership positions in these activities.

Melinda was struck by their interactions—how they negotiated the rules of their games and how three students moved seamlessly between English and Korean. It dawned on her that she did not really know her students. Of course, she knew about their reading levels; she knew that Maria was a T, Tommy was an M, and Darius was a P pushing Q. And she knew the reading strategies they had at their disposal when she worked with them in guided reading groups. However, she did not really know about their interests, social lives, fears, or triumphs. She did not really know them as people. As the bell rang and recess drew to a close, the students quickly folded up their notes and stowed away their games as they prepared to re-enter "classroom time." In a flash they returned to their desks and transformed back into the readers she knew so well.

After school, while chatting with a colleague, Melinda wondered out loud what she was missing: "I'm beginning to think that with all of my assessments, guided reading, writing prompts, test prep—ugh, can't wait till that's over—I've forgotten that they are just kids. They're people." Her colleague agreed and related a story about a recent home visit she conducted to meet and talk with the parents of a student, and Melinda made a mental note to consider doing this as well. As she continued observing her students during indoor recess that winter, she came to enjoy the less structured time, and when outdoor recess resumed, she missed it. With state testing wrapping up, she decided that the extra instructional time she had devoted to test prep would be devoted to "activity time" at the end of each day: 20 minutes during which her students needed to be involved in some activity, such as games, writing, reading, or even note-writing. During this time, Melinda made the decision to go back to school for her master's degree.

Fast-forward 4 more years. Melinda has completed her master's in reading, and with her reading specialist certification she has stepped into a new role as a literacy coach. In this new position, she coordinates the school's reading assessment data and works with teachers as they implement the district's new curriculum—reading and writing workshop.

Melinda was part of the district task force that advised the administration and school board's adoption of a workshop approach. In graduate school, she learned more about reading and writing workshop. She understood it as creating a space for literacy development that invited students to read and write about their own interests and lives while also enabling teachers to know their students beyond reading level. As a literacy coach, she emphasizes peer interaction and teacher discourse as they mediate students' development, and she encourages teachers to find out about students' linguistic and cultural funds of knowledge and to recruit those strengths in their instruction. It is not lost on Melinda that this means advising teachers against the independent seatwork and skills worksheets that she herself had students doing only a few years previously. Instead, she works with them to design instruction that invites peer interaction and collaboration and to support them as they differentiate their instruction within a workshop approach.

While Melinda feels confident sharing her understandings of teaching and learning with teachers in her new role as a coach, she is cognizant of how these interactions also support her own constantly shifting understandings about teaching, learning, and literacy. As she works with a third-year 2nd-grade teacher whose students use iPads for multimodal writing, for example, she has begun thinking more deeply about how technology mediates literacy practices and teaching. As Melinda navigates her way through this complex profession, building her own repertoires of expertise, she has become increasing aware of how much more she still has to learn.

In this extended vignette, Melinda's theoretical understandings about literacy learning and teaching shift in tandem with her practices. While initially viewing reading as a cognitive process, in which readers apply strategies and access prior knowledge to support comprehension, she revises her thinking toward a view of reading as a sociocultural-historical process. She comes to understand the importance of social interaction and getting to know students' cultural and linguistic strengths in order to recruit this knowledge in the classroom. This includes recognizing that her students do not lack schemata, and making efforts to find out what her students know and then building on that knowledge to support student learning.

Importantly, Melinda's theoretical shift did not begin in graduate school, nor did it emerge out of some transcendental process of enlightenment. Rather, it was sparked in the context of her everyday work. Even as this work took on different qualities with policy changes and her new role as a literacy coach, it was in her own practice of teaching and coaching that her understandings continued to morph. Indeed, Melinda engaged in both informal, or everyday, inquiry, as well as more systematic inquiry through continued education. She then moved into a position in which her primary role is to support other teachers in inquiring about their teaching.

TEACHER INQUIRY

Inquiry is often thought of as synonymous with research. However, inquiry takes many forms, ranging from formal and systematic research to brief instances in which we question our practices (sometimes in the moment), interpret those events, and then shift our practice accordingly. Indeed, I designed Chapters 6 through 10 of this book to prompt readers to inquire into the relationship between theory and practice—to engage in praxis. I intentionally included vignettes in which the process of everyday inquiry either lurks behind the scenes of practice or more directly guides practice in the moment. Like practice, inquiry is inseparable from theory and permeates several aspects of teaching, professional development, and classroom-based research. In this section, I discuss literacy coaching and approaches to classroom research that can foment inquiry to support praxis and pedagogical innovation.

Literacy Coaching

Coaching is considered to be a crucial approach to professional development and implementing local curriculum reform efforts (International Reading Association, 2004). A wealth of professional texts and research exist delineating coaches' roles and the kinds of practices coaches might engage in as they work in schools and classrooms. While coaches increasingly take on the role of managing school literacy achievement data, particularly since the implementation of No Child Left Behind (2001) and Race to the Top (2011), they are also often responsible for working with teachers as they implement new local curricular initiatives targeted toward state standards or the CCSS. However, coaches may fulfill a variety of roles that can support teacher inquiry and professional development, including coach as encourager, facilitator, and demonstrator (Vanderburg & Stephens, 2010) and as someone who supports teachers in engaging in critical reflection on their teaching (MacPhee, 2013; Stover, Kissel, Haag, & Shoniker, 2011).

However, literacy coaching involves more than simply fulfilling a professional role. While coaches are typically expected to assume identities as expert teachers and purveyors of "best practices," these roles and coaches' work are constantly negotiated during their daily work in schools and are impacted by the contexts in which they are situated (Hibbert, Heydon, & Rich, 2008). Within political climates characterized by high-stakes assessment and teacher accountability, coaches may encounter tensions between assigned roles as curricular experts, a position of power with respect to classroom teachers, and their own recognition of the complexities of teaching, learning, and assessment. Such tensions add to the challenges of coaches' work, which involves a complex negotiation of power structures, professional relationships, and conflicting expectations (Rainville & Jones, 2009). Indeed, researchers have recently documented how interactions between coaches and teachers are infused with emotion as teachers and coaches negotiate this complex terrain (Hunt & Handsfield, 2013; Jones & Rainville, 2014).

However, as Melinda's experiences in the above vignette make clear, coaching is not a one-way street with only the coach passing on knowledge to teachers. Because their work happens from both inside and outside the classroom, coaches stand to gain a broader perspective on teaching and learning within their professional contexts. For Melinda, for example, coaching is a reciprocal process. While she supports teachers as they implement new curricular initiatives, her work as a coach also pushes her own professional development and pedagogical knowledge. This is evident as she begins to consider how digital technologies such as iPads might mediate students' literacy development—something she had not previously devoted significant thought to.

With these considerations in mind, literacy coaching can be conceptualized as a *collaborative and dialogic* activity involving inquiry as critical reflection as teachers and coaches engage together to examine both their tacit and explicit theoretical assumptions about literacy, teaching, and learning (Jewett & MacPhee, 2012; Stephens & Mills, 2014; Stover et al., 2011). Conceptualized this way, literacy coaching becomes a space of praxis in which teachers and coaches push the boundaries of both literacy instruction and theory.

However, teachers need not participate in formal coaching interactions or relationships in order to engage in such collaborative inquiry. Rather, this kind of inquiry may happen in more impromptu ways, in the teachers' workroom during lunch, or (as in the case of Melinda and her colleague) after school, as teachers reflect on their instruction, make their theoretical assumptions and pedagogical rationales explicit, and consider alternatives for future practice. Similar spaces for critical inquiry and praxis are also made available through approaches to classroom-based research.

Classroom-Based Research

Most school systems are not set up to support teachers in conducting formal classroom research. And yet, many teachers do, and the process of engaging in systematic research on instruction can pave the way for theoretically rich pedagogical innovation. Classroom research is often embedded within graduate coursework, in which teachers carry out systematic inquiry in their own classrooms and schools. In other cases, teachers may collaborate with university-based researchers. Baumann and Duffy-Hester (2000) refer to this kind of classroom-based research as "teacher research" (p. 78), intentional and systematic investigations of classroom practices involving reflection and action. They identified five characteristics of this type of inquiry: (1) Research questions are generated in response to real problems that teachers face in their own classrooms; (2) research questions may shift as teachers engage in classroom inquiry; (3) existing theories drive and inform teachers in the inquiry process; (4) inquiry is generative of theories of teaching, learning, and schooling; and (5) teacher-researchers are reflective about their instruction (2000, p. 83). Note the reciprocal relationship between theory and practice in numbers 3 and 4, as well as the close relationship between research, theory, and practice. In short, teacher research is grounded in *praxis*. It is pragmatic and action-oriented (Cochran-Smith & Lytle, 1993), and holds promise for generating both pedagogical and theoretical innovation. These themes are especially characteristic of two approaches to classroom research: action research and design-based research.

In action research, teachers conduct systematic inquiry in their own classrooms with the purpose of improving or honing their own instruction while adding to the knowledge base in the field (Noffke, 1997). The emphasis of action research is practical, and teachers' own understandings and self-knowledge, including their theoretical orientations to literacy, teaching, and learning, are privileged (Kemmis & McTaggart, 2000). Typically, in action research, university-based researchers may be involved only in supporting roles, taking an advocacy stance or consulting on research processes. In Participatory Action Research (PAR), university researchers may take a more significant role, collaborating with teacher-researchers in the design and conduct of the study. Such arrangements make sense given the compartmentalization of K–12 teachers' and university faculty's work, which makes it challenging for teachers to carry out full-fledged research studies without support in the way of time and funding. PAR may also involve collaboration with families and community members. In PAR, the tasks of inquiry, including data collection and analysis, are shared.

Patricia Valente (whose teaching I spotlighted in Chapter 9) and I engaged in a PAR project exploring how Patricia and her students' discursive positioning of one another was related to students' meaning-making in the classroom and their comprehension achievement. She and I collaboratively developed research questions and procedures, and we have worked together to analyze the data. Behind these research processes was the intention of promoting social change and social justice within Patricia's classroom and her students' immediate community.

Additional examples of action research in literacy abound. Gerald Campano (2007), for example, inquired into his own instruction in his 5th-grade classroom in an urban California school district. He weaves his own understandings of himself and his family's immigrant history into his interpretations of his students' cultural, linguistic, and literate strengths. He uses the insights gleaned from his research to inform his own teaching and to make recommendations for the field of literacy studies as a whole.

Action research studies such as these address real problems in the immediate contexts of teachers' own classrooms and generate findings that are significant both for teachers' own instruction and for students and the field at large. A central element of action research is becoming aware of one's own theoretical commitments and how those are manifested in the classroom. As such, this form of classroom inquiry creates space for praxis as teacher-researchers experiment with both practices and theories in reflexive ways. Design-based research is a framework for inquiry that offers similar potential for praxis.

Design-based research, also referred to as *formative* or *design* experiments, involves teachers as key stakeholders and decisionmakers in the inquiry process. This form of classroom inquiry has gained favor in part because of concerns in the literacy education community regarding the value of experimental research (Reinking, 2011). Typically, experimental research requires participating teachers to carry out with fidelity instructional practices that include materials and approaches designed for the purposes of the study, but not necessarily attuned to the specifics of their classroom contexts or students (Bradley & Reinking, 2011). At the other end of the spectrum, teachers may not be drawn to naturalistic qualitative studies, which may focus more on understanding classroom practices in their "natural" state than on improving instruction in the immediate context of the study. This can turn off teachers interested in developing new practices and experimenting with alternative pedagogies in an ongoing way to benefit their students in the here and now.

Design-based research responds to these concerns by anchoring systematic inquiry in the contingencies of classrooms. Because of the contextualized nature of such studies, researchers external to the school and classroom context rely on collaborating teachers' understandings and expertise with respect to factors that can impact the effectiveness of instructional interventions or programs. Teacher-researchers and external researchers collaborate to design, carry out, and modify interventions in flexible ways to positively impact student learning (Bradley & Reinking, 2011). This iterative process of inquiry lends itself to exploring how both theories regarding literacy and teaching as well as pedagogical approaches may be tested, taken up, and modified within the classroom context.

There are several examples of design-based research in language and literacy studies. Baumann, Ware, and Edwards (2007), for instance, explored the impact of a yearlong program to develop 5th-graders' vocabulary knowledge. In this research, Donna Ware was also the classroom teacher. In their article, they explain their relative engagements with instruction within the study: "Donna provided most of the vocabulary instruction, with Jim [Baumann] and Elizabeth [Edwards] (university collaborators) teaching occasional lessons and assuming responsibility for much of the data gathering" (p. 109). And in other design-based research studies, teachers have worked collaboratively with researchers without taking on research roles but consulting with researchers on the interventions used in the study (e.g., Ivey & Broaddus, 2007). In sum, design-based research enables teachers to not only impact formal research but also to engage in reflective and collaborative inquiry that is theoretically informed and, in turn, has the potential to inform theories of reading and literacy.

CONCLUDING THOUGHTS: PRAXIS AND USEFUL INQUIRY

A common underpinning of teacher inquiry, whether we are talking about literacy coaching, informal and even momentary reflection and pedagogical experimentation, or teacher research, is its _catalytic validity_. Patti Lather

(1991) described catalytic validity as the extent to which inquiry positively impacts research participants and contexts. This is different from traditional conceptions of validity in research, in which studies are judged according to whether analytical measurements are accurate and reliable. Catalytic validity gets not only at whether research findings are reliable but also whether they are pedagogically viable and desirable. In other words, inquiry that has catalytic validity is also inquiry that is *useful*. Such inquiry is constantly in motion, just like Melinda's professional growth.

Inquiry that has catalytic validity also requires *useful* theory; it will not abide theory that is pretentious or elegant while ignoring the messiness of real classrooms and the complexities of teaching and learning. Rather, theoretically rich teaching and inquiry live in everyday moments in classrooms, in teachers' lounges, in summer reading groups, in the interactions between students and teachers, and in the daily reflections and moment-by-moment pedagogical activity that comprises engaged teaching. These are the spaces that are generative of praxis.

QUESTIONS FOR PRAXIS

1. What if Melinda had been teaching in a different professional context, with different curricular policies and expectations? How might working within a different curricular context have shaped her professional development trajectory differently?
2. In what ways have your understandings and practices changed over longer periods of time—a year, several years, or your entire career? To what extent have policy and reform initiatives challenged or solidified your changing understandings about literacy, teaching, and learning, and classroom practices?

RESOURCES AND ADDITIONAL READINGS

Baumann, J. F., Ware, D., & Edwards, E. C. (2007). "Bumping into spicy, tasty words that catch your tongue": A formative experiment on vocabulary instruction. *The Reading Teacher, 61*(2), 108–122.

Ivey, G., & Broaddus, K. (2007). A formative experiment investigating literacy engagement among adolescent Latina/o students just beginning to read, write, and speak English. *Reading Research Quarterly, 42*, 512–545.

Jones, S., & Rainville, K. N. (2014). Flowing toward understanding: Suffering, humility, and compassion in literacy coaching, *Reading & Writing Quarterly: Overcoming Learning Difficulties, 30*(3), 270–287. doi:10.1080/10573569.2014.909270

Stover, K., Kissel, B., Haag, K., & Shoniker, R. (2011). Differentiated coaching: Fostering reflection with teachers. *Reading Teacher, 64*(7), 498–509.

References

Adams, M. J. (2013). Modeling the connections between word recognition and reading. In D. E. Alvermann, N. J. Unrau, & R. B. Ruddell (Eds.), *Theoretical models and processes of reading* (6th ed., pp. 783–806). Newark, DE: International Reading Association.

Afflerbach, P., Pearson, P. D., & Paris, S. G. (2008). Clarifying differences between reading skills and reading strategies. *The Reading Teacher, 61*(5), 364–373. doi:10.1598/RT.61.5.1

Alarcón, W., Cruz, C., Jackson, L. G., Prieto, L., & Rodriguez-Arroyo, S. (2011). Compartiendo nuestras historias: Five testimonios of schooling and survival. *Journal of Latinos & Education, 10*(4), 369–381.

Alexander, P. A., & Fox, E. (2013). A historical perspective on reading research and practice, redux. In D. E. Alvermann, N. J. Unrau, & R. B. Ruddell (Eds.), *Theoretical models and processes of reading* (6th ed., pp. 3–46). Newark, DE: International Reading Association.

Alvermann, D. E., Unrau, N. J., & Ruddell, R. B. (Eds.) (2013). *Theoretical models and processes of reading* (6th ed.). Newark, DE: International Reading Association.

American Psychiatric Association. (2013). *Diagnostic and statistical manual of mental disorders* (5th ed.). Washington, DC: Author.

Anderson, R. C. (2013). Role of the reader's schema in comprehension, learning, and memory. In D. E. Alvermann, N. J. Unrau, & R. B. Ruddell (Eds.), *Theoretical models and processes of reading* (6th Ed., pp. 476–488). Newark, DE: International Reading Association.

Anderson, R. C., & Pearson, P. D. (1984). A schema-theoretic view of basic processes in reading comprehension. In P. D. Pearson, R. Barr, M. L. Kamil, & P. B. Mosenthal (Eds.), *Handbook of reading research* (pp. 37–55). White Plains, NY: Longman.

Andrews, R., Torgerson, C., Beverton, S., Locke, T., Low, G., Robinson, A., Zhu, D. (2004). *The effect of grammar teaching (syntax) in English on 5 to 16 year olds' accuracy and quality in written composition.* London, England: EPPI-Centre, Social Science Research Unit, Institute of Education.

Appleman, D. (2009). *Critical encounters in high school English: Teaching literary theory to adolescents* (2nd ed.). New York, NY: Teachers College Press.

Au, K. H., & Jordan, C. (1981). Teaching reading to Hawaiian children: Finding a culturally appropriate solution. In H. T. Trueba, G. P. Guthrie, & K. H. Au (Eds.), *Culture and the bilingual classroom: Studies in classroom ethnography* (pp. 139–152). Rowley, MA: Newbury House.

Aukerman, M. (2007). When reading it wrong is getting it right: Shared evaluation pedagogy among struggling fifth grade readers. *Research in the Teaching of English, 42*(1), 56–103.

Baer, D. R., Invernizzi, M., Templeton, S., & Johnston, F. (2011). *Words their way: Word study for phonics, vocabulary and spelling instruction* (5th ed.). Upper Saddle River, NJ: Pearson.

Bakhtin, M. M. (1981). *The dialogic imagination: Four essays.* (M. Holquist, Ed. & Trans.; C. Emerson, Trans.). Austin: University of Texas Press.

Bakhtin, M. (1984). *Problems of Dostoevsky's poetics.* (C. Emerson, Ed. & Trans.). Minneapolis: University of Minnesota Press.

Bandura, A. (2001). Social cognitive theory: An agentic perspective. *Annual Review of Psychology, 52*(1), 1–26.

Barch, D., & Yarkoni, T. (2013). Introduction to the special issue on reliability and replication in cognitive and affective neuroscience research. *Cognitive, Affective, & Behavioral Neuroscience, 13*, 687–689.

Bartlett, F. (1932). *Remembering: A study in experimental and social psychology.* London, England: Cambridge University Press.

Baumann, J., & Duffy-Hester, A. M. (2000). Making sense of classroom worlds: Methodology in teacher research. In M. Kamil, P. Mosenthal, P. D. Pearson, & R. Barr (Eds.), *Handbook of reading research* (Vol. 3, pp. 77–98). Mahwah, NJ: Erlbaum.

Baumann, J. F., Edwards, E. C., Boland, E. M., Olejnik, S., & Kame'enui, E. (2003). Vocabulary tricks: Effects of instruction in morphology and context on fifth-grade students' ability to derive and infer word meanings. *American Educational Research Journal, 40*(2), 447–494.

Baumann, J. F., Ware, D., & Edwards, E. C. (2007). "Bumping into spicy, tasty words that catch your tongue": A formative experiment on vocabulary instruction. *The Reading Teacher, 61*(2), 108–122.

Bautista, M. A., Bertrand, M., Morrell, E., Scorza, D., & Matthews, C. (2013). Participatory action research and city youth: Methodological insights from the Council of Youth Research. *Teachers College Record, 115*(10), 1–23.

Bazerman, C. (2009). Issue brief: Discourse communities. Urbana, IL: National Council of Teachers of English. Retrieved from www.ncte.org/college/briefs/dc

Beck, I. L., McKeown, M. G., & Kucan, L. (2013). *Bringing words to life: Robust vocabulary instruction* (2nd ed.). New York, NY: Guilford.

Bell, D. (1980). *Brown. v. Board of Education* and the interest-convergence dilemma. *Harvard Law Review, 93*(3), 518–533.

Bennett, C. M., & Miller, M. B. (2010). How reliable are the results from functional magnetic resonance imaging? *Annals of the New York Academy of Sciences, 1191*, 133–155.

Bereiter, C., & Engelmann, S. (1966). *Teaching disadvantaged children in the preschool.* Englewood Cliffs, NJ: Prentice Hall.

Beverley, J. (2000). Testimonio, subalternity, and narrative authority. In N. K. Denzin & Y. S. Lincoln (Eds.), *Handbook of qualitative research* (2nd ed., pp. 555–565). Thousand Oaks, CA: Sage.

Bishop, R. S. (1997). Selecting literature for a multicultural curriculum. In V. J. Harris (Ed.), *Using multiethnic literature in the K–8 classroom* (pp. 1–19). Norwood, MA: Christopher Gordon.

Blommaert, J. (2005). *Discourse: Key topics in sociolinguistics.* New York, NY: Cambridge University Press.

Blommaert, J., & Rampton, B. (2011). Language and superdiversity: A position paper. *Working Papers in Urban Language and Literacies, 70*. Retrieved from www.kcl.ac.uk/ldc

Bomer, R., Dworin, J. E., May, L., & Semingson, P. (2008). Miseducating teachers about the poor: A critical analysis of Ruby Payne's claims about poverty. *Teachers College Record, 110*(12), 2497–2531.

Bornkessel-Schlesewsky, I., Schlesewsky, M., & Small, S. L. (2014). Implementation is crucial but must be neurobiologically grounded: Comment on "Toward a computational framework for cognitive psychology: Unifying approaches from cognitive neuroscience and comparative cognition" by W. Tecumseh Fitch. *Physics of Life Reviews, 11*, 365–366.

Bourdieu, P., & Wacquant, L. J. D. (1992). *An invitation to reflexive sociology.* Chicago, IL: University of Chicago Press.

Bourke, R. T. (2008). First graders and fairy tales: One teacher's action research of critical literacy. *The Reading Teacher, 62*(4), 304–312.

Boushey, G., & Moser, J. (2006). *The daily five: Fostering literacy independence in the elementary grades.* Portland, ME: Stenhouse.

Boushey, G., & Moser, J. (2009). *The CAFE book: Engaging all students in daily literacy assessment and instruction.* Portland, ME: Stenhouse.

Bowling, D. (2014). Cognitive theory and brain fact: Insights for the future of cognitive neuroscience. Comment on "Toward a computational framework for cognitive psychology: Unifying approaches from cognitive neuroscience and comparative cognition" by W. Tecumseh Fitch. *Physics of Life Reviews, 11*, 377–379.

Bradley, B. A., & Reinking, D. (2011). Revisiting the connection between research and practice using design research and formative experiments. In N. Duke & M. Mallette (Eds.), *Literacy research methodologies* (2nd ed., pp. 188–212). New York, NY: Guilford Press.

Bronfenbrenner, U., & Morris, P. A. (2006). The bioecological model of human development. In W. Damon (Series Ed.) & R. M. Lerner (Vol. Ed.), *Handbook of child psychology: Vol. 1 Theoretical models of human development* (pp. 793–828). New York, NY: John Wiley & Sons.

Brown, R. (2008). The road not yet taken: A transactional strategies approach to comprehension instruction. *The Reading Teacher, 61*(7), 538–547. doi:10.1598/RT.61.7.3

Brown, R., Pressley, M., Van Meter, P., & Schuder, T. (1996). A quasi-experimental validation of transactional strategies instruction with low-achieving second grade readers. *Journal of Educational Psychology, 88,* 18–37.

Button, K. S., Ioannidis, J. P. A., Mokrysz, C., Nosek, B. A., Flint, J., Robinson, E. S. J., & Munafo, M. R. (2013). Power failure: Why small sample size undermines the reliability of neuroscience. *Nature Reviews Neuroscience, 14*(5), 365–376.

Cabrera, N. L., Meza, E. L., Romero, A. J., & Rodríguez, R. C. (2013). "If there is no struggle, there is no progress": Transformative youth activism and the school of ethnic studies. *Urban Review, 45*(1). doi:10.1007/s11256-012-0220-7

Calkins, L. (1994). *The art of teaching writing.* Portsmouth, NH: Heinemann.

Calkins, L. (2003). *Units of study for primary writing.* Portsmouth, NH: Heinemann.

Calkins, L. (2014). *Units of study in opinion, information, and narrative writing.* Portsmouth, NH: Heinemann. Retrieved from www.heinemann.com/shared/onlineresources/E04717/CalkinsSam_LoRez.pdf

Calkins, L., & Oxenhorn, A. (2003). *Small moments: Personal narrative writing.* Portsmouth, NH: Heinemann.

Campano, G. (2007). *Immigrant students and literacy: Reading, writing, and remembering.* New York, NY: Teachers College Press.

Camus, A. (1947). *The plague.* New York, NY: Vintage Books.

Cazden, C. B. (2001). *Classroom discourse: The language of teaching and learning* (2nd ed.). Portsmouth, NH: Heinemann.

Chall, J. S. (1983). *Stages of reading development.* New York, NY: McGraw-Hill.

Chinn, C., Anderson, R. C., & Waggoner, M. (2001). Patterns of discourse during two kinds of literature discussion. *Reading Research Quarterly, 36*(4), 378–411.

Clay, M. M. (1966). *Emergent reading behavior.* Unpublished doctoral dissertation. University of Auckland, New Zealand.

Clay, M. M. (1972). *Reading: The patterning of complex behavior.* Auckland, NZ: Heinemann.

Clay, M. M. (1993a). *An observation survey of early literacy achievement.* Auckland, NZ: Heinemann.

Clay, M. M. (1993b). *Reading recovery: A guidebook for teachers in training.* Auckland, NZ: Heinemann.

Clay, M. M. (2000). *Concepts about print: What have children learned about the way we print language?* Portsmouth, NH: Heinemann.

Cobb, P. (1990). A constructivist perspective on information-processing theories of mathematical activity. *International Journal of Educational Research, 14*(1), 67–92.

Cochran-Smith, M., & Lytle, S. L. (Eds.). (1993). *Inside/outside: Teacher research and knowledge.* New York, NY: Teachers College Press.

Cole, M., & Scribner, S. (1978). Introduction. In L. S. Vygotsky, *Mind in society* (pp. 1–14). Cambridge, MA: Harvard University Press.

Collins, J., & Blot, R. (2003). *Literacy and literacies: Texts, power, and identity.* New York, NY: Cambridge University Press.

Coltheart, M. (2005). Modeling reading: The dual-route approach. In M. J. Snowling & C. Hulme (Eds.), *The science of reading: A handbook* (pp. 6–23). Malden, MA: Blackwell.

Crumpler, T. P., & Wedwick, L. (2011). Readers, texts, and contexts in the middle: Re-imagining literature education for young adolescents. In S. Woolf, K. Coats, P. Enciso, & C. Jenkins (Eds.), *Handbook of research on children's and young adult literature* (pp. 63–75). New York, NY: Routledge.

Cunningham, J. W., & Fitzgerald, J. (1996). Epistemology and reading. *Reading Research Quarterly, 31*(1), 3660.

Daniels, H. (1994). *Literature circles: Voice and choice in the student-centered classroom.* Portland, ME: Stenhouse.

Davis, B. (2004). *Inventions of teaching: A genealogy.* Mahwah, NJ: Erlbaum.

Davis, B., Sumara, D., & Luce-Kapler, R. (2008). *Engaging minds: Changing teaching in complex times* (2nd ed.). New York, NY: Routledge.

de Certeau, M. (1984). *The practice of everyday life.* Berkeley: University of California Press.

Dekker, S., Lee, N. C., Howard-Jones, P., & Jolles, J. (2012). Neuromyths in education: Prevalence and predictors of misconceptions among teachers. *Frontiers in Psychology, 3,* 429. doi:10.3389/fpsyg.2012.00429

Delgado, R., & Stefancic, J. (Eds.). (2000). *Critical race theory: The cutting edge* (2nd ed.). Philadelphia, PA: Temple University Press.

Dewey, J. (1904). *The Educational Situation.* Chicago, IL: University of Chicago Press.

Dewey, J., & Bentley, A. F. (1949). *Knowing and the known.* Boston, MA: Beacon.

DiCamillo, K. (2006). *The miraculous journey of Edward Tulane.* Somerville, MA: Candlewick Press.

Dixon-Krauss, L. (1996). *Vygotsky in the classroom: Mediated literacy instruction and assessment.* White Plains, NY: Longman.

Dodge, B. (1995). WebQuests: A technique for Internet-based learning. *Distance Educator, 1*(2), 10–13.

Draper, R. J., Broomhead, P., Jensen, A. P., Nokes, J., & Siebert, D. (Eds.). (2010). *(Re)imagining literacies for content-area classrooms.* New York, NY: Teachers College Press.

Draper, R. J., & Siebert, D. (2010). Rethinking texts, literacies, and literacy across the curriculum. In R. J. Draper, P. Broomhead, A. P. Jensen, J. Nokes, & D. Siebert (Eds.), *(Re)imagining literacies for content-area classrooms* (pp. 20–39). New York, NY: Teachers College Press.

Draper, S. (2010). *Out of my mind.* New York, NY: Atheneum Books.

Dressman, M. (2007). Theoretically framed: Argument and desire in the production of general knowledge about literacy. *Reading Research Quarterly, 42*(3), 332–363.

Du Bois, W. E. B. (1903). *The souls of Black folk.* New York, NY: Bantam Classic.

Durkin, D. (1978–1979). What classroom observation reveals about reading comprehension instruction. *Reading Research Quarterly, 14,* 481–533.

Dyson, A. H., & Genishi, C. (2013). Social talk and imaginative play: Curricular basics for young children's language and literacy. In D. E. Alvermann, N. J. Unrau, & R. B. Ruddell (Eds.), *Theoretical models and processes of reading* (6th ed., pp. 164–181). Newark, DE: International Reading Association.

Edelsky, C., & Cherland, M. R. (2006). A critical issue in critical literacy: The 'popularity effect.' In K. Cooper & R. E. White (Eds.), *The practical critical educator* (pp. 3–16). Dordrecht, Netherlands: Springer.

Edmiston, B. (2007). Mission to Mars: Using drama to make a more inclusive classroom for literacy learning. *Language Arts, 84*(4), 337–346.

Edmiston, B. (2013). *Transforming teaching and learning through active dramatic approaches: Engaging students across the curriculum.* New York, NY: Routledge.

Edwards, P. A., & Schmidt, P. A. (2006). Essay book review: Critical race theory: Recognizing the elephant and taking action. *Reading Research Quarterly, 41*(3), 404–415.

Ehri, L. C., & McCormick, S. (2013). Phases of word learning: Implications for instruction with delayed and disabled readers. In D. E. Alvermann, N. J. Unrau, & R. B. Ruddell (Eds.), *Theoretical models and processes of reading* (6th ed., pp. 339–361). Newark, DE: International Reading Association.

Engeström, Y. (1987). *Learning by expanding: An activity-theoretical approach to developmental research.* Helsinki, Finland: Orienta-Konsultit.

Erskine, K. (2010). *Mockingbird.* New York, NY: Philomel Books.

Escamilla, K., Loera, M., Ruiz, O., & Rodríguez, Y. (1998). An examination of sustaining effects in Descubriendo La Lectura programs. *Literacy Teaching and Learning: An International Journal of Early Reading and Writing, 3*(2), 59–81.

Fecho, B., & Meacham, S. (2007). Learning to play and playing to learn: Research sites as transactional spaces. In C. Lewis, P. Enciso, & E. B. Moje (Eds.), *Reframing sociocultural research on literacy: Identity, agency, and power* (pp. 163–188). Mahwah, NJ: Erlbaum.

Fedorenko, E., Nieto-Castañón, A., & Kanwisher, N. (2013). Syntactic processing in the human brain: What we know, what we don't know, and a suggestion on how to proceed. *Brain and Language, 120,* 187–207.

Fingeret, L. (2008). *March of the penguins:* Building knowledge in a kindergarten classroom. *The Reading Teacher, 62*(2), 96–103.

Fish, S. (1980). *Is there a text in this class?* Cambridge, MA: Harvard University Press.

Fisher, D. & Frey, N. (2014). Content area vocabulary learning. *The Reading Teacher, 67*(8), 594–599.

Fitch, W. T. (2014). Toward a computational framework for cognitive psychology: Unifying approaches from cognitive neuroscience and comparative cognition. *Physics of Life Reviews, 11,* 329–364.

Flynt, E. S., & Brozo, W. G. (2008). Developing academic language. Got words? *The Reading Teacher, 61*(6), 500–502.

Foster, M. (1989). "It's cookin' now": A performance analysis of the speech events of a Black teacher in an urban community college. *Language in Society, 18,* 1–29.

Freebody, P., & Luke, A. (1990). Literacies programs: Debates and demands in cultural context. *Prospect: Australian Journal of TESOL, 5*(7), 7–16.

Freire, P. (1970). *Pedagogy of the oppressed.* New York, NY: Continuum.

Freire, P., & Macedo, D. (1987). *Literacy: Reading the word and the world.* New York, NY: Bergin & Garvey.

García, O., Flores, N., & Woodley, H. (2012). Transgressing monolingualism and bilingual dualities: Translanguaging pedagogies. In A. Yiakoumetti (Ed.), *Harnessing linguistic variation to improve education* (pp. 45–75). Bern, Switzerland: Peter Lang.

Gee, J. P. (1991). Socio-cultural approaches to literacy (literacies). *Annual Review of Applied Linguistics, 12,* 31–48.

Gee, J. P. (1996). *Social linguistics and literacies* (2nd ed.). Philadelphia, PA: Routledge/Falmer.

Genesee, F., Lindholm-Leary, K., Saunders, W. M., & Christian, D. (Eds.). (2006). *Educating English language learners: A synthesis of research evidence.* New York, NY: Cambridge University Press.

Gentry, J. R. (1982). An analysis of developmental spelling in *GMYS at WRK. The Reading Teacher, 36,* 192–200.

Gentry, J. R. (2000). A retrospective on invented spelling and a look forward. *The Reading Teacher, 54*(3), 318–332.

Glover, M. (2009). *Engaging young writers, preschool-Grade 1.* Porstmouth, NH: Heinemann.

Godley, A. J., Carpenter, B. D., & Werner, C. A. (2007). "I'll speak in proper slang": Language ideologies in a daily editing activity. *Reading Research Quarterly, 42*(1), 100–131.

Goldenberg, C., Tolar, T. D., Reese, L., Francis, D. J., Bazán, A. R., & Mejía-Arauz, R. (2014). How important is teaching phonemic awareness to children learning to read in Spanish? *American Educational Research Journal, 51*(3), 604–633.

González, N., Moll, L. C., & Amanti, C. (Eds.). (2005). *Funds of knowledge: Theorizing practices in households, communities, and classrooms.* Mahwah, NJ: Lawrence Erlbaum.

Goodman, K. S. (Ed.). (1979). *Miscue analysis: Applications to reading instruction.* Urbana, IL: National Council of Teachers of English.

Goodman, K. S., & Burke, C. L. (1973, April). *Theoretically based studies of patterns of miscues in oral reading performance* (Project No. 9-0375). Washington, DC: U.S. Office of Education.

Goodman, K. S., & Goodman, Y. M. (1979). Learning to read is natural. In L. B. Resnick & P. A. Weaver (Eds.), *Theory and practice of early reading* (Vol. 1, pp. 137–154). Hillsdale, NJ: Erlbaum.

Goodman, Y. M. (1996). Revaluing readers while readers revalue themselves: Retrospective miscue analysis. *The Reading Teacher, 49,* 600–609.

Goodman, Y. M., & Goodman, K. S. (2013). To err is human: Learning about language processes by analyzing miscues. In D. E. Alvermann, N. J. Unrau, & R. B. Ruddell (Eds.), *Theoretical models and processes of reading* (6th ed., pp. 525–543). Newark, DE: International Reading Association.

Goswami, U., Ziegler, J. C., Dalton, L., & Schneider, W. (2003). Nonword reading across orthographies: How flexible is the choice of reading units? *Applied Psycholinguistics, 24,* 235–247.

Gough, P. B. (1972). One second of reading. In J. F. Kavanagh & I. G. Mattingly (Eds.), *Language by ear and by eye: The relationships between speech and reading* (pp. 331–358). Cambridge, MA: MIT Press.

Gow, P. (2014, March 3). What's dangerous about the grit narrative, and how to fix it [Education Week Blog post]. Retrieved from blogs.edweek.org/edweek/independent_schools/2014/03/whats_dangerous_about_the_grit_narrative_and_how_to_fix_it.html

Graves, D. H. (1983). *Writing: Teachers and children at work.* Exeter, NH: Heinemann.

Greene, J. (1990). Knowledge accumulation: Three views on the nature and role of knowledge in social science. In E. Guba (Ed.), *The paradigm dialog* (pp. 227–245). Newbury Park, CA: Sage.

Greene, M. (1995). *Releasing the imagination: Essays on education, the arts, and social change.* San Francisco, CA: Jossey-Bass.

Guerra, J. (2012). From code segregation to code switching to code meshing: Finding deliverance from deficit thinking through language awareness and performance. In P. J. Dunstron, S. K. Fullerton, C. C. Bates, K. Headley, & P. M. Stecker (Eds.), *61st yearbook of the Literacy Research Association* (pp. 108–118). Oak Creek, WI: Literacy Research Association.

Gumperz, J. J. (1982). *Discourse strategies.* New York, NY: Cambridge University Press.

Guthrie, J. T., & Wigfield, A. (2000). Engagement and motivation in reading. In M. Kamil, P. Mosenthal, P. D. Pearson, & R. Barr (Eds.), *Handbook of reading research* (Vol. 3, pp. 403–422). Mahwah, NJ: Erlbaum.

Gutiérrez, K. D., & Orellana, M. F. (2006). The "problem" of English learners: Constructing genres of difference. *Research in the Teaching of English, 40,* 502–507.

Gutiérrez, K., Rymes, B., & Larson, J. (1995). Script, counterscript, and underlife in the classroom: James Brown versus Brown v. Board of Education. *Harvard Educational Review, 65*(3), 445–471.

Haddix, M., & Rojas, M. A. (2011). (Re)framing teaching in urban classrooms: A poststructural (re)reading of critical literacy as curricular and pedagogical practice. In V. Kinloch (Ed.), *Urban literacies* (pp. 111–124). New York, NY: Teachers College Press.

Handsfield, L. J. (2007). From discontinuity to simultaneity: Mapping the "what ifs" in a classroom literacy event using rhizoanalysis. In D. W. Rowe & R. T. Jiménez (Eds.), *56th yearbook of the National Reading Conference* (pp. 216–234). Oak Creek, WI: National Reading Conference.

Handsfield, L. J. (2011). Disruptive comprehension instruction: Tools for constructing, deconstructing, and reconstructing meaning. *Theory Into Practice, 50*(2), 125–132.

Handsfield, L. J. (2012). Mediating learning and negotiating curricular ideologies in a fourth grade bilingual classroom. In B. Yoon & H. K. Kim (Eds.), *Teachers' roles in second language learning: Classroom applications of sociocultural theory* (pp. 41–61). Charlotte, NC: Information Age.

Handsfield, L. J., & Crumpler, T. P. (2013). "Dude, it's not a appropriate word": Negotiating word meanings, language ideologies, and identities in a literature discussion group. *Linguistics and Education, 24*(2), 112–130.

Handsfield, L. J., Crumpler, T. P., & Dean, T. R. (2010). Tactical negotiations and creative adaptations: The discursive production of literacy curriculum and teacher identities across space-times. *Reading Research Quarterly, 45*(4), 405–431.

Handsfield, L. J., Dean, T. R., & Cielocha, K. M. (2009). Becoming critical consumers and producers of text: Teaching literacy with Web 1.0 and Web 2.0. *The Reading Teacher, 63*(1), 40–50.

Handsfield, L. J., & Jiménez, R. T. (2008). Revisiting cognitive strategy instruction in culturally and linguistically diverse classrooms: Cautions and possibilities. *Language Arts, 85*(6), 450–458.

Handsfield, L. J., & Jiménez, R. T. (2009). Cognition and misrecognition: A Bourdieuian analysis of cognitive strategy instruction in a linguistically and culturally diverse classroom. *Journal of Literacy Research, 42*(2), 151–195.

Harré, R., & Van Langenhove, L. (Eds.). (1999). *Positioning theory: Moral contexts of intentional action.* Malden, MA: Blackwell.

Harvey, S., & Goudvis, A. (2000). *Strategies that work: Teaching comprehension to enhance understanding.* Portsmouth, NH: Stenhouse.

Heath, S. B. (1983). *Ways with words: Language, life, and work in communities and classrooms.* New York, NY: Cambridge University Press.

Heitzeg, N. A. (2009). Education or incarceration? Zero tolerance policies and the school to prison pipeline. *Forum on Public Policy Online, 2,* 121. Retrieved from forumonpublicpolicy .com/summer09/archivesummer09/heitzeg.pdf

Helmuth, L. (May, 2011). Top 10 myths about the brain. *Smithsonian.* Retrieved from www .smithsonianmag.com/science-nature/top-ten-myths-about-the-brain-178357288

Hibbert, K. M., Heydon, R. M., & Rich, S. J. (2008). Beacons of light, rays, or sun catchers? A case study of the positioning of literacy teachers and their knowledge in neoliberal times. *Teaching and Teacher Education, 24,* 303–315.

Hiebert, E. H., & Raphael, T. E. (1996). Psychological perspectives on literacy and extensions to educational practice. In D. C. Berliner & R. C. Calfee (Eds.), *Handbook of educational psychology* (pp. 550–602). New York, NY: Macmillan.

Hilgard, E. R. (1948). *Theories of learning.* East Norwalk, CT: Appleton-Century-Crofts.

Hodson, D. (2003). Time for action: Science education for an alternative future. *International Journal of Science Education, 25*(6), 645–670.

Holdaway, D. (1979). *The foundations of literacy.* Sydney, Australia: Ashton Scholastic.

Hoover, W. A., & Gough, P. B. (1990). The simple view of reading. *Reading and Writing: An Interdisciplinary Journal, 2,* 127–160.

Houston, J. W., & Houston, J. D. (1973). *Farewell to Manzanar.* Boston, MA: Houghton Mifflin.

Hruby, G. G. (2001). Sociological, postmodern, and new realism perspectives in social constructionism: Implications for literacy research. *Reading Research Quarterly, 36,* 48–62.

Hruby, G. G., & Goswami, U. (2011). Neuroscience on reading: A review for reading education researchers. *Reading Research Quarterly, 46*(2), 156–172.

Hruby, G. G., & Hynd, G. W. (2006). Decoding Shaywitz: The modular brain and its discontents [Book review essay on "Overcoming dyslexia"]. *Reading Research Quarterly, 41,* 544–556.

Hull, G., & Schultz, K. (2001). Literacy and learning out of school: A review of theory and research. *Review of Educational Research, 71*(4), 575–611.

Hunt, C. S., & Handsfield, L. J. (2013). The emotional landscapes of literacy coaching: Issues of identity, power, and positioning. *Journal of Literacy Research, 45*(1), 47–86.

Husband, T. (2010). He's too young to learn about that stuff: Anti-racist pedagogy and early childhood social studies. *Social Studies Research and Practice, 5*(2), 61–75.

Hymes, D. (1996). *Ethnography, linguistics, narrative inequality: Toward an understanding of voice.* London, England: Taylor & Francis.

International Reading Association. (2004). *The role and qualifications of the reading coach in the United States: A position statement of the International Reading Association.* Newark, DE: Author.

Iser, W. (1978). *The act of reading: A theory of aesthetic response.* Baltimore, MD: Johns Hopkins University Press.

Iser, W. (1993). *The fictive and the imaginary: Charting literary anthropology.* Baltimore, MD: Johns Hopkins University Press.

Ivey, G., & Broaddus, K. (2007). A formative experiment investigating literacy engagement among adolescent Latina/o students just beginning to read, write, and speak English. *Reading Research Quarterly, 42,* 512–545.

Jadallah, M., Anderson, R. C., Nguyen-Jahiel, K., Miller, B. W., Kim, I., Kuo, L., Dong, T., & Wu, X. (2010). Influence of a teacher's scaffolding moves during child-led small group discussions. *American Educational Research Journal, 48*(1), 194–230.

Jewett, P. (2011). Multiple literacies gone wild. *The Reading Teacher, 64*(5), 341–344.

Jewett, P., & MacPhee, D. (2012). Adding collaborative peer coaching to our teaching identities. *The Reading Teacher, 66*(2), 105–110.

Jiménez, R. T., David, S., Fagan, K., Risko, V. J., Pacheco, M., Pray, L., & Gonzales, M. (2015). Using translation to drive conceptual development for students becoming literate in English as an additional language. *Research in the Teaching of English, 49*(3), 248–271.

Jiménez, R. T., García, G. E., & Pearson, P. D. (1996). The reading strategies of bilingual Latina/o students who are successful English readers: Opportunities and obstacles. *Reading Research Quarterly, 31,* 90–112.

Jones, S. (2004). Living poverty and literacy learning: Sanctioning topics of students' lives. *Language Arts, 81*(6), 461–469.

Jones, S., Clarke, L. W., & Enriquez, G. (2010). *The reading turn-around: A five-part framework for differentiated instruction.* New York, NY: Teachers College Press.

Jones, S., & Rainville, K. N. (2014). Flowing toward understanding: Suffering, humility, and compassion in literacy coaching, *Reading & Writing Quarterly: Overcoming Learning Difficulties, 30*(3), 270–287. doi:10.1080/10573569.2014.909270

Kalman, J. (1999). *Writing on the plaza: Mediated literacy practices among scribes and clients in Mexico City.* Cresskill, NJ: Hampton Press.

Kamberelis, G., & de la Luna, L. C. (1996). Constructing multiculturally relevant pedagogy: Signifying on the basal. In D. J. Leu, C. K. Kinzer, & K. A. Hinchman (Eds.), *Literacies for the 21st century: Research and practice* (pp. 329–344). Chicago, IL: National Reading Conference.

Kamberelis, G., & Dimitriadis, G. (2005). *Qualitative inquiry: Approaches to language and literacy research.* New York, NY: Teachers College Press.

Keats, E. J. (1976). *The snowy day.* New York, NY: Penguin Group.

Kemmis, S., & McTaggart, R. (2000). Participatory action research. In N. K. Denzin & Y. S. Lincoln (Eds.), *Handbook of qualitative research* (2nd ed., 567–606). Thousand Oaks, CA: Sage.

Kiesling, S. (2004). Dude. *American Speech, 79*(3), 281–305.

King, Jr., M. L. (1994). *Letter from the Birmingham jail.* New York, NY: HarperCollins.

Kinloch, V. (2010). *Harlem on our minds: Place, race, and the literacies of urban youth.* New York, NY: Teachers College Press.

Kintsch, W. (1988). The role of knowledge in discourse comprehension: A construction-integration model. *Psychological Review, 95*(2), 163–182.

Kintsch, W. (1998). *Comprehension: A paradigm for cognition.* New York, NY: Cambridge University Press.

Kintsch, W. (2013). Revisiting the construction–integration model of text comprehension and its implications for instruction. In D. E. Alvermann, N. J. Unrau, & R. B. Ruddell (Eds.), *Theoretical models and processes of reading* (6th ed., pp. 807–839). Newark, DE: International Reading Association.

Kliebard, H. M. (1995). *The struggle for the American curriculum: 1893–1958.* New York, NY: Routledge.

Kress, G., & Van Leeuwen, T. (1996). *Reading images: The grammar of visual design.* New York, NY: Routledge.

Labbo, L. D. (1996). A semiotic analysis of young children's symbol making in a classroom computer center. *Reading Research Quarterly, 31*(4), 356–385.

LaBerge, D., & Samuels, S. J. (1974). Towards a theory of automatic information processing in reading. *Cognitive Psychology, 6,* 293–323.

Labov, W. (1972). *Language in the inner city: Studies in the Black English vernacular.* Philadelphia, PA: University of Pennsylvania Press.

Ladson-Billings, G., & Tate, W. F. (1995). Toward a critical race theory of education. *Teachers College Record, 97*(1), 47–68.

Langer, J. A. (1990). The process of understanding: Reading for literary and informative purposes. *Research in the Teaching of English, 24*(3), 229–260.

Langer, J. A. (1998). Thinking and doing literature: An eight-year study. *The English Journal, 87*(2), 16–23.

Lankshear, C., & Knobel, M. (2003). *New literacies.* Maidenhead, Berkshire, England: Open University Press.

Larson, J., & Marsh, J. (2005). *Making literacy real: Theories and practices for learning and teaching.* London, England: Sage.

Lather, P. (1991). *Getting smart: Feminist research and pedagogy with/in the postmodern.* New York, NY: Routledge.

Lave, J., & Wenger, E. (1991). *Situated learning: Legitimate peripheral participation.* Cambridge, England: Cambridge University Press.

Lee, C. D. (2007). *Culture, literacy, and learning: Taking bloom in the midst of the whirlwind.* New York, NY: Teachers College Press.

Lee, H. (1960). *To kill a mockingbird.* Philadelphia, PA: Lippincott.

Lemke, J. (2000). Across the scales of time: Artifacts, activities, and meanings in ecosocial systems. *Mind, Culture, and Activity, 7*(4), 273–290.

Leontiev, A. N. (1978). *Activity, consciousness, and personality.* Englewood Cliffs, NJ: Prentice Hall.

Leontiev, A. N. (1981). *Problems of the development of the mind.* Moscow, Soviet Union: Progress.

Leu, D. J., Kinzer, C. K., Coiro, J., Castek, J., & Henry, L. (2013). New literacies: A dual-level theory of the changing nature of literacy, instruction, and assessment. In D. E. Alvermann, N. J. Unrau, & R. B. Ruddell (Eds.), *Theoretical models and processes of reading* (6th ed., pp. 1150–1181). Newark, DE: International Reading Association.

Lewis, C., Enciso, P., & Moje, E. B. (Eds.). (2007). *Reframing sociocultural research on literacy.* Mahwah, NJ: Erlbaum.

Literacy Resources, Inc. (2013, June 25). Phonemic awareness research. Retrieved from www.literacyresourcesinc.com/research

Lotherington, H., & Chow, S. (2006). Rewriting "Goldilocks" in the urban, multicultural elementary school. *The Reading Teacher, 60*(3), 242–252.

Luke, A. (2000). Critical literacy in Australia: A matter of context and standpoint. *Journal of Adolescent and Adult Literacy, 43*(5), 448–461.

Luke, A., & Freebody, P. (1999). A map of possible practices: Further notes on the four resources model. *Reading Online.* Retrieved from www.readingonline.org/research/luke-freebody.html

MacPhee, D. (2013). Professional development as the study of self: Using self-knowledge to mediate the act of teaching. In P. J. Dunston, S. K. Fullerton, C. C. Bates, P. M. Stecker, M. W. Cole, A. H. Hall . . . K. N. Headley (Eds.), *62nd yearbook of the Literacy Research Association* (pp. 311–323). Altamonte Springs, FL: Literacy Research Association.

Martínez, R. A. (2013). Reading the world in *Spanglish*: Hybrid language practices and ideological contestation in a sixth-grade English language arts classroom. *Linguistics & Education, 24*(3), 276–288. dx.doi.org/10.1016/j.linged.2013.03.007.

Martínez, R. A., Orellana, M. F., Pacheco, M., & Carbone, P. (2008). Found in translation: Connecting translating experiences to academic writing. *Language Arts, 85,* 421–431.

Marzollo, J., & Pinkney, B. (1993). *Happy birthday, Martin Luther King.* New York, NY: Scholastic.

Mason, J. (1980). When do children learn to read? An exploration of four-year-old childrens' letter and word reading competencies. *Reading Research Quarterly, 15,* 202–227.

McIntyre, A. (2000). Constructing meaning about violence, school and community: Participatory action research with urban youth. *The Urban Review, 32*(2), 123–154.

McKeown, M. G., Beck, I. L., & Blake, R. G. K. (2009). Rethinking reading comprehension instruction: A comparison of instruction for strategies and content approaches. *Reading Research Quarterly, 44*(3), 218–251.

McLaughlin, M., & DeVoogd, G. (2004). Critical literacy as comprehension: Expanding reader response. *Journal of Adolescent and Adult Literacy, 48*(1), 52–62.

McVee, M., Dunsmore, K., & Gavelek, J. R. (2005). Schema theory revisited. *Review of Educational Research, 75,* 531–566.

Meacham, S., & Buendia, E. (1999). Modernism, post-modernism, and poststructuralism and their impact on literacy. *Language Arts, 76,* 510–516.

Merchant, G. (2007). Writing the future in the digital age. *Literacy, 41*(3), 118–128.

Moje, E. B. (2008). Foregrounding the disciplines in secondary literacy teaching and learning: A call for change. *Journal of Adolescent & Adult Literacy, 52*(2), 96–107.

Moje, E. B., & Lewis, C. (2007). Examining opportunities to learn literacy: The role of critical sociocultural literacy research. In C. Lewis, P. Enciso, & E. B. Moje (Eds.), *Reframing sociocultural research on literacy* (pp. 15–48). Mahwah, NJ: Erlbaum.

Moll, L. C. (2014). *L. S. Vygotsky and education.* New York, NY: Routledge.

Moll, L. C., Amanti, C., Neff, D., & González, N. (1992). Funds of knowledge for teaching: Using a qualitative approach to connect homes and classrooms. *Theory Into Practice, 31,* 132–141.

Montes, M. (2003). *Get ready for Gabí: A crazy mixed-up Spanglish day.* New York, NY: Scholastic.

Moorman, G., Blanton, W., & McLaughlin, T. (1994). The rhetoric of whole language. *Reading Research Quarterly, 29*(4), 308–329.

Morrell, E. (2008). *Critical literacy and urban youth: Pedagogies of access, dissent, and liberation.* New York, NY: Routledge.

Morrell, E., & Duncan-Andrade, J. M. R. (2002, July). Promoting academic literacy with urban youth through engaging hiphop culture. *English Journal,* pp. 88–92.

Morson, G. S., & Emerson, C. (1990). *Mikhail Bakhtin: Creation of a prosaics.* Stanford, CA: Stanford University Press.

Moss, B. J. (2001). From the pews to the classrooms: Influences of the African American church on academic literacy. In J. L. Harris, A. G. Kamhi & K. E. Pollock (Eds.), *Literacy in African American communities* (pp. 195–211). Mahwah, NJ: Lawrence Erlbaum Associates.

Munsch, R. (1980). *The paper bag princess.* Buffalo, NY: Annick Press.

NAACP Legal Defense and Education Fund, Inc. (2005). *Dismantling the school to prison pipeline.* Retrieved from www.naacpldf.org/publication/dismantling-school-prison-pipeline

National Reading Panel. (2000). *Report of the National Reading Panel. Teaching Children to Read: An Evidence-Based Assessment of the Scientific Research Literature on Reading and Its Implications for Reading Instruction.* Washington, DC: National Institute of Child Health and Human Development.

New London Group. (1996). A pedagogy of multiliteracies: Designing social futures. *Harvard Educational Review, 66*(1), 60–92.

No Child Left Behind Act of 2001, Pub. L. No. 107-110 [H.R. 10], 115 Stat. 1425 (Jan. 08, 2002).

Noffke, S. E. (1997). Professional, personal, and political dimensions of action research. In M. W. Apple (Ed.), *Review of research in education* (Vol. 22, pp. 305–343). Washington, DC: American Educational Research Association.

O'Neill, C. (1995). *Drama worlds: A framework for process drama.* Portsmouth, NH: Heinemann.

Orellana, M. F., Reynolds, J., Dorner, L., & Meza, M. (2003). In other words: Translating or "para-phrasing" as a family literacy practice in immigrant households. *Reading Research Quarterly, 38*(1), 12–34.

Palincsar, A. S. (2007). Reciprocal teaching 1982 to 2006: The role of research, theory, and representation in the transformation of instructional research. In D. Rowe, R. Jiménez, D. Compton, D. Dickinson, Y. Kim, K. Leander, & V. Risko (Eds.), *56th yearbook of the National Reading Conference* (pp. 41–52). Oak Creek, WI: National Reading Conference.

Palincsar, A. S., & Brown, A. L. (1984). Reciprocal teaching of comprehension-fostering and monitoring activities. *Cognition and Instruction, 1,* 117–175.

Palincsar, A., & Schutz, K. M. (2011). Reconnecting strategy instruction with its theoretical roots. *Theory Into Practice, 50*(2), 1–8.

Pantaleo, S., & Sipe, L. R. (2008). Postmodernism and picturebooks. In L. R. Sipe and S. Pantaleo (Eds.), *Postmodern picturebooks* (pp. 1–8). New York, NY: Routledge.

Paris, S. G. (2005). Reinterpreting the development of reading skills. *Reading Research Quarterly, 40*(2), 184–202.

Paulson, E. J., & Armstrong, S. L. (2010). Situating reader stance within and beyond the efferent–aesthetic continuum. *Literacy Research and Instruction, 49,* 86–97. doi:10.1080/19388070902736821

Paxton, T. (1990). *Belling the cat and other Aesop's fables.* New York, NY: William Morrow.

Payne, R. K. (2013). *A framework for understanding poverty: A cognitive approach* (5th ed.). Highlands, TX: aha Process.

Pennington, J. L., Obenchain, K. M., & Brock, C. H. (2014). Reading informational texts: A civic transactional perspective. *The Reading Teacher, 67*(7), 532–542.

Pennycook, A. (2001). *Critical applied linguistics: A critical introduction.* Mahwah, NJ: Erlbaum.

Peters, M., & Burbules, N. (2004). *Poststructuralism and educational research.* Lanham, MD: Rowman & Littlefield.

Philips, S. U. (1972). Participant structures and communicative competence: Warm Springs children in community and classroom. In C. B. Cazden, V. P. John, & D. Hymes (Eds.), *Functions of language in the classroom* (pp. 370–394). New York, NY: Teachers College Press.

Piaget, J. (1950). *The psychology of intelligence.* London, England: Kegan Paul, Trench, & Trubner.

Piaget, J. (1954). *The construction of reality in the child.* New York, NY: Basic Books.

Piercy, M. (1982). To be of use. In *Circles on the Water: Selected poems* (p. 106). New York, NY: Alfred A. Knopf.

Pressley, M. (2000). What should comprehension instruction be the instruction of? In M. Kamil, P. Mosenthal, P. D. Pearson, & R. Barr (Eds.), *Handbook of reading research* (vol. 3, pp. 545–562). Mahwah, NJ: Lawrence Erlbaum.

Pressley, M., El-Dinary, P. B., Gaskins, I., Schuder, T., Bergman, J. L., Almasi, J., & Brown, R. (1992). Beyond direct explanation: Transactional instruction of reading comprehension strategies. *Elementary School Journal, 92,* 513–555.

Purcell-Gates, V. (2012). Epistemological tensions in reading research and a vision for the future. *Reading Research Quarterly, 47*(4), 465–471. doi:10.1002/RRQ.031.

Rainville, K. N., & Jones, S. (2009). Situated identities: Power and positioning in the work of a literacy coach. *The Reading Teacher, 61*(6), 440–448.

RAND Reading Study Group. (2002). *Reading for understanding: Towards an R&D program in reading comprehension.* Washington, DC: Office of Educational Research and Improvement (OERI), U.S. Department of Education.

Rasinski, T. V. (2010). *The fluent reader: Oral reading strategies for building word recognition, fluency, and comprehension* (2nd ed.). New York, NY: Scholastic.

Ray, K. W. (1999). *Wondrous words: Writers and writing in the elementary classroom.* Urbana, IL: National Council of Teachers of English.

Ray, K. W., & Glover, M. (2008). *Already ready: Nurturing writers in preschool and kindergarten.* Portsmouth, NH: Heinemann.

Razfar, A., & Gutiérrez, K. (2003). Reconceptualizing early childhood literacy: The sociocultural influence. In N. Hall, J. Larson, & J. Marsh (Eds.), *Handbook of early childhood literacy* (pp. 34–47). London, England: Sage.

Reinking, D. (2011). Beyond the laboratory and lens: New metaphors for literacy research. In P. J. Dunston, L. B. Gambrell, K. N. Headley, S. K. Fullerton, P. M. Stecker, V. R. Gillis, & C. C. Bates (Eds.), *60th yearbook of the Literacy Research Association* (pp. 1–17). Oak Creek, WI: Literacy Research Association.

Reutzel, D. R., Smith, J. A., & Fawson, P. C. (2005). An evaluation of two approaches for teaching reading comprehension strategies in the primary years using science information texts. *Early Childhood Research Quarterly, 20*(3), 276–305.

Reynolds, R. E., & Sinatra, G. (2005). The cognitive revolution in scientific psychology: Epistemological roots and impact on reading research. In J. M. Royer (Ed.), *The cognitive revolution in educational psychology* (pp. 13–40). Greenwich, CT: Information Age.

Reznitskaya, A., Anderson, R. C., McNurlen, B., Nguyen-Jahiel, K., Archodidou, A., & Kim, S. (2001). Influence of oral discussion on written argument. *Discourse Processes, 32*(2&3), 155–175.

Riedel, B. W. (2007). The relationship between DIBELS, reading comprehension, and vocabulary in urban first grade students. *Reading Research Quarterly, 42*(4), 546–567.

Roberts, T. A., Christo, C., & Shefelbine, J. A. (2011). Word recognition. In M. L. Kamil, P. D. Pearson, E. B. Moje, & P. P. Afflerbach (Eds.), *Handbook of reading research* (Vol. 4, pp. 229–258). New York, NY: Routledge.

Rogers, R., & Mosley, M. (2006). Racial literacy in a second-grade classroom: Critical race theory, whiteness studies, and literacy research. *Reading Research Quarterly, 41*(4), 462–495.

Rogoff, B. (1995). Observing sociocultural activity on three planes: Participatory appropriation, guided participation, and apprenticeship. In J. V. Wertsch, P. del Rio, & A. Alvarez (Eds.), *Sociocultural studies of mind* (pp. 139–164). New York, NY: Cambridge University Press.

Rogoff, B. (2003). *The cultural nature of human development*. Oxford, England: Oxford University Press.

Rosenblatt, L. M. (1978). *The reader, the text, and the poem*. Carbondale, IL: Southern Illinois University Press.

Rosenblatt, L. M. (2004). The transactional theory of reading and writing. In R. B. Ruddell & N. J. Untrau (Eds.), *Theoretical models and processes of reading* (5th ed., pp. 1363–1398). Newark, DE: International Reading Association.

Roth, W., & Lee, Y. (2007). "Vygotsky's neglected legacy": Cultural-historical activity theory. *Review of Educational Research, 77*(2), 186–232.

Rubin, R., & Carlan, V. G. (2005). Using writing to understand bilingual children's writing development. *The Reading Teacher, 58*(8), 728–739.

Rumelhart, D. E. (1980). Schemata: The building blocks of cognition. In R. J. Spiro, B. C. Bruce, & W. F. Brewer (Eds.), *Theoretical issues in reading comprehension* (pp. 38–58). Hillsdale, NJ: Lawrence Erlbaum Associates.

Rumelhart, D. E. (1994). Toward an interactive model of reading. In R. B. Ruddell, M. R. Ruddell, & H. Singer (Eds.), *Theoretical models and processes of reading* (4th ed., 864–894). Newark, DE: International Reading Association.

Rumelhart, D. E., & McClelland, J. L. (1986). On learning the past tenses of English verbs. In J. L. McClelland & D. E. Rumelhart (Eds.), *Parallel distributed processing, Vol. 2: Psychological and biological models* (pp. 216-271). Cambridge, MA: MIT Press.

Rymes, B. (2014) *Communicating beyond language: Everyday encounters with diversity*. New York, NY: Routledge.

Samuels, S. J. (1994). Toward a theory of automatic information processing in reading, revisited. In R.B. Ruddell, M.R. Ruddell, & H. Singer (Eds.) *Theoretical models and processes of reading* (4th ed., pp. 816–837). Newark, DE: International Reading Association.

Samuels, S. J. (2006). Looking backward: Reflections on a career in reading. *Journal of Literacy Research, 38*(3), 327–344.

Samuels, S. J. (2007). Commentary: The DIBELS tests: Is speed of barking at print what we mean by reading fluency? *Reading Research Quarterly, 42*(4), 563–566.

Saussure, F. (1959). *Course in general linguistics*. (W. Baskin, Trans.). New York, NY: Philosophy Library.

Serafini, F. (2011). When bad things happen to good books. *The Reading Teacher, 65*(4), 238–241.

Shanahan, C., & Shanahan, T. (2014). Does disciplinary literacy have a place in elementary school? *The Reading Teacher, 67*(8), 636–639.

Shanahan, T., & Barr, R. (1995). Reading Recovery: An independent evaluation of the effects of an early instructional intervention for at-risk learners. *Reading Research Quarterly, 30,* 958–996.

Sipe, L. R. (1999). Children's response to literature: Author, text, reader, context. *Theory Into Practice, 38*(3), 120–129.

Skinner, B. F. (1954). The science of learning and the art of teaching. *Harvard Educational Review, 24,* 86–97.

Smagorinsky, P. H. (2009). Essay review: The culture of Vygotsky. *Reading Research Quarterly, 44*(1), 85–95. dx.doi.org/10.1598/RRQ.44.1.4

Smith, F. (1971). *Understanding reading: A psycholinguistic analysis of reading and learning to read*. New York, NY: Holt, Rinehart & Winston.

Smith, F., & Goodman, K. S. (2011). On the psycholinguistic method of teaching reading. In J. B. Cobb & M. K. Kallus (Eds.), *Historical, theoretical, and sociological foundations of reading in the United States* (pp. 264–269). Boston, MA: Pearson.

Sousa, D. A. (2006). *How the brain learns* (3rd ed.). Thousand Oaks, CA: Corwin Press.

Spiegel, D. L. (1998). Silver bullets, babies, and bath water: Literature response groups in a balanced literacy program. *The Reading Teacher, 52*(2), 114–124.

Spivey, N. N. (1987). Constructing constructivism: Reading research in the United States. *Poetics, 16,* 169–192.

Spivey, N. N. (1997). *The constructivist metaphor: Reading, writing, and the making of meaning*. San Diego, CA: Academic Press.

Stahl, S. A. (1999). Why innovations come and go (and mostly go): The case of whole language. *Educational Researcher, 28,* 13–22. doi:10.3102/0013189X028008013

Stahl, S. A., Duffy-Hester, A. M., & Stahl, K. D. (1998). Theory and research into practice: Everything you wanted to know about phonics (but were afraid to ask). *Reading Research Quarterly, 33*(3), 338–355.

Stahl, S. A., & Fairbanks, M. (1986). The effects of vocabulary instruction: A model-based meta-analysis. *Review of Educational Research, 56,* 72–110.

Stahl, S. A., & Heubach, K. M. (2005). Fluency oriented reading instruction. *Journal of Literacy Research, 37*(1), 25–60.

Stahl, S. A., & McKenna, M. C. (2000). The concurrent development of phonological awareness, word recognition, and spelling. Center for Improvement of Early Reading Achievement. Retrieved from www.ciera.org/library/archive/2001-07/200107.htm

Stephens, D., & Mills, H. (2014). Coaching as inquiry. *Reading/Writing Quarterly, 30*(1), 1–17.

Stover, K., Kissel, B., Haag, K., & Shoniker, R. (2011). Differentiated coaching: Fostering reflection with teachers. *Reading Teacher, 64*(7), 498–509.

Street, B. (1984). *Literacy in theory and practice.* Cambridge, England: Cambridge University Press.

Street, B. (1995). *Literacy in theory and practice.* Cambridge, MA: Cambridge University Press.

Street, B. (2003). What's "new" in new literacy studies? Critical approaches to literacy in theory and practice. *Current Issues in Comparative Education, 5*(2), 77–91.

Sumara, D. J., & Davis, B. A. (2006). Correspondence, coherence, complexity: Theories of learning and their influences on processes of literary composition. *English Teaching: Practice and Critique, 5*(2), 34–55.

Teale, W., & Sulzby, E. (1986). *Emergent literacy: Writing and reading.* Norwood, NJ: Ablex.

Thorndike, E. L. (1903). *Educational psychology.* New York, NY: Teachers College, Columbia University.

Thorndike, E. L. (1912). The measurement of educational products. *The School Review, 20*(5), 289–299.

Tough, P. (2012). How children succeed: Grit, curiosity, and the hidden power of character. New York, NY: Houghton Mifflin Harcourt.

Tracey, D. H., & Morrow, L. M. (2012). *Lenses on reading: An introduction to theories and models* (2nd ed.). New York, NY: Guilford Press.

Turbill, J. (2001, July/August). Getting kindergarteners started with technology: The story of one school. *Reading Online, 5*(1). Retrieved from www.readingonline.org/international /inter_index.asp?HREF=turbill2/index.html

Unrau, N. J., & Alvermann, D. E. (2013). Literacies and their investigation through theories and models. In D. E. Alvermann, N. J. Unrau, & R. B. Ruddell (Eds.), *Theoretical models and processes of reading* (6th ed., pp. 47–90). Newark, DE: International Reading Association.

Urrieta Jr., L. (2010). *Working from within Chicana and Chicano activist educators in Whitestream Schools.* Tucson, AZ: University of Arizona Press.

Valencia, R. R. (2010). *Dismantling contemporary deficit thinking: Educational thought and practice.* New York, NY: Routledge.

Vanderburg, M., & Stephens, D. (2010). The impact of literacy coaches: What teachers value and how teachers change. *Elementary School Journal, 111*(1), 141–163.

Van der Veer, R. (2007). Vygotsky in context: 1900–1935. In H. Daniels, M. Cole, & J. V. Wertsch (Eds.), *The Cambridge companion to Vygotsky* (pp. 21–49). New York, NY: Cambridge University Press.

Vasquez, V. (2004). *Negotiating critical literacies with young children.* Mahwah, NJ: Erlbaum.

Vélez-Ibáñez, C. G. (1988). Networks of exchange among Mexicans in the U.S. and Mexico: Local level mediating responses to national and international transformations. *Urban Anthropology, 17*(1), 27–51.

Vul, E., Harris, C., Winkielman, P., & Pashler, H. (2009). Puzzlingly high correlations in fMRI studies of emotion, personality, and social cognition. *Perspectives in Psychological Science, 4,* 274–290.

Vygotsky, L. S. (1978). *Mind in society: The development of higher psychological processes.* (M. Cole, V. John-Steiner, S. Scribner, & E. Souberman, Eds. & Trans.). Cambridge, MA: Harvard University Press.

Vygotsky, L. S. (2012). *Thought and language: Revised and expanded edition.* Cambridge, MA: MIT Press.

Walberg, H. J., & Haertel, G. D. (1992). Educational psychology's first century. *Journal of Educational Psychology, 84*(1), 6–19.

Watson, J. B. (1913). Psychology as the behaviorist views it. *Psychological Review, 20,* 158–177.

Weaver, C. (1996). *Teaching grammar in context.* Portsmouth, NH: Heinemann.

Weber, P. H. (1920). Behaviorism and indirect response. *The Journal of Philosophy, Psychology and Scientific Methods, 17*(24), 663–667.

Weber, P. H. (1922). Discussions: General examinations. *Educational Review, 63*(5).

Weisberg, D. S., Keil, F. C., Goodstein, J., Rawson, E., & Gray, J. R. (2008). The seductive allure of neuroscience explanations. *The Journal of Cognitive Neuroscience, 20,* 470–477.

Wertsch, J. V. (1991). *Voices of the mind: A sociocultural approach to mediated action.* Cambridge, MA: Harvard University Press.

Wheeler, R. S., & Swords, R. (2004). Codeswitching: Tools of language and culture transform the dialectally diverse classroom. *Language Arts, 81,* 470–480.

White, E. B. (1952). *Charlotte's web.* New York, NY: HarperCollins.

Wiesner, D. (2001). *The three pigs.* New York, NY: Clarion Books.

Williams, V. (1982). *A chair for my mother.* New York, NY: Greenwillow Books.

Wolfe, P., & Nevills, P. (2009). *Building the reading brain, preK–3* (2nd ed.). Thousand Oaks, CA: Corwin.

Zamudio, M., Russell, C., Rios, F., & Bridgeman, J. L. (2011). *Critical race theory matters.* New York, NY: Routledge.

Zhang, J., & Stahl, K. D. (2011). Collaborative reasoning: Language-rich discussions for English learners. *The Reading Teacher, 65*(4), 257–260.

Ziegler, J. C., & Goswami, U. (2005). Reading acquisition, developmental dyslexia, and skilled reading across languages: A psycholinguistic grain size theory. *Psychological Bulletin, 131*(1), 3–29.

Ziegler, J. C., & Goswami, U. (2006). Becoming literate in different languages: Similar problems, different solutions. *Developmental Science, 9*(5), 429–436.

Index

AUTHORS

Adams, M. J., 28, 29f, 122, 126
Afflerbach, P., 40–41
Alarcón, W., 171
Alexander, P. A., 18, 21, 31
Almasi, J., 40
Alvermann, D. E., 3, 5
Amanti, C., 63, 64, 65–66, 128
American Psychiatric Association, 31
Anderson, R. C., 11t, 41, 42, 44, 65, 133–134, 143
Andrews, R., 101
Appleman, D., 140
Archodidou, A., 65
Armstrong, S. L., 52
Au, K. H., 67
Aukerman, M., 43

Baer, D. R., 33, 35
Bakhtin, M., 89, 108
Bandura, A., 59
Barch, D., 32
Barr, R., 73
Bartlett, F., 21, 43
Baumann, J. F., 44, 195, 197
Bautista, M. A., 11t, 78
Bazán, A. R., 30
Beck, I. L., 122, 123
Bell, D., 95, 150
Bennett, C. M., 32
Bentley, A. F., 50
Bereiter, C., 18, 68
Bergman, J. L., 40
Bertrand, M., 11t, 78
Beverley, J., 95, 172
Beverton, S., 101
Bishop, R. S., 97
Blake, R. G. K., 123
Blanton, W., 48
Blommaert, J., 67
Blot, R., 86, 91

Boland, E. M., 44
Bomer, R., 64
Bornkessel-Schlesewsky, I., 32
Bourdieu, P., 4
Bourke, R. T., 82
Boushey, G., 19
Bowling, D., 32
Bradley, B. A., 197
Bridgeman, J. L., 95, 96, 171
Broaddus, K., 197
Brock, C. H., 175
Bronfenbrenner, U., 32
Broomhead, P., 86
Brown, A. L., 44
Brown, R., 11t, 40
Brozo, W. G., 122
Buendia, E., 82
Burbules, N., 77
Burke, C. L., 45, 135
Button, K. S., 32

Cabrera, N. L., 96
Calkins, L., 11t, 60–61, 159, 160, 161
Campano, G., 196
Camus, A., 145
Carbone, P., 66, 102
Carlan, V. G., 35
Carpenter, B. D., 102
Castek, J., 40, 87, 113
Cazden, C. B., 66, 67, 69, 107, 180, 181
Chall, J. S., 33, 34
Cherland, M. R., 93
Chinn, C., 65
Chow, S., 82
Christian, D., 122
Christo, C., 26–27, 29
Cielocha, K. M., 53, 113
Clarke, L. W., 91, 123
Clay, M. M., 11t, 70, 71, 72, 73, 166

Cobb, P., 20, 21, 26
Cochran-Smith, M., 195
Coiro, J., 40, 113
Cole, M., 57, 58
Collins, J., 86, 91
Coltheart, M., 11t, 22t, 25–26
Coriro, J., 87
Crua, C., 171
Crumpler, T. P., 54, 55, 91, 108, 129
Cunningham, J. W., 6

Dalton, L., 28
Daniels, H., 53, 103
David, S., 40
Davis, B., 6, 8, 9, 15, 21, 36–37, 38, 39, 57, 60, 75, 76, 80
Davis, B. A., 15, 38, 39
Dean, T. R., 53, 91, 113
de Certeau, M., 91
Dekker, S., 31
de la Luna, L. C., 65
Delgado, R., 92
DeVoogd, G., 52, 123
Dewey, J., 50
DiCamillo, K., 45
Dimitriadis, G., 3, 5, 7f, 80, 90
Dixon-Krauss, L., 58
Dodge, B., 88
Dong, T., 65
Dorner, L., 40, 66
Draper, R. J., 69, 86, 174
Draper, S., 151
Dressman, M., 2
Du Bois, W. E. B., 145
Duffy-Hester, A. M., 47–48, 101, 195
Duncan-Andrade, J. M. R., 65, 81
Dunsmore, K., 42, 43, 56

Durkin, D., 40
Dworin, J. E., 64
Dyson, A. H., 71

Edelsky, C., 93
Edmiston, B., 54, 140
Edwards, E. C., 44, 197
Edwards, P. A., 96
Ehri, L. C., 11t, 33, 34, 35, 106, 127
El-Dinary, P. B., 40
Emerson, C., 90
Enciso, P., 11t, 89
Engelmann, S., 18, 68
Engëstrom, Y., 59
Enriquez, G., 91, 123
Erskine, K., 139
Escamilla, K., 73

Fagan, K., 40
Fairbanks, M., 122
Fawson, P. C., 123
Fecho, B., 51
Fedorenko, E., 32
Fingeret, L., 44
Fish, S., 53, 119
Fisher, D., 122
Fitch, W. T., 32
Fitzgerald, J., 6
Flint, J., 32
Flores, N., 102
Flynt, E. S., 122
Foster, M., 107
Fox, E., 18, 21, 31
Francis, D. J., 30
Freebody, P., 52, 77, 81, 93
Freire, P., 4, 11t, 79–80, 93, 96, 170–171, 188, 189
Frey, N., 122

García, G. E., 40
García, O., 102
Gaskins, I., 40
Gavelek, J. R., 42, 43, 56
Gee, J. P., 31, 84, 89, 137, 175
Genesee, F., 122
Genishi, C., 71
Gentry, J. R., 11t, 33, 34, 35, 36, 106, 165
Glover, M., 163
Godley, A. J., 102
Goldenberg, C., 30
Gonzales, M., 40
González, N., 63, 64, 65–66, 128

Goodman, K. S., 11t, 22t, 36, 41, 45, 47, 48, 135, 181
Goodman, Y. M., 11t, 22t, 41, 45, 47, 181
Goodstein, J., 31
Goswami, U., 7, 11t, 22t, 28, 29–30, 32
Goudvis, A., 123
Gough, P. B., 11t, 22, 22t, 23–24
Gow, P., 92
Graves, D. H., 61, 159
Gray, J. R., 31
Greene, J., 76
Greene, M., 160
Guerra, J., 102
Gumperz, J. J., 11t, 67, 180
Guthrie, J. T., 55–56
Gutiérrez, K., 70, 112, 128, 140

Haag, K., 194, 195
Haddix, M., 93
Haertel, G. D., 18
Handsfield, L. J., 53, 89, 91, 103, 108, 113, 123, 129, 176, 194
Harré, R., 89
Harris, C., 32
Harvey, S., 123
Heath, S. B., 11t, 64, 68, 83, 123
Heitzeg, N. A., 95
Helmuth, L., 31
Henry, L., 40, 87, 113
Heubach, K. M., 121, 165
Heydon, R. M., 194
Hibbert, K. M., 194
Hiebert, E. H., 17
Hilgard, E. R., 17
Hodson, D., 81
Holdaway, D., 70, 72, 112, 166
Hoover, W. A., 11t, 22t, 23–24
Houston, J. D., 183
Houston, J. W., 183
Howard-Jones, P., 31
Hruby, G. G., 9, 15, 31, 32, 39, 57, 76
Hull, C. S., 84
Hunt, C. S., 194
Husband, T., 145
Hymes, D., 66
Hynd, G. W., 31

International Reading Association, 194
Invernizzi, M., 33, 35
Ioannidis, J. P. A., 32
Iser, W., 11t, 41, 53, 55
Ivey, G., 197

Jackson, L. G., 171
Jadallah, M., 65
Jensen, A. P., 86
Jewett, P., 88, 195
Jiménez, R. T., 26, 40, 103, 123
Johnston, F., 33, 35
Jolles, J., 31
Jones, S., 91, 123, 171, 194
Jordan, C., 67

Kalman, J., 158
Kamberelis, G., 3, 5, 7f, 65, 80, 90
Kame'enui, E., 44
Kanwisher, N., 32
Keil, F. C., 31
Kemmis, S., 196
Kiesling, S., 137
Kim, I., 65
Kim, S., 65
Kinloch, V., 11t, 87
Kintsch, W., 11t, 41, 48–49, 50, 135–136, 187–188
Kinzer, C. K., 40, 87, 113
Kissel, B., 194, 195
Kliebard, H. M., 15, 17, 26
Knobel, M., 11t, 87, 88, 102–103, 113
Kress, G., 102
Kucan, L., 122
Kuo, L., 65

Labbo, L. D., 113
LaBerge, D., 11t, 22t, 24, 33, 126
Labov, W., 67–68
Ladson-Billings, G., 11t, 95
Langer, J. A., 52
Lankshear, C., 11t, 87, 88, 102–103, 113
Larson, J., 62, 140
Lather, P., 197–198
Lave, J., 62
Lee, C. D., 65, 66, 102
Lee, H., 114
Lee, N. C., 31
Lee, Y., 59
Lemke, J., 190

Leontiev, A. N., 59
Leu, D. J., 40, 87, 113
Lewis, C., 11t, 89, 90
Lindholm-Leary, K., 122
Locke, T., 101
Loera, M., 73
Lotherington, H., 82
Low, G., 101
Luce-Kapler, R., 8, 9, 15, 21, 36–37, 38, 39, 57, 75, 76, 80
Luke, A., 52, 77, 81, 93, 94
Lytle, S. L., 195

Macedo, D., 80
MacPhee, D., 194, 195
Marsh, J., 62
Martínez, R. A., 66, 102
Mason, J., 34
Matthews, C., 11t, 78
May, L., 64
McClelland, J. L., 11t, 22t, 28, 106
McCormick, S., 11t, 33, 34, 35, 106, 127
McIntyre, A., 78
McKenna, M. C., 165
McKeown, M. G., 122, 123
McLaughlin, M., 52, 123
McLaughlin, T., 48
McNurlen, B., 65
McTaggart, R., 196
McVee, M., 42, 43, 56
Meacham, S., 51, 82
Mejía-Arauz, R., 30
Merchant, G., 102–103, 112
Meza, E. L., 96
Meza, M., 40, 66
Miller, B. W., 65
Miller, M. B., 32
Mills, H., 195
Moje, E. B., 11t, 89, 90, 102
Mokrysz, C., 32
Moll, L. C., 58, 63, 64, 65–66, 72, 128
Montes, M., 129
Moorman, G., 48
Morrell, E., 4, 11t, 65, 76, 78, 79, 80, 81, 85, 94
Morris, P. A., 32
Morrow, L. M., 8
Morson, G. S., 90
Moser, J., 19
Mosley, M., 145
Moss, B. J., 67

Munafo, M. R., 32
Munsch, R., 97

NAACP, 95
National Reading Panel, 47
Neff, D., 63, 64
Nevills, P., 31
New London Group, 11t, 87, 88, 113, 155, 156
Nguyen-Jahiel, K., 65
Nieto-Castañon, A., 32
No Child Left Behind, 101, 191
Noffke, S. E., 196
Nokes, J., 86
Nosek, B. A., 32

Obenchain, K. M., 175
Olejnik, S., 44
O'Neill, C., 54, 140
Orellana, M. F., 40, 66, 102, 128
Oxenhorn, A., 160, 161

Pacheco, M., 40, 66, 102
Palincsar, A. S., 44, 123
Pantaleo, S., 77
Paris, S. G., 40–41, 121
Pashler, H., 32
Paulson, E. J., 52
Pearson, P. D., 11t, 40–41, 42, 133–134
Pennington, J. L., 175
Pennycook, A., 86
Peters, M., 77
Philips, S. U., 67
Piaget, J., 21, 35, 39
Piercy, M., 1
Pray, L., 40
Pressley, M., 11t, 40, 123
Prieto, L., 171
Purcell-Gates, V., 32

Rainville, K. N., 194
Rampton, B., 67
RAND Reading Study Group, 123
Raphael, T. E., 17
Rasinski, T. V., 33, 121, 122
Rawson, E., 31
Ray, K. W., 65, 159, 163
Razfar, A., 70, 112
Reese, L., 30
Reinking, D., 196–197
Reutzel, D. R., 123
Reynolds, J., 40, 66

Reynolds, R. E., 8, 18, 21, 26, 36
Reznitskaya, A., 65
Rich, S. J., 194
Riedel, B. W., 33
Rios, F., 95, 96, 171
Risko, V. J., 40
Roberts, T. A., 26–27, 28, 29
Robinson, A., 101
Robinson, E. S., 32
Rodríguez, R. C., 96
Rodríguez, Y., 73
Rodriguez-Arroyo, S., 171
Rogers, R., 145
Rogoff, B., 11t, 62, 63, 119, 127, 144
Rojas, M. A., 93
Romero, A. L., 96
Rosenblatt, L., 11t, 41, 50–52, 53, 119, 120, 149
Roth, W., 59
Rubin, R., 35
Ruddell, R. B., 5
Ruiz, O., 73
Rumelhart, D. E., 11t, 21, 22t, 24–25, 26, 28, 106
Russell, C., 95, 96, 171
Rymes, B., 67, 140

Samuels, S. J., 11t, 21, 22, 22t, 24, 33, 46, 126, 158
Saunders, W. M., 122
Saussure, F., 38
Schlesewsky, M., 32
Schmidt, P. A., 96
Schneider, W., 28
Schuder, T., 11t, 40
Schultz, K., 84
Schutz, K. M., 123
Scorza, D., 11t, 78
Scribner, S., 57, 58
Semingson, P., 64
Serafini, F., 123, 140
Shanahan, C., 174, 175
Shanahan, T., 73, 174, 175
Shefelbine, J. A., 26–27, 29
Shoniker, R., 194, 195
Siebert, D., 69, 86, 174
Sinatra, G., 8, 18, 21, 26, 36
Sipe, L. R., 52, 77, 149
Skinner, B. F., 11t
Smagorinsky, P. H., 57–78, 58, 60, 127, 128

Small, S. L., 32
Smith, F., 22t, 41, 48
Smith, J. A., 123
Sousa, D. A., 31
Spiegel, D. L., 101
Spivey, N. N., 42, 57
Stahl, K. D., 47–48, 65, 101,
    121, 122
Stahl, S. A., 47–48, 101, 165
Stefancic, J., 92
Stephens, D., 194, 195
Stover, K., 194, 195
Street, B., 11t, 83, 84
Sulzby, E., 11t, 112
Sumara, D., 8, 9, 15, 21,
    36–37, 38, 39, 57, 75,
    76, 80
Sumara, D. J., 15, 38, 39
Swords, R., 69, 102

Tate, W. F., 11t, 95
Teale, W., 11t, 112
Templeton, S., 33, 35
Thorndike, E. L., 17

Tolar, T. D., 30
Torgerson, C., 101
Tough, P., 92
Tracey, D. H., 8
Turbill, J., 71, 112

Unrau, N. J., 3, 5
Urrieta, L., Jr., 92

Valencia, R. R., 64, 68
Vanderburg, M., 194
Van der Veer, R., 59
Van Langenhove, L., 89
van Leeuwen, T., 102
Van Meter, P., 11t, 40
Vasquez, V., 93, 145
Vélez-Ibañez, C. G., 63
Vul, E., 32
Vygotsky, L. S., 57–58, 69,
    72, 89, 127, 136

Wacquant, L. J. D., 4
Waggoner, M., 65
Walberg, H. J., 18

Ware, D., 197
Watson, J. B., 11t
Weaver, C., 102
Weber, P. H., 20
Wedwick, L., 54, 55
Weisberg, D. S., 31
Wenger, E., 62
Werner, C. A., 102
Wertsch, J. V., 11t, 62, 119
Wheeler, R. S., 69, 102
White, E. B., 84
Wigfield, A., 55–56
Winkielman, P., 32
Wolfe, P., 31
Woodley, H., 102
Wu, X., 65

Yarkoni, T., 32

Zamudio, M., 95, 96, 171
Zhang, J., 65
Zhu, D., 101
Ziegler, J. C., 7, 11t, 22t, 28,
    29–30

SUBJECTS

Ability differences, 155. See also
    Differentiated instruction
About this book, 1, 7–10
Academic identity, 136–137, 144
Academic language, 86, 102, 122, 181
Accountability pressures, 191
Accuracy and fluency, 122
Achievement testing, 17
Action research, 195–196
Activating prior knowledge, 44, 126
Activity-based learning, 68–69, 176
Adult literacy, 80
Aesthetic stance, 51–52, 119, 149
African American funds of knowledge, 65
African American Vernacular English
    (AAVE), 68
Agency, 89, 90–92, 98
Alphabetic cues, 34
Alphabetic literacy, 109
Analogy approach, 161, 162
Analytic phonics, 47
Apprenticeship, 62–63, 64, 72, 119, 128,
    144, 165
Appropriateness of topics, 142–143,
    144–145, 148
Approximation, 36, 70, 72, 112, 165
Arizona and ethnic studies programs, 96
Artifacts of culture, 142, 144
Artificial intelligence, 21, 26

Assessment, 17, 18, 49, 72, 97, 122, 191
Association and conditioning, 17–18
Attention, 24, 127
Attitude toward text. See Stance
Audience, 159, 160, 169–172
Authenticity: literature/texts, 47, 61, 65,
    101–102, 103, 109, 165; writing
    activities, 140, 165, 169–172, 179–181
Authoring lives/texts, 160
Author's purpose, 81, 82, 91–92, 94
Automatic information processing model,
    11t, 22t, 24, 33. See also Information-
    processing theories
Automaticity, 24, 28, 30, 33, 34, 35, 127
Autonomous model of literacy, 83–84

Background knowledge, 44
"Back-up" capacity of phonological
    processor, 28
Balanced literacy approach, 191
"Banking model" of teaching, 80
"Barking at print," 46
Basic skills programs, 18
Bazerman, C., 84
Behaviorism, 17–20, 36–37, 106. See also
    Correspondence theories
Behavior modification, 18, 19
Behavior study, 18
Best practices, 194

Bilingual classroom examples, 129–137, 166–173, 176–182
Bilingual education, 68–69, 129
Bilingualism, 169
Bottom-up information-processing theories, 21, 24. *See also* Gough's information processing model
"Brain-based" education, 31
Brain processing capacity, 24
Brain's role in learning, 15
Brown, M., 145
Brown v. Board of Education, 95
Bubonic plague outbreak (1940s), 145
Bullying/cyberbullying, 151, 153

C.A.F.E. (Comprehension, Accuracy, Fluency, and Expanding vocabulary), 19
Call-and-response structure, 107
CAP (concepts about print), 71–73, 101–102, 112
Capitalism and dehumanization, 80
Carolina Piedmont literacy practices, 83
Catalytic validity, 197–198
CCSS (Common Core State Standards). *See* Common Core State Standards (CCSS)
Chair for My Mother, A (Williams), 161, 165
Change and human development, 58
Charting observations, 177, 179, 180
CHAT (cultural-historical activity theory), 62
Chronotypes, 90–91
Classical conditioning, 17–18. *See also* Behaviorism
Classism, 96
Classroom-based research, 195–197
Classroom behavior management, 103
Closure in process drama, 54
Coaching as reciprocal process, 194
"Code book," 22
Codemeshing/codemixing, 102, 181
Codeswitching, 69, 102
Cognates, 175
Cognitive constructivism, 31–32, 39–41, 56. *See also* Construction–integration model; Psycholinguistic theory; Schema theory; Transactional/reader response theory
Cognitive processes, 21
Coherence/incoherence, 75, 77–78
Coherence theories. *See also* Cognitive constructivism; Social constructivism: about, 38–39, 57; and Calkins's *Units of Study*, 61–62; and emergent literacy, 73; and incoherence, 75; small moments praxis example, 165;

and social constructionism, 97–98; and social constructivism, 60, 62; and sociolinguistic theory, 69
Collaborative dialogue, 53
Collaborative inquiry, 195
Collaborative learning, 62–63, 65
Collaborative Reasoning (CR), 65
Collective activity, 59, 62–63
Colorblind racism, 95
Commitment to theory, 3
Common Core State Standards (CCSS), 60, 166, 174, 194
Community change, 83
Community change research, 78–79
Compensatory capabilities in processing, 28
Complex text and active problem solving, 175, 187–188
Comprehension. *See also* Praxis examples—meaning construction: autobiographical-writing example, 166–173; and correspondence theories, 15, 19, 23–24; definition (RAND Group), 123; and disciplinary literacy, 174, 187–188; and high-quality literature, 139; and social constructivism, 40–41, 42–44, 48–50; teacher inquiry, 191
Comprehension, Accuracy, Fluency, and Expanding vocabulary (C.A.F.E.), 19
Computer exposure, 110–111
Computer metaphor, 21, 26
Concepts about print (CAP), 71–73, 101–102, 112
Concepts of screen, 71–72, 112
Concepts transfer, 15
Conditioned behavior, 17–18
Connectionism, 17, 28, 30. *See also* Behaviorism
Conscientizaçao (conscientization), 80, 170–171, 189
Consolidated-alphabetic developmental stage, 34
Constructing meaning. *See* Comprehension
Construction–integration model, 48–50, 135–136, 187
Content area reading, 86, 174, 175. *See also* Disciplinary literacies
Context processor, 28, 29f
Contextualized skill instruction, 101–102
Controlled learning environment, 106
Conventional forms of language, 73, 79, 112, 161, 162, 163, 165
Conventional stage of spelling development, 34
Cooperative grouping. *See* Collaborative learning

"Correct" understandings, 43, 53
Correspondence theories, 15–16, 83–84, 97–98, 106–107. *See also* Automatic information processing model; Behaviorism; Correspondence theories; Dual route cascaded model; Gough's information processing model; Grain size theory; Information-processing theories; Interactive model; Parallel distributed processing model; Stage theories
Counternarratives, 95–96, 97
CR (Collaborative Reasoning), 65
Critical analysis of texts, 166
Critical as concept, 76
Critical consciousness, 96, 145
Critical framing, 88, 156
Critical inquiry, 78–79
Critical literacy framework, 93
Critical literacy pedagogy. *See* Critical literacy theory
Critical literacy theory, 79–83, 170–171, 188–189. *See also* Social constructionism
Critical media literacy, 155
Critical race theory (CRT), 92, 95–97, 144–145, 150, 171–172. *See also* Social constructionism
Critical reflection, 195
Critical social science, 76–77, 91–92. *See also* Social constructionism
Critical sociocultural theory (CST), 89–92, 108–109, 136–137. *See also* Social constructionism
Critical stance, 52, 188
Cueing systems, 134–135, 181
Cultural-historical activity theory (CHAT), 62
Cultural history, 63–64
Cultural knowledge, 172
Cultural mediation, 128
Culture: communities of, 58, 63, 64, 68; context of, 94, 108; and identity, 144; and memory, 43; practices related to, 63, 128; relevance of, 144
Curricular models and instructional strategies: behaviorism, 18–19, 36–37
Curricular models concept, 5
Curriculum design, 87, 88

Daily Five, 19
Daily practice introduction, 99
Data collection, 176
Decoding, 22, 24, 48. *See also* Gough's information processing model; Information-processing theories
Deconstruction, 77, 97

Deep structure, 45
Deficit assumptions, 64, 167
Dehumanization and capitalism, 80
Democracy ideal, 95
Descriptive writing, 160, 165, 168
Design-based research, 195, 196–197
Design experiments, 196–197
Designing as concept, 156
Detail in writing, 160, 165, 168
Dewey, J., 39, 55
Diagnosing reading difficulties, 30, 31, 33
Diagnostic Indicators of Basic Early Literacy Skills (DIBELS), 30, 33
Dialect, 67–68
Dialogic language, 89–90
Dialogue/discourse, 79, 80, 94, 170, 171, 188–189
DIBELS (Diagnostic Indicators of Basic Early Literacy Skills), 30, 33
Dictionary use, 134
Differentiated instruction, 101–102, 109
Digital literacies, 112, 113, 155
Digital tools of practice, 88–89, 128, 194–195
Directed Reading-Thinking Activity (DR-TA), 44
Direct instruction approaches, 15, 16–17, 18–19, 33. *See also* Explicit language instruction
Direct Instruction System for Teaching and Remediation (DISTAR), 18–19, 68
Disabilities, 155
Disciplinary literacies, 86. *See also* Praxis examples—disciplinary literacies
Discourses construct, 84, 86, 89–92, 137
"Discourses" versus discourses, 84
Discursive orientation, 76
Discursive positioning, 89, 91–92, 196
DISTAR (Direct Instruction System for Teaching and Remediation), 18–19, 68
Distributed model, 106
"Double consciousness," 145
Drama. *See* Process drama
Drill and practice, 18
DR-TA (Directed Reading-Thinking Activity), 44
Dual route cascaded model, 28, 33. *See also* Information-processing theories

Eagle Friends, 153
Early literacy, 70. *See also* Emergent literacy theory
Ebola outbreak (2014), 146, 149, 150
Economic context, 76
Education policy, 4
Efferent stance, 51–52, 149

Emergent literacy theory, 70–73, 112–113, 165–166
Emotional development, 128
Empathy, 155
Empiricism, 15, 18, 20, 21
English language arts praxis examples, manipulating sentences, 114–120; other people's shoes, 151–156; world literature, 145–151
Enlightenment period, 77
Environmental control/manipulation, 18
Environmental print, 72, 109
Epistemology concept, 6
Examples of praxis. *See entries beginning* Praxis examples—
Executive Order 9066, 183
Experiential learning, 39, 40
Expert teachers, 194
Explicit language instruction: code-cracking, 101–102; and coherence theories, 40, 44, 69, 72; and correspondence theories, 16–17, 19, 33, 106; disciplinary literacy, 69, 187; and meaning construction, 121, 127, 136, 165; writing, 165
Expressed interpretations, 51, 154–155
Expressed responses, 51, 154–155
External attention, 24
External researchers, 197
Extinction, 18

Facebook, 151–156
Fairy tale genre, 82, 89–90
Fakebook web tool, 151–156
"Feature extraction device," 25
Feedback to students, 19
Ferguson, MO, fatal shooting, 142, 143, 145
Fidelity instructional practices, 197
Field trip, 176
Figurative language, 134, 135, 136, 175
Finding Nemo, 168
Fishbowl discussion, 146, 147, 149
Fluency, 28, 121, 122, 165
Fordism, 87
Formalist approach, 119, 120
Formative experiments, 196–197
Forms of writing, 167–168
Four resources model of reading, 81, 93
Frankfurt School, 76
Freire, P., 170
Full-alphabetic developmental stage, 34
Funds of knowledge, 63–66, 68, 128, 144, 172. *See also* Prior knowledge

Gentrification, 78–79
Gentry's model, 34–35, 36

Geocaching example, 88
Get Ready for Gabí (Montes), 129
Global discourse practices, 84
Global economy, 87
"Goldilocks and the Three Bears," 82
Gough's information processing model, 22–24, 33. *See also* Information-processing theories
Grade-level examples of praxis: PreK–1st-grade, 109–114; 1st grade, 160–166; 3rd grade, 103–106, 124–128; 4th grade, 129–137, 166–173, 176–182; 6th grade, 151–156; 9th grade, 114–120; 10th grade, 182–189; 11th and 12th grades, 145–151
Grain size theory, 28–30, 106. *See also* Information-processing theories
Grammar instruction, 102–103
Grapheme-phoneme consistency, 29–30
Graphic organizers, 44
Graphophonemic rule system route, 26–27
Graphophonics cueing system, 34, 45, 46, 106
Graphophonics instruction, 107
Greek roots, 175
"Grit narrative," 92
Guided participation format, 63, 144

Handmade books, 164
Hands-on instruction, 176
Happy Birthday, Martin Luther King (Marzollo & Pinkney), 141, 143, 145
Harlem and gentrification, 78–79
Heteronormativity, 95–96
Hierarchy of skills, 19, 182
High-frequency words, 23, 122
High-stakes testing, 114
Historical context, 62–63, 76, 89, 108, 128
History classroom praxis example, 182–189
Humanism, 77
Human psychological development. *See* Psychological development

Idea units, 188
Identity, 82, 89–94, 108–109, 160, 181
Ideological model of literacy, 83–84
Ideological nature of schooling, 76–77
Imagery, 175
Imagination, 54–55
Implicit skills instruction, 101
Inappropriate classroom behavior, 103
Incremental progression, 16–17
Independent reading, 90, 103
Individual experience, 42
Inequality/inequity, 76, 77, 80, 82–83, 96. *See also* Racism/racial injustice

Inference, 154–155
Information-processing theories, 20, 21,
    22t, 30–33, 36–37, 106, 126–127. *See
    also* Automatic information processing
    model; Correspondence theories;
    Dual route cascaded model; Gough's
    information processing model; Grain
    size theory; Interactive model; Parallel
    distributed processing model
Initiation-Response-Evaluation (IRE), 67, 107
Initiation-Response-Feedback (I-R-F), 67
Inquiry. *See* Inquiry learning (Dewey);
    Participatory Action Research
    (PAR); Teacher development:
    inquiry; WebQuests; Y-PAR (Youth
    Participatory Action Research)
Inquiry learning (Dewey), 39, 55
Institute for Social Research, Frankfurt
    University, 76
Instructional strategies concept, 5
Integration and construction–integration
    model, 49
Intelligence testing, 17
Intentional cognitive activity, 40
Interactive model, 25–26, 28, 106. *See also*
    Information-processing theories
Interactivity, 26
Interest convergence, 95, 150
Internal attention, 24
Internal coherence, 39, 42
Internal-development processes, 58
Internalization, 15, 19, 58, 63, 128
Internet, 88, 113, 169, 181
Interpreting text, 96, 123
Interrelated aspects of language, 70–71
Invented spelling, 36, 72, 73, 161, 165, 166
Involuntary response, 17–18
Iran literacy practices, 83
IRE (Initiation-Response-Evaluation), 67, 107
I-R-F (Initiation-Response-Feedback), 67
Irony, 175
Isolated skills instruction, 17, 35, 36, 102,
    103
Isolating theory from practice, 4–5

Journals, 53, 124, 128, 178, 179, 180

K–2 instruction, 16–17
Kernel sentences, 116–118
King, Martin Luther, Jr., 145
Knowing one's students, 191–192
Knowledge. *See also* Funds of knowledge;
    Prior knowledge: acquisition of literacy,
    15, 25, 33–34, 38–39, 75, 77–78, 97;
    and epistemology, 6; sources of, 15,
    18, 19, 20–21, 38, 57, 78; specific,

25, 122–128, 134, 137, 164–165,
    174–175, 191

Language context, 108
Language cueing systems, 45
Language-in-use, 66, 180
Language levels, 45
Language mediation. *See* Semiotic mediation
Language variation, 103–106, 180
Latino critical theory (LatCrit), 95, 168,
    171, 172
Latin roots, 175
Law of readiness, 17, 19, 20
Learning assumptions, 3
Legal language, 186
Letter-by-letter process, 22
Letter from a Birmingham Jail (King), 175
Letter recognition, 22
Letter–sound correspondence. *See*
    Graphophonics cueing system
Letter writing, 168
Lexical knowledge, 25
Lexical route from print to pronunciation,
    25–26
"Librarian," 22
Linear processing, 16, 24–25
Linguistic comprehension. *See* Gough's
    information processing model
Linguistic context, 108
Linguistic diversity. *See* Language variation
Linguistic flexibility, 180
Linguistic scaffolding, 181
"Literacies," 83
Literacy coaching, 194–195
Literacy community, 128
"Literacy practices," 83
Literacy Resources, Inc., 16
Literacy technologies, 155
Literary stance, 82
Literature circles, 141–143
Literature-engagements praxis examples.
    See Praxis examples—literature
    engagements
Literature study: analysis, interpretation,
    critique, 119, 140; approaches,
    139–140; formats, 53, 68–69,
    115–116, 129, 141–143; and inquiry,
    139–140; participation structures,
    66–67, 68, 107, 108, 140; relation to
    comprehension instruction, 139
Literature use and stage theories, 36
Lived experiences, 80
Living systems theory of literacy, 32
Local curricular initiatives, 194
Local discourse practices, 84
Local economies, 87

Locke, J., 20
Logographic elements, 34

Male privilege, 95–96
Marginalized peoples, 95
Marx, K., 58, 59, 76
Marxism, 59
Meaning construction, 166–173. *See also* Comprehension; Praxis examples—meaning construction
Meaning processor, 28, 29f
Mechanical processing, 25–26
Media attention and neuroscience research, 31, 32
Memoir genre, 171
Memory, 24, 42
Mentor texts, 165
Meritocracy, 92
"Merlin," 23
Metacognition, 40–41, 44
Mexican American funds of knowledge, 63–64
Mexican American Studies (MAS) programs, 96
Micro-/macrostructures in text, 49
Mid-workshop, 61
Minilessons, 61, 161, 168, 169, 180, 186
Minority representations in literature, 140
Miscues and miscue analysis, 45–47, 178, 181–182
Mockingbird (Erskine), 139–140
Model construct, 5
Modeling as instructional practice, 40, 65, 155, 165, 169, 177
Momentos de cambio (moments of change), 166–170
Morpheme instruction, 127
Multilingual classroom examples, 103–106, 129–137, 166–173
Multilingual speakers and grain size theory, 29
Multiliteracies/new literacies theory, 86–89, 113–114, 155–156. *See also* Social constructionism
Multimodality in literacy, 87, 155
Multiple processors, 28

Narratives and power structures, 90, 95–97, 171
Narrative writing, 160–166. *See Units of Study for Primary Writing* (Calkins); *Units of Study in Opinion, Information, and Narrative Writing* (Calkins)
Naturalistic qualitative studies, 197
Neuroscience and literacy, 31–32
New literacy studies (NLS), 83–86, 89, 172–173, 179–180. *See also* Social constructionism
New London Group, 86–88, 155
"New times," 87
Nominalizations, 175
Nonlexical route from print to pronunciation, 25–26
Nonlinear processing, 24–25, 26
Nonsense-word reading, 27

Objective knowledge, 15, 19, 20
Observation and learning. *See* Empiricism
Observation as instructional practice, 72
Observation journals, 176, 177
Observation Survey of Early Literacy Achievement, An (Clay), 72, 73, 158
One-minute reading assessments, 122
One-on-one tutoring example, 124–128
Operant conditioning, 18, 19. *See also* Behaviorism
Oppression, 80, 82
Oral practice, 172
Oran, Algeria, and plague outbreak, 145
Orthographic phase. *See* Consolidated-alphabetic developmental stage
Orthographic processor, 28, 29f
Orthography, 25–30, 34, 106, 120–127
Out of My Mind (Draper), 151–156
Out-of-school literacy practices, 85
Overt instruction. *See* Explicit language instruction

Paperbag Princess, The (Munsch), 97
Parallel distributed processing (PDP) model, 28, 29f. *See also* Information-processing theories
Paraphrasing, 187–188
Partial-alphabetic developmental stage, 34
Participation structures, 66–67, 68, 107, 108, 140
Participatory Action Research (PAR), 78–79, 196
Participatory appropriation, 63, 144
Partner work, 148
Passive learning, 17
Passive voice, 175
Paternalism, 82
"Pattern synthesizer," 25, 26
Pavlov's dogs, 18
PDP (parallel distributed processing) model. *See* Parallel distributed processing (PDP) model
"Pedagogy of Multiliteracies, A," 86–87
Pedagogy of the Oppressed (Freire), 80
Peer interaction. *See* Participation structures
Peer modeling, 62

Persuasive writing, 169, 170
Phenomena of interest, 3
Phonemes, 17, 22–23, 27, 29–30, 101
Phonemic Awareness Curriculum, 16–17,
    19, 30
Phonetic stage of spelling development, 34
Phonics, 36, 47, 101, 103
Phonological processor, 28, 29f
Phonology, 24, 165
Plague, The (Camus), 145–150
Play, 58, 72
Pokémon example, 84–86
Police brutality, 142
Ponle el Cascabel al Gato (Belling the Cat)
    (Paxton), 168
Positioning and power structure, 78, 89, 91,
    94, 108–109
Post-Fordism, 87
"Postmodern picture books," 77
Postracial narrative, 145
Poststructuralism, 76, 77–78. *See also* Social
    constructionism
Power relationships: and content of this
    book, 7; and pedagogical choices, 4;
    and social constructionism, 76–78,
    82–84, 89–95, 108, 137, 140, 171
Practice of theory, 1, 3–4. *See also entries*
    beginning Praxis examples—
Pragmatic cueing system, 45
Praxis construct, 4, 5–6, 7t
Praxis examples—disciplinary literacies:
    about, 174–176; Japanese internment,
    182–189; charting plant growth,
    176–182
Praxis examples—literature engagements:
    about/introduction, 139–141; civil
    rights, 141–145; stepping into role,
    151–156; world literature, 145–151
Praxis examples—meaning construction:
    about/introduction, 121–124; fluency
    instruction, 124–128; strategic reading,
    129–137
Praxis examples—skills/concepts of
    literacy: about/introduction, 101–103;
    manipulating sentences, 114–120;
    valentines making, 109–114; word
    sorting, 103–106
Praxis examples—writing development:
    about/introduction, 158–160;
    autobiographical writing, 166–173;
    small moments, 160–166
Pre-alphabetic developmental stage, 34
Precommunicative stage of spelling
    development, 34
Predetermined scope and sequence, 16–17,
    101, 106

Prediction, 44
Predictive value of theory, 3
Prelude writing component, 61
Prereading activities, 49–50, 174
Preservice teachers event, 169–170
"Primary memory," 22–23
Primary source documents, 183–185
Print-rich classrooms, 72, 109
Print-to-speech processing model, 25–26.
    See also Dual route cascaded model;
    Information-processing theories
Prior knowledge, 42–44, 49, 126, 134, 136,
    188. *See also* Funds of knowledge
Problem-solving approach, 80
Process drama, 54–55
Process writing, 61–62
Professional journals, 32
Proliferation of language/literacy practices,
    87
Propositions, 48–49, 136, 188
Protagonists of color, 97
Pseudoword reading, 27
Psycholinguistic theory, 22t, 45–48, 55,
    134–135, 181. *See also* Cognitive
    constructivism; Top-down information-
    processing theories
Psychological development, 57–58
Public speaking events, 167, 170–173
Publishing, 162–164
"Put It on the Train" vignette, 103

Questioning stance, 81

Racism/racial injustice, 92, 143, 144–145,
    147–150, 171
Radical empiricism, 20. *See also* Empiricism
Radio broadcast, 125
RAND Reading Study Group, 123
Read-alouds, 103, 126, 161
Reader purposes, 49–50, 53, 149
Reader-response activities, 53
Readers' theater, 6, 121
Readiness. *See* Law of readiness
Reading comprehension. *See* Comprehension
Reading difficulties diagnosis. *See*
    Diagnosing reading difficulties
Reading levels, 66
Reading miscue analysis (RMA), 47. *See also*
    Miscues and miscue analysis
Reading program development, 18
Reading-rate emphasis, 122
Reading readiness, 17
Reading Recovery, 72
Reading response activity, 151–156
Reading specialist, 160
Reading success prediction, 16–17

"Reading the word," 188
"Reading the world," 80, 93, 188
Reciprocal teaching, 44
Reductionist view of reading, 31
Reflection on practice, 4
Register, 66–67, 69, 86, 102
Reinforcement, 18
Repeated reading, 33, 121, 125–128, 165
Research, 79, 176, 178
Resistance stance, 52, 149, 150
Responses to text, 51
Responsive-collaborative participation
    structures, 140
Retelling/summary, 141–142
Retrospective miscue analysis (RMA), 47
Rhyming words, 103–104
RMA (retrospective miscue analysis), 47. See
    also Miscues and miscue analysis
"Roaming about the known," 72, 165
Rogoff, B., 59
Roosevelt, F. D., 183
Rubin and Carlan's stage theory, 35
Russian social theory, 59

Schema concept and functions, 42–43, 155
Schema theory, 42–44, 143, 133–134. See
    also Cognitive constructivism
"Scholastic point of view," 4
"School to prison pipeline," 92, 95
Science experiments, 176
Scribing, 158
Second-stream responses, 51
Self-correction, 182
Self-monitoring, 40–41, 43–44, 47, 49, 53,
    182
Semantic cueing system, 45, 46
Semantic mapping, 44
Semantic memory, 24, 127
Semantics, 25
Semiotic mediation, 57–58, 60, 89, 102,
    118, 128, 144
Semiphonetic stage of spelling development,
    34
Sense data. See Empiricism
Sensitive topics, 142–143, 144–145, 148
Sexism, 96, 97
Share component of process writing, 61
Shared reading, 72, 121–122
Shifting nature of technology, 87
Shifting use of theory in research, 2–3
Sight vocabulary, 34
"Signifiers"/words as "signifiers," 38
"Signifying" versus representation, 38–39
Situated practice, 88, 89, 113, 144, 155,
    172
Situation model, 49–50, 135–136, 187, 188

Skills/concepts of literacy practice and
    theory. See Praxis examples—skills/
    concepts of literacy
Skills focus, 18, 33, 36
Skills instruction, 67, 79, 81, 98, 101, 102
Skinner, B. F., 18, 20
Slavery, 97
Snowy Day, The (Keats), 161, 165
Social change. See Critical literacy theory
Social-cognitive theory. See Social
    constructivism
Social constructionism, 7, 76–79,
    97–98. See also Critical literacy
    theory; Critical race theory (CRT);
    Critical sociocultural theory (CST);
    Multiliteracies/new literacies; New
    literacy studies
Social constructivism, 57–62, 73, 75, 165.
    See also Emergent literacy theory;
    Sociocultural-historical theory;
    Sociolinguistic theory
Social context of development, 57–60
Social media, 151–155
Socio-cognitive theory. See Social
    constructivism
Sociocultural-historical theory, 62–66,
    89, 118–119, 144. See also Social
    constructivism
Sociocultural theory, 62. See also Social
    constructivism
Socioeconomic diversity, 114
Sociolinguistic theory: 66–70, 107–108, 180
Space for literacy development, 192
Spanish speakers and literacy development,
    30, 35, 36
Spelling development, 34–35, 70–73
Spelling instruction, 29–30, 34, 103–104,
    106, 127, 161, 164–165
Stage theories, 33–36, 106, 127, 164–165.
    See also Correspondence theories
Stance, 50–52, 53, 94, 149–150
Standardized assessments, 191
State standards, 194
Stimulus and response, 17, 18, 20
Student-centered approaches, 55, 128
Student engagement, 56
Student interactions. See Participation
    structures
Student interests, 125, 126
Students in role, 54
Subjective experience, 149
Subjective knowledge, 15, 19, 78
Subject-object reciprocity, 50
Summary/retelling, 141–142
Surface structure, 45
Syntactic context, 25

Syntactic cueing system, 45, 46
Syntactic features of content area text, 175
Syntactic knowledge, 25
Synthetic phonics, 47
Systems of oppression, 80, 170–171

Tableau, 54–55
Taking dictation, 158
Teacher collaboration, 195
Teacher development: about, 190; shifting
     pedagogies, 190–193; inquiry, 193–198
Teacher in role, 54
"Teacher research," 195
Technology, 87, 113, 182
Testimonios, 95, 97, 168–169, 171–172
Testing, 18, 197
Textbase, 49, 135–136, 187, 188
Text complexity, 48–50
Text features, 186
Text processors, 25
Text support for one's ideas, 146, 153
Text-to-world connections, 141–145, 146,
     187
Theme-based student selection, 141
Theoretical grounding in teaching, 3
Theories, graphic overview, 11t, 22t
Theory concepts, 1–2, 5–6
Theory-to-practice examples. See entries
     beginning Praxis examples—
"The Place Where Sentences Go When They
     Are Understood," 23
Thought and Language (Vygotsky), 70
"Three Billy Goats Gruff, The," 82
Three Pigs, The (Wiesner), 77
"To Be of Use" (Piercy), 1
To Kill a Mockingbird (Lee), 114
Tools of practice, 86–87, 88–89, 113
Tool use, 59, 64
Top-down information-processing
     theories, 21, 24. See also Cognitive
     constructivism; Psycholinguistic theory
"TPWSGWTAU," 23
"Training" in literacy, 16–17, 19
Transactional/reader response theory, 50–53,
     119–120, 154–155, 149–150
Transactional strategies instruction (TSI),
     40–41, 52–53, 123
Transactional view of reading, 50
Transferability of literacy skills, 83–84
Transformative action, 78–79, 80, 82, 156,
     170–171, 189
Transformed practice, 88
Transitional stage of spelling development, 34
Translanguaging, 102, 181
TSI (transactional strategies instruction).

See Transactional strategies instruction
     (TSI)
Tucson Unified School District, 96

UNIDOS (United Non-Discriminatory
     Individuals in Demanding Our Studies),
     96
Units of Study for Primary Writing
     (Calkins), 60–62, 64, 160
Units of Study in Opinion, Information, and
     Narrative Writing (Calkins), 60–62, 64
Universal learning/expectations, 20, 62, 78,
     83–84, 107, 118
Urban classroom examples, 141–145
Useful inquiry/theory, 198

Values, 77–78, 81, 84
Varieties of English, 103
Vegetable garden, 176
"Visual information store," 25, 26
Visual memory, 24
Vocabulary and meaning making, 121, 122
Vocabulary development, 124, 125, 128,
     175, 176, 180
Vocabulary instruction, 101, 122
Voices of people of color, 95, 170–171
VoiceThread, 125, 126
Volcano research, 125
Vygotsky's impact on teaching and learning:
     and social constructionism, 89, 118,
     127, 136; and social constructivism,
     57–60, 62–63, 70

Watson, J. B., 18, 20
Ways with Words (Heath), 68
WebQuests, 88, 182–187, 189
West Africa ebola outbreak, 146
White privilege, 94, 95–96
Whole-class instruction, 16–17, 101
Whole language philosophy/curricular
     approach, 47–48, 55
Whole text emphasis, 47
Wiesner, D., 77
Word families, 106
Word identification. See Word recognition
Word knowledge, 122, 164, 165
Word morphology, 175
Word recognition: information processing
     theories, 22, 24, 26–30; and stage
     theory, 34, 35, 164–165
Words Their Way (Baer et al.), 35
Word tiers, 122
Word wall, 161
Word writing/spelling. See Spelling
     development

Worldviews and histories of inequity, 92
World Wide Web, 88
Writing: emergent literacy, 71–73; process/
    writing workshop, 60–62, 64, 161–162,
    165, 168, 192; as a transaction, 51–52
Writing development praxis. *See* Praxis
    examples—writing development

Y-PAR (Youth Participatory Action
    Research), 78–79, 81, 96

Zone of proximal development (ZPD), 58,
    60, 66, 127–128
ZPD (zone of proximal development). *See*
    Zone of proximal development (ZPD)

About the Author

Lara J. Handsfield is associate professor in the School of Teaching and Learning at Illinois State University in Normal, Illinois, where she teaches literacy methods courses for undergraduates and graduate courses in theoretical foundations of literacy. Lara's research critically examines comprehension instruction in culturally and linguistically diverse classrooms, how teachers negotiate multiple and conflicting pedagogical demands in their work, and implications for student and teacher identities. Her work has been funded by the Spencer Foundation and published in several academic and professional journals, including *Reading Research Quarterly*, *Language Arts*, the *Journal of Literacy Research*, *The Reading Teacher*, *Harvard Educational Review*, and *Theory into Practice*. She is currently co-editor of the journal *Action in Teacher Education*.